WELSH HISTORY

Wales between the Wars

Wales between the Wars

Edited by

Trevor Herbert
Gareth Elwyn Jones

Cardiff
University of Wales Press
1988

University of Wales Press, 6 Gwennyth Street, Cathays, Cardiff CF2 4YD

British Library Cataloguing in Publication Data

Wales between the Wars.
1. Wales, 1919–1939
I. Herbert, Trevor   II. Jones, Gareth Elwyn
942.9082

ISBN 0-7083-0989-5

Cover design : Cloud Nine Design

The publishers wish to acknowledge the advice and assistance given by the Design Department of the Welsh Books Council which is supported by the Welsh Arts Council.

Typeset by Megaron, Cardiff
Printed in Wales by Graham Harcourt (Printers) Ltd, Swansea

Welsh History and its Sources

Welsh History and its Sources is a project conducted at the Open University in Wales from 1985 to 1988 and funded by a Welsh Office Research Development grant. The project gratefully acknowledges the financial support made available by the Secretary of State for Wales.

Project Director: Dr Trevor Herbert

Senior Visiting Fellow: Dr Gareth Elwyn Jones

Steering Committee: Mr O.E. Jones, H.M.I. (Chairman)
Professor R.R. Davies, History Department,
    University College of Wales, Aberystwyth
Mr N. Evans, Coleg Harlech
Mr D. Maddox, Adviser, Mid Glamorgan LEA
Mr A. Evans, Head of History Department,
    Y Pant Comprehensive School, Pontyclun

Secretary to the Project at the
Open University in Wales: Mrs Julia Williams

Contents

Illustrations

Maps and Diagrams

The Contributors

TREVOR HERBERT is Sub-Dean, Senior Lecturer in Music and Arts Staff Tutor at the Open University in Wales. He is the author of various Open University course materials and specializes in British music history.

GARETH ELWYN JONES is Reader in History Education in the Department of Education, University College of Swansea. He has taught various courses for the Open University in Wales and is currently an arts foundation course tutor-counsellor and assistant staff tutor.

DAVID SMITH is Professor of the History of Wales at University College, Cardiff, and was formerly an Open University tutor. He has also contributed to another volume in this series.

DEIAN HOPKIN is Senior Lecturer in the Department of History at the University College of Wales, Aberystwyth. He was formerly a tutor-counsellor for the Open University's Aberystwyth study centre and a post-foundation tutor in the Faculty of Social Sciences.

KENNETH O. MORGAN is Fellow and Praelector in History, The Queen's College, Oxford. He has contributed to Open University television programmes on history and has also contributed to another volume in this series.

PETER STEAD is Senior Lecturer in History at the University College of Swansea. He has formerly tutored Open University history courses.

DENNIS THOMAS is a Lecturer in the Economics Department of the University College of Wales, Aberystwyth.

DEIRDRE BEDDOE is Reader in History at the Polytechnic of Wales, Pontypridd, and has been a tutor for Open University history courses.

Preface

This series gives an insight into Welsh history by examining its sources and the ways in which some leading historians use those sources. It is not formally a history of Wales. This volume, for instance, is not a chronological history of Wales in the period 1918–1939, neither is it a comprehensive history in the sense that its themes embrace all of the major issues and events that were important in that period. Readers of this book will, we hope, learn a great deal about Wales between the first and second world wars, but they will learn as much about the way in which professional historians interpret the raw materials of history.

The choice of topics reflects the editors' view of central themes in the period. Those themes also tell us much about the nature of the evidence available to the historian. The economic transformation in Wales between the wars could hardly have been more dramatic. Dennis Thomas's exploration of the decline is an essential prelude. It leads logically to Deian Hopkin's discussion of the ways in which individuals and communities reacted to the economic disasters which befell them. Kenneth O. Morgan explores the reasons why organized, conventional politics remained impotent in the face of disaster. We then move to a more neglected area of historiography, women's history, illuminated by Deirdre Beddoe as she looks not only at the effects of the Depression but also at the mythology and reality of attitudes towards women. Rarer still in interpretations of the history of the twentieth century is reference to the way in which individuals, communities and nations are interpreted in non-literary media. Peter Stead's essay shows how, in its tragedy, Wales got caught up, incongruously, in a world symbolized by Hollywood. Literature is the theme of the final section of material. Probably in no period of Welsh history have so many talented writers reacted so immediately and positively to the economic and social stress that scarred community consciousness. David Smith's essay and sources provide, therefore, a unique and, in terms of history books, unconventional, view. We normally expect poets and novelists to provide an insight into the inner realities of individual or national tragedies, to some degree retrospectively. We expect politicians to react more immediately and practically.

At one level *Wales between the Wars* is simply a book about one period in the history of Wales, and about the ways in which historians interpret that period. However, the series of which this volume is a part has been designed to serve a number of functions for anyone who is formally or informally engaged in a study of Welsh history. Those studying with a tutor, for instance extra-mural, university or sixth-form students, will find that it is a resource which will form a basis for, or enhance, a broader study of Welsh history. Those who are studying in a more remote location, far from formal classes in Welsh history, will find that the contents of the book are so ordered as to guide them through a course of study similar, but not analogous, to the methods which have proved successful in continuing education programmes of the Open University. The main feature of this method is that it attempts to combine a programmatic approach with something more flexible and open-ended.

Central to this book are Sections A to F which contain three different but closely related and interlinked types of material. Each of the six essays is written on a clearly-defined topic. Each essay is immediately followed by a collection of source material which is the basis of the evidence for the essay. Within each essay, reference is made to a particular source document by the inclusion of a reference number in the essay text; this reference number is also placed in the left hand margin of the essay.

The Sources section of each topic is followed by a section called 'Debating the Evidence'. The primary purpose here is to highlight the special features, weaknesses and strengths of each collection of sources and to question the way in which the author of the essay has used them. It is worth pointing out that we have not attempted here simply to act as *agents provocateurs*, setting up a series of artificial controversies which can be comfortably demolished. The purpose is to raise the sorts of questions which the essayists themselves probably addressed before they employed these sources. In doing this we hope to expose the types of issues that the historian has to deal with. The 'Debating the Evidence' sections pose a number of questions about the sources. They do not provide model answers and neatly tie up all of the loose ends concerning each source. The discipline of history does not allow that approach. If it did, there would be no need for a book of this type. The 'discussions' which round off each section simply put forward a number of ideas which will cause readers to consider and reconsider the issues which have been raised. The purpose is to breed the kind of healthy scepticism about historical sources which underlies the method of approach of the professional historian.

Other parts of the book support these central sections. The Introduction poses basic problems about the difficulties of coping with historical sources, points which are consolidated in the 'Debating the Evidence' sections. The intention of the opening essay, *Wales between the Wars*, is to outline the principal changes which took place in Wales during this period and to hint at the issues that motivated those changes.

At the end of the book is a glossary which explains briefly a number of the more technical terms and concepts arising out of the essays/ sources collection. Although a glossary is properly a list of explanations of words and terms, we have additionally included brief details of persons who are prominent in the essay and document material. Such words are *italicized* (thus) in the text and will be explained in the glossary.

Readers will, of course, decide how best to profit from the different constituent elements in the book. The first two chapters should certainly be read first, as these provide a context for the rest of the book. It is also important to read the six essays (with or without reference to the source collections) before reading the 'Debating the Evidence' sections. It is necessary to have this broad framework for examining and re-examining the collections of sources. The 'Debating the Evidence' sections refer both forward and back to various sources on the assumption that you have familiarized yourself with the material in this way.

The open-ended nature of the book serves to highlight the extent to which it has been our intention to do no more than *contribute* to an understanding of Welsh history. Different editors would have chosen different topics. The essays here should be seen within the framework of a much wider range of writings which over the past few decades has become available. The greatest success which a book like this can meet with is that it imparts to its readers an insatiable desire to know more about Welsh history and to do so from a standpoint which is constantly and intelligently questioning the ways in which historians provide that knowledge.

Acknowledgements

The development of the Welsh History and its Sources project was made possible by the support of the Secretary of State for Wales and I am happy to have made formal acknowledgement to the Secretary of State and individuals connected with the project elsewhere in this book.

Funding from the Open University made possible the development of the initial ideas that were eventually nurtured by a Welsh Office grant. The assistance of various individuals and departments of the Open University has been frequently and freely given. In particular, I am grateful to Wynne Brindle, Richard McKracken and Barry Hollis. Also my colleagues at the Open University in Wales, where the project was based, have been constantly helpful. Julia Williams, secretary to the Arts Faculty of the Open University in Wales, acted as secretary to the project. As well as word-processing the texts for the entire series she was immensely efficient in the administration of the project.

University College of Swansea were kind enough to allow the part secondment of Dr Gareth Elwyn Jones to work on the project. Without him the project would not have progressed beyond being an idea as I have relied entirely on his widely respected expertise for overseeing the academic content of the series.

Diverse contributions have enhanced the effectiveness of the material. John Hunt of the Open University drew the maps and diagrams, often from a jumble of data and instructions. Photographic research and administration was done by Rhodri Morgan. Annette Musker compiled the index. Anne Howells of the University of Wales Press copy-edited the series and made many useful suggestions for improvement. I am grateful to Dr D.A.T. Thomas of the Open University in Wales for advice on and translation of certain Welsh language passages.

My major debt of gratitude is to the contributors, each of whom was asked to write to a prescribed topic, format, word length and submission date. Each fulfilled the brief with absolute accuracy, punctuality and co-operation. The format was prescribed by me. Any shortcomings that remain can be put down to that prescription and to the consequences that emanated from it.

TREVOR HERBERT

Cardiff
March 1987

Introduction

The essays contained in this book have been written not only by specialist historians, but also by specialists in the particular topic on which they have written. They are authorities on their subject and they make pertinent, informed and professional observations. Each essay is an important contribution to the historiography of Wales.

As specialists they know the sources for their topics intimately. They have included extracts from a cross-section of these sources to indicate on what evidence they base the generalizations and conclusions in their essays. We hope that the essays will interest you and that the documents will bring you into contact with the kind of primary sources which you may not have encountered before. Historians face a variety of problems when they consult source material and face even more difficulties when they have to synthesize the material collected into a coherent narrative and analysis of the events they are describing. In doing so, even the best historians make mistakes. Sometimes these are trivial (or not so trivial!) errors of fact. You may even spot factual discrepancies between information given in the various essays and the documents in this book.

At the end of each essay/sources section there is a short discussion section. By the time you reach it you will have read the essay and the sources on which the essay is based.

The discussion section is concerned with problems of interpretation. It is an attempt to conduct a debate with the author about the way in which the essay relates to the sources. This is partly achieved by asking pertinent questions about the nature of the sources. The intention is that you are stimulated to think about the validity of the exercise of writing history and the methodology of the study of history which is essentially what distinguishes it from other disciplines. The dialogue is a complex one and the questions posed do not, generally, have any 'right' answers.

But they do have some answers which make more sense than others. We feel that the historians who have written the essays have provided answers which are reasonable. But historians are not infallible, however eminent they may be. Their conclusions are open to debate and discussion, as, for that matter, is their whole procedure of working. As you work through the discussion and questions you will notice that there is specific cross-referencing to the relevant section of the essay (or essays) and to documents. It is important that you use these cross-references since the success of the exercise depends vitally on taking into account the relationship between the primary source material and what the historian makes of it.

At the heart of the historian's task is the search for and subsequent use of evidence, much of it of the sort you will encounter here. The crucial distinction in the nature of this evidence is that between primary and secondary sources. There is no completely watertight definition of what constitutes a primary source but a reasonable working definition would be that primary sources consist of material which came into existence during the particular period which the historian is researching, while secondary sources came into existence after that period. Another important point is that the extent to which a source can be regarded as primary or secondary relies as much on the topic of research as it does on the date of that source.

These distinctions between primary and secondary sources hold good, and remain useful, even for the historian dealing with the recent past, though the nearer we come to the present the less straightforward is the classification.

For example, one of Dr Kenneth O. Morgan's sources is comment on a 1933 by-election fought by Arthur Horner. He recalls the election in his autobiography, written in 1960. Since our period of study is the history of Wales in the inter-war period, 1918–1939, this source should be a secondary source. However, oral reminiscences recalled on tape and transcribed, or autobiography, are generally taken to be primary sources when they relate specifically to the period under consideration. This is because those recalling the events were active participants in them. There would be no problem of classification if the historian's topic was different. If, for example, the research was to produce a biography of the life and work of Arthur Horner then his autobiography would, indubitably, be a primary source.

The interpretation of historical sources is extremely complex. It was once believed by highly reputable historians that if they mastered all the sources they could write 'true' history. There is at least one eminent historian who argues this now. You might like to consider on which side of the debate you stand at the moment.

Most historians would argue that this is impossible. Because we are removed from the time and place of the event, we are influenced by prejudices of nationality, religion or politics. However, there is some compensation for this because we know, usually, what the results were of actions which occurred during the period of a given topic and this benefit of hindsight is enormously useful in trying to analyse the interplay of various factors in a situation and their influence on subsequent events. As you read the essays and documents in this collection, consider the degree of objectivity and subjectivity displayed by the authors. To do this you will need to consider what you would like to know about the authors before coming to a decision and how far the authors are entitled to their own interpretations. Of course, you, too, may come to the material with your own prejudices.

There is a similar pattern of presentation for each essay and its related documents. There are specific questions involving comprehension, evaluation, interpretation and synthesis, with synthesis, arguably, the highest level of the skills. However, there can be no rigid demarcation of historical skills such as interpretation and synthesis and some questions will overlap the various categories. Neither is there a standard form of 'answer', as the discussions demonstrate. What the questions do provide is guidance for a structured pattern of study which will enhance your understanding of the essays and documents.

Above all, there is dialogue and discussion about the way in which each historian has handled the complexities of writing about and interpreting the past. That such interpretation is as skilled, informed and mature as is conceivably possible is essential to our well-being as a society. In that these books are about the history of Wales they contribute fundamentally to that end. That vitality depends on debate, analytical, informed, structured debate. It is the purpose of this book to stimulate your involvement in that debate in a more structured way than has been attempted before in the study of the history of Wales.

Timechart

Wales		Other significant events
	1914–18	The Great War
South Wales coalfield taken over by the government.	**1916**	
	1918	Coupon Election. Enormous coalition majority. Liberals divided.
Royal Commission on coal industry recommends nationalization of the industry.	**1919**	Treaty of Versailles.
Disestablishment of the Church in Wales.	**1920**	British Communist Party formed.
Coal industry handed back to the coal-owners, followed by miners' defeat in lock-out and reduced wages.	**1921**	Anglo-Irish Treaty with Ulster opting out.
	1921/22	Beginning of the post-war trade slump.
Urdd Gobaith Cymru (the Welsh League of Youth) founded.	**1922**	Coalition government of Lloyd George falls. Andrew Bonar Law becomes Prime Minister. Geddes' Axe — cuts in education and social services.

| | 1923 | Stanley Baldwin replaces Bonar Law as Prime Minister. Matrimonial Causes Act puts women in slightly less disadvantageous position in divorce cases. |

| | 1924 | (January to November) First Labour Government. Ramsay MacDonald Prime Minister, replaced in November by Baldwin. |

Plaid Genedlaethol Cymru (the Welsh Nationalist Party) founded.   **1925**   Return to the Gold Standard.

Creation of South Wales Miners' Industrial Union.   **1926**   General Strike and Miners' Lock-out ends in defeat for miners, reduced wages and longer hours.
Imperial Conference recognizes that the British Commonwealth is a voluntary organization of members with equal status.

The first Hunger March against unemployment leaves south Wales.   **1927**

1929   MacDonald Prime Minister of Labour Government. Stock market crash.

Height of mass unemployment in south Wales and emigration from the area.   **1930**

| | 1931 | Economic/political crisis. MacDonald Prime Minister of national government with massive Conservative support. Sir Oswald Mosley forms a new political party of Fascists. |

Struggle between South Wales Miners' Federation and company unionism at its height. **1934**

Stay-down strikes at south Wales collieries. **1935** Baldwin becomes Prime Minister.

Peace Pledge Union founded — Britain's largest pacifist organization. **1936** The Abdication crisis. Edward VIII abdicates. George VI becomes king.

Substantial numbers of Welsh volunteers join the International Brigade to fight in the Spanish Civil War. **1936–38** Spanish Civil War.

Symbolic burning of bombing school at Penyberth, Llŷn. **1936**

1937 Neville Chamberlain becomes Prime Minister.

1937–39 Policy of Appeasement.

1938 Czechoslovakian crisis/ Munich.

First Welsh language primary school started. **1939** Anglo-Polish Agreement.

1939–45 Second World War.

Wales between the Wars

DAVID SMITH

No period in recent British history has been the subject of more intense debate and disagreement than the inter-war years. Those who lamented in the 1980s that the number unemployed were as many as those in the 'locust years' of the 1930s were quickly reminded that the 1930s were also a decade of remarkable economic growth. At various stages since the Second World War historians and other commentators have sought to understand the Depression or the Slump in the light of their own contemporary circumstances. It is, then, a crucial period for the subsequent debates on welfarism, on industrial relations, on social disorder, on governmental responsibilities, on the concept of 'two nations' and on the quest for economic regeneration. It was an argument that was well underway before 1939: were the regions of north-west and north-east England, of south-east Scotland, northern Ireland, south Wales the Special Areas the government designated in 1934 for care and attention to their problems of ailing, heavy industry and social deprivation or were they human disaster areas where whole communities were left to rot?

For a time it was those who asserted the latter who won the day. The economic management and social welfare policies that successive administrations fostered after 1945 underlined the validity of inter-ventionism and gave credibility to the popular wisdom about the pre-war years. The 1930s, in particular, were imagined (by poets, novelists and painters) and documented (by journalists, sociologists, photo-graphers and film-makers) as no other decade had ever been. The images were often heart-rending — wide-eyed children in ragged clothes, disconsolate groups of men shuffling around the streets in idleness, desperate women amidst the worn-out clutter of damp, bug-infested kitchens, the defiance of a *Hunger March* — and, in their human immediacy, made to seem so natural as to be absolutely real. The age of the documentary, in art as well as in life, was stamped with the mark of authenticity.

'This book', wrote the novelist James Hanley (1901–86) of his *Grey Children* (1937), a compilation of oral testimony on life in south Wales, 'is a result of my own desire to go and see what has now become generally known as a "special area" . . . [but] . . . when the late Prime Minister [Stanley Baldwin] described this area as a "special area" he was rather wide of the mark. On his own assumption it would imply that being so it would have the consideration due to it . . . [and that] . . . swinging on the full tide of a vast re-armament programme, things are beginning to brighten up in south Wales . . . In fact, I should say things are worse and not better. A special area is a new kind of social hell, with nothing special about it except the demoralization of a whole people, physical and moral, the breaking-up of family life, the vast amount of malnutrition not only amongst the adult population, but amongst the children.

The unemployment problem does not mean that men are idle only; it means that throughout the length and breadth of south Wales social tragedies of many kinds are being played out. It is not only lack of bread and scandalous housing conditions, it is the terrible feeling of not being wanted, of being useless and carrying on one's back the social stigma that now attaches to all idle men. If it went on for another few years they might well forget what human beings are like . . .'

And then the War came, and after it the insistence, on all sides, that 'Never Again' was the only worthwhile lesson to be learned. However, as the more prosperous post-war years caused individual and impressionistic memories to dim so, from the 1960s, both the authenticity and the general applicability of those inter-war images were questioned. Historians stressed that they did not indicate the extension of social services, the rise in consumerism and the availability of consumer durable goods, the coming of electricity and the family car, a rise in real incomes for the majority in work, the provision of paid holidays, a building boom from 1932 to the War, new arterial roads and light industries, leisure pursuits in sport or at the cinema and, in essence, the affluence-in-embryo of 'the Midlands' and the 'Home Counties' which would become the more general condition of the 1950s.[1] Mass unemployment and social misery receded under this historiographical bombardment to the margins and fringes which were neither central nor, for most, home. Even the history of Wales in these years — one that could not be easily accommodated in any of the rooms of this historical mansion — was depicted as more of a deviation from the usual Welsh pattern than a normative feature.[2] The concentration on that economic abyss into which the Welsh had fallen was seen as an ineradicable folk-memory that had coloured, and perhaps twisted, the politics and social policies of Wales for too long. It was, in short, irrelevant in longer-term perspective to the needs and aspirations of the people of Wales.

Maybe, in the 1980s, our own contemporary engagement with our history will yield a fresh view of the significance for Wales of this period. What is already undeniable is that the hypnotic fascination of what occurred within Wales and its wider implications are, again, centre stage. 'What Wales experienced between the two Wars', wrote Gwyn A. Williams, 'was a major reconstruction of the British and world economy, which left it a battered, sub-standard and lopsided region under a peculiarly rigid economic regime',[3] and Kenneth O. Morgan insisted in 1981 that though 'Some historians . . . have tended to paint a more cheerful picture of the thirties than once used to be prevalent . . . in south Wales, this verdict cannot possibly be accepted . . . a whole society was crucified by mass unemployment and near-starvation'.[4] It is then not only the relationship of the historiography of Wales to that of Britain but also that of Wales to its own history which is thrown into high relief by study of the 1920s and 1930s.

From this angle it would be wise not to consider the period as a whole, but rather as a series of time-zones in which the different spaces of Welsh society often collided in mutual lack of recognition. Thus the relative prosperity of part of north-east Wales (steel, rayon, building) and the development of coastal tourism (Rhyl, Llandudno, Bangor, Caernarfon) can be contrasted very sharply with the huge decline in bituminous coal exports and steel-making in the south-east and the concomitant withering of the great docks at Cardiff and Barry where, in addition, a leisure industry remained frozen in the concrete ugliness of the early 1920s from that day to this. Or we could consider the amazing vitality of cultural life in inter-war Swansea (the painters Alfred Janes and Mervyn Levy, the composer Daniel Jones and his friend, Dylan Thomas) and wonder how far it is connected to the comparative well-being of the south west's trade in anthracite coal (peak production year — 1934) whilst in the more populous valleys to the east the huge output of 1913 when south Wales dominated the world's export trade in coal seemed a dream time that, in the phrase of Rhymney poet, Idris Davies, had become 'a swift disaster'. Cardiff, that coal metropolis, shrank back into provinciality until it found a new role as a service capital in the 1960s. Certainly the city did not appear to be central to any Welsh mainstream after it lost its economic primacy in the early 1920s and until it found its eventual focus as a cultural nexus.

National and social unity were already intertwined and problematic for Wales in 1920. The paradox was that, at first sight, the material developments of the Victorian and Edwardian years had succoured an indigenous Welsh population and boosted, immeasurably, a Welsh-language culture at many levels of appreciation and attainment. The concentration of population in the south was not, for a time, perceived as a threat to the balance of Welsh life because, after all, the bulk of immigrants to 1900 were straightforwardly Welsh and, thereafter, absolute numbers of Welsh-speakers increased to 1914 despite non-Welsh incomers. After the First World War all changed and, more importantly, is seen to change. The census of 1921 reveals what that of 1931 will confirm: the percentage of Welsh-speakers has begun an absolute and percentage decline (36.8 per cent in 1931). Nor was there any real comfort in the fact that the very icon of Victorian Wales, the Nonconformist religion, could still attract in the 1920s some 400,000 adherents since it was starkly clear that the fabric of chapels, the stipends of ministers and the efficacy of the faith as a public instrument were straws held against the wind of an increasingly secular society. The Liberal Party, which had espoused the great and traditional causes of Wales in the areas of civil and religious liberties, might point to the final disestablishment of the Church under the premiership of David Lloyd George in 1920 but a surer sign of political desire was that expressed in the return of half of Wales's 36 MPs in 1922 — with Lloyd George in voluntary retreat and, involuntarily, sidelined forever — for the newly organized Labour Party under the widest franchise made available by the democratizing *Representation of the People Act* in 1918. Despite minor fluctuations, gains from and losses to Liberals in the north and west or Conservatives in the coastal extremities, border and towns, Labour's grip on the political life of Wales was to be unshakeable until the apogee of 1966 (32 out of 36 MPs returned) had been passed.

That political domination did not, in the inter-war years, spell national togetherness because it was, in effect, the delayed by-product of the gathering of a working-class population in the southern valleys. The

4

work-force occupied by the coal industry alone was 274,000 in 1921 and the slashing in half of that body of men by the early 1930s had repercussions far beyond the economic distress of the mining areas and coal ports. The linking of rural to industrial Wales by common roots, religions and language was, to an extent, broken in this generation. The 'Atlantic of the spirit that separates the Teifi from the Bronx', in Gwyn Thomas's barbed phrase, now put the Rhondda on the other side of the ocean. The woollen mills of west Wales had been directly dependent 'on the industrial market of south Wales'[5] and prices had rocketed between 1914 and 1918. Along with their market they now collapsed and in Drefach and Felindre alone almost half of the 50 mills in operation in 1900 closed in the years immediately after the War. Neither market nor escape route for landless labourers existed any more. Life on the land in this Wales was only an idyll in the evocative memoirs of those whose emigration or professionalization removed them from its toil. The tenant farmers into whose hands the land went after the break-up of the great landed estates after 1918 — itself a sale encouraged by inflated prices as much as impelled by crippling costs — were the recipients of a nineteenth-century legacy they had long wanted to inherit but their path to prosperity was, overshadowed by debt and agricultural difficulties and only lubricated to ease by the coming of the Milk Marketing Board in 1933, a stony one. Mechanization ended the existence of farm labour in any numbers just as surely as the railways had drained away the rural working class to the towns and industries. What was left behind was a rate-paying political class of farmers and professionals in the small towns whose neglect and indolence in the face of socially preventable diseases (especially 'the Welsh scourge' — *tuberculosis*) was indicted by the Ministry of Health's comprehensive survey in 1939. Labour politics in the stricken valleys had effected, via its imperfect democracy, action which a stagnant rural Wales could not, or would not, take.

The divisiveness was more acute in this decline than the fracture between regions and occupations had been when the boom was on. The 1890s have been plausibly interpreted in British economic history as 'a climacteric' or ending which only the 1930s turned around; in Wales no such phasing existed, for the 1890s were still expansionist and it is the 1920s which, for Wales, marks this climax and the 1960s that sees a new shift. Lloyd George had speculated in 1907 that south Wales might 'develop into one of the greatest manufacturing centres in the whole Empire' but that was not, as L. J. Williams observes, 'the kind of question that could have been posed with any sense of tact — or credibility — in . . . Merthyr or Blaenau Ffestiniog in the 1930s.'[6] The latter was, in common with the rest of the slate quarrying industry which had been declared 'non-essential' in the War, a forlorn remnant of that quintessentially Welsh extractive industry. The former, too, insofar as its existence as iron and steel manufacture was concerned, was well set on its career as myth and legend in fiction and historical writing. Merthyr's population plummetted in inverse proportion to its un-employment rate and, with a thousand people leaving the borough every year in the 1920s, government commissioners investigating in the mid-1930s and P.E.P. (Political and Economic Planning) thinkers in 1938 concluded it was time to close it all down. The President of *Plaid Cymru*, *Saunders Lewis* (1893–1985), who wrote in his scathing poem 'The Deluge, 1939' that 'Here once was Wales . . .' would have agreed.

'Here once', but no longer in *Lewis*'s eyes, for industrial Wales had forfeited its Welshness not only by virtue of its majority use of the English language but also by overthrowing all hierarchies of culture and taste in a loathsome embrace of popular culture and mass politics that masqueraded as democracy. Unemployment for him, and the youthful *Plaid Cymru* (founded in 1925 in Pwllheli) which largely agreed that south Wales needed to be 'de-industrialized', was the sad, rotten fruit of bourgeois exploitation and proletarian materialism. *Plaid Cymru* was a response to the soft, cultural or sentimental nationalism of the Edwardian era but it remained a culture-group until after 1945 with no discernible influence on Welsh politics. Its heart-felt wish to unify a broken-bodied Wales by the healing touch of linguistic shamanism was diametrically opposed to the much more influential politics of the Communist Party which enjoyed considerable support in south Wales. The Communist Party saw the immiseration of the Welsh working-class as stout evidence of its 'proletarian internationalism' to be harnessed to the cause of oppressed workers on Clydeside or in India or, dramatically, in Spain. No parliamentary seat was won in Wales but Rhondda East almost fell in 1933 and, more narrowly still, in 1945, whilst the Communist Party's deep influence can be better traced in local council elections and union activities. Most of the 118 from the mining valleys who fought on the Republican side in the *Spanish Civil War* went under the aegis of the Communist Party.[7] Their heroism and sacrifice are not to be gainsaid, but, once more, it has been endowed retrospectively with a weightiness that it did not have in its own day. The social and economic

6

extremities to which parts of Wales had been driven, elicited and
encouraged extremist views as well as utopian visions of a radically
altered future. Reality was more circumspect, politics generally more
pragmatic. No less than nationalists or communists did the Labour Party
abhor the Wales for which it became *the* party (as had the Liberals before
it) but it continued to advocate *collectivist* policies of a reformist nature
and to administer the derelict towns and villages it had inherited as best
it could. On the whole it was a thankless task performed with more
compassion than imagination. And, on the whole, it was widely
supported for, in addition to the radical/liberal outlook and pre-1920
cultural characteristics of most Welsh Labour MPs, they and the people
they represented had come to share, via wartime controls and economic
dislocation, the view that only a centralized state planning and managing
the economy could usher in any kind of tangible improvement in their
own lifetimes. The seeds of the 1945 Labour general election victory and
its far-ranging policy commitments were as much rooted in this popular
consciousness as in the books of *Keynes* and *Beveridge*.

Many of these disparate strands only came together from the mid-
1930s. Perhaps it was only then that the full realization of what had
occurred since the War, and how intractable the problems were, finally
dawned on everyone. By then any talk of recovery was clearly laughable.
The unemployment figures, worse than for any other region of Britain
in the case of south Wales, were affected neither by the government's
feeble industrial transference policy of 1928 nor by the voluntary out-
migration of what ended up as more than 450,000 people in less than
twenty years nor yet by the late and inadequate siting of industrial estates
(notably in Treforest after 1938) or new steel works provision in Ebbw
Vale (1938). It would only be the next war that inspired a fresh (indeed
insatiable and impossible) demand for coal and coal miners and only the
war, with its ordnance factories in Wales, which gave large-scale paid
employment to women. At the same time it would be mistaken to equate
an acceptance of the situation with a passivity of spirit. Despair,
individual and public, certainly existed, and boosted the suicide rate to
cite only the most obvious indicator of the phenomenon as a social
manifestation. Yet, alongside it, there was resistance whose struggle
was, in quite significant ways, channelled institutionally.

It is, again, to a longer time span that we must turn for explanation.
The events that culminated in the *General Strike* in 1926 had their origins
in 1909–10. It has been shown that Liberalism, alternately dressed in the

clothes of *Progressivism* or Lib-Labism, had so penetrated the whole
culture of Wales that before 1914 its political sway was not seriously at
question. Yet, unarguably too, the industrial militancy and social
discontent that erupted in riots and strikes was symptomatic of
dissatisfactions that would, after 1918, sweep a new generation of
leaders to power. The press of the early 1920s, as the miners reel from
one national confrontation to another (1919, 1920, 1921) is full of bitter
diatribes conducted between such men as Noah Ablett (1883–1935),
chief *Marxist* guru in the coalfield and then miners' agent in Merthyr,
and the youthful Frank Hodges (1887–1947), who had moved from the
Garw valley to become a compromising General Secretary of the *MFGB*
(Miners' Federation of Great Britain) until he entered the first Labour
government of 1923–24; between Vernon Hartshorn (1872–1931), MP
for Ogmore since 1918, a prominent figure in that same government and
President of the *South Wales Miners' Federation* until he resigned because
of '*Bolshevism*' in the coalfield led by his arch enemy 'Emperor' A. J.
Cook (1884–1931), Rhondda miners' agent who succeeded Hodges as
General Secretary of all the British miners whom he led with passion and
blind conviction through the *General Strike* of May 1926 and the six
months they stood alone until driven to defeat in December. A chapter
of hope in direct action, undertaken by industrial unions exercising an
unparalleled sway over the loyalty of their members, ended there.

The men who succeeded them — whether Aneurin Bevan (1897–
1960) who entered Parliament as Ebbw Vale's Labour MP in 1929 or
Arthur Horner (1894–1969) who led the *SWMF (South Wales Miners'*
Federation) with skill and brilliance as their first Communist leader from
1936 — had to operate within narrower confines. Down to 1934 the
SWMF, still the single most important organization in Wales, lost half
its membership to unemployment, proved unable to organize more than
half those left into the union, saw its funds and capacities in educational
and welfare work destroyed, suffered the indignity of two further wage
cuts (including the infamous Schiller Award of 1931 which assessed a
man's wages by means of a pitiful 'family supplement' of 6*d.* for wife and
3*d.* for a child) and saw a rival union, fostered by the owners in certain
pits, challenge successfully its once unrivalled rule. In these years, even
within the *SWMF*, former colleagues (Labour and Communist),
quarrelled bitterly in mutual, and self-destructive, recrimination.

The tide turned when the anthracite coalfield in the west exerted its
growing authority and elected Jim Griffiths (1890–1975) as overall

President. Before he left to become Llanelli's MP in 1936 Griffiths oversaw the re-organization (by streamlining and rank and file involvement) of *the Fed* and equipped it for·the dramatic episodes of stay-down strikes (1935) and social boycotts (1934–38) by which it extirpated its rival and regained prestige and membership.[8] 1935 was a crucial year, for it was then that the National Government, abandoning the pretence of being able to 'solve' the unemployment problem, introduced its new bill whose net result would be to reduce the benefit paid by making payment more uniform, more bureaucratically assessed and more severely means-tested.

The mass community demonstrations of January and February 1935 in south Wales have now re-entered the public memory in Wales and their impact by forcing the government to slap a stand-still order on the Act (subsequently introduced in less harsh form) has, rightly, been acknowledged as a vital political intervention. Historians have been too ready, though, to pounce on relatively minor episodes like the scuffle at the assistance offices in Merthyr in which communists and women were involved and which Merthyr's 'marxist' Labour MP, S.O. Davies (1886–1972) roundly condemned. This is to read the current desires of some activists backwards. What *was* overwhelming in 1935 was the peaceful, mass action of up to 300,000 people on weekend after weekend and, as much to the point, the impetus to action which *only* a re-vitalized *SWMF* could supply for that society. The later *Popular Front* activities were, as *Horner* knew full well, dependent on the Communist Party acting as no more than an accredited minority: and it was the *SWMF* which stood for the bedrock of that politics and of that society. By 1939, 13 out of the 18 Labour MPs in south Wales were nominees of *the Fed*. It was this story which can affirm that the area was indeed and not just 'perhaps the most militant area in Britain during this period'.[9]

There were many aspects of Welsh life which were relatively untouched by this drama in the south, untouched in ways that made the area hermetically sealed in its economic decline where it had been expansive and all-embracing in its economic rise. Newer aspects of Welsh unity were being seen in the spread of grammar schools and the shared days of those with scholarships at the university colleges, with the growing protectiveness for Welsh-language culture that saw constant demands for an all-Welsh rule to be introduced at the National Eisteddfod, and, in contradistinction, with the permeation of Welsh life by newspapers, movies and radio, by sporting events and retail (advertised) goods which imposed their own cultural logic on all the others. Time and space intersected here, too, and broke down, in daily affairs no less than in political and economic ones, the more separate features of pre-1900 Wales.

The stormy times to which Wales was subjected in the inter-war years did not, for a long while yet, permit a longer-term reading of this history. Instead, the 'legend' was embellished until the rhetoric and novels of Red Rhondda and valleys once green cluttered up our understanding with their clichés of guilt, betrayal and redemption. Then forgotten was a literature, mainly though not exclusively in English for the poetry of *Gwenallt* was a notable fusion from the Swansea Valley of *Marxism* and Christianity, which sought to fashion a form that could be faithful to this collective drama. Gradually we have come to recognize that in the panoramic novels of Jack Jones (1884–1970), the surreal Marx Brothers comedies of Gwyn Thomas (1913–1981) and the epic political romances of Lewis Jones (1897–1939) we possess a literature of thunderous historical resonance.[10] These were the years, too, in which the poets Alun Lewis (1915–44) and Dylan Thomas (1914–53), both from middle-class backgrounds in Aberdare and Swansea, oddly out of touch with the world erupting all around them, found voices as fine as any in the poetry of these islands this century. They, and their more involved, older contemporaries — Glyn Jones (b.1905) and Idris Davies (1905–53) — were given a platform in the magazines of this new 'Anglo-Welsh' school, in Gwyn Jones's (b.1906) *Welsh Revival* (1939–48) and Keidrych Rhys's *Wales* (1937–49). Already the fierce determination to comprehend fully — beyond the document or the voiced testimony — the total nature of these disturbing Welsh times was being eloquently expressed. Alun Lewis, non-Welsh speaking son of a Welsh-speaking professional family planted in the heart of the steam coalfield, wrote home from war service in India in 1944:

I regret my lack of Welsh very deeply. I really will learn it when I come home again. I know more Urdu than Welsh: it's very sad . . . If I could live my life over again one of the things I'd do would be to learn Welsh: another to do an English degree at Oxford or London: a third to work underground for a year . . . When I come back I shall always tackle my writing through Welsh life and ways of thought: it's my only way; but I must get to grips with the details of life as I haven't yet done: the law, the police, the insurance, the hospitals, the employment exchanges, the slums . . .[11]

Alun Lewis, of course, never came back but, in a sense, his detailed list of things-to-do was the one that the Welsh did adopt after 1945. They were pushed to do so by a belief that their fragmented world needed some kind of mending and, more, by the disgust which those like James Hanley felt when they contemplated the waste of inter-war Wales. For, when all the statistics have been massaged to indicate growth in care and improvement in services, Wales still serves to indict the callous indifference that condemned two generations to live in a social hell in which an 'allowance of 3*d*. a meal for an adult may have been adequate to ward off an Ethiopian extreme of starvation, but it would not buy a pint of milk, costing at that time 3 1/2*d*.' and where dependence 'on benefit rates committed the unemployed to a humiliating and meagre subsistence'. Nutritional minimum standards were met by less than half the unemployed and within families it was 'the universal cry of commentators that the full impact of malnutrition was being staved off by the sacrifice of mothers'.[12] As late as 1939 only 2 per cent of the British school population enjoyed free school meals as Medical Officers of Health continued, by and large, to ignore the effects of malnutrition and the *Means Test* continued to be applied harshly. A malnutrition rate of 25 per cent in the Pontypridd area in 1934 and 1935 did not see a meals scheme introduced. Clothes deteriorated along with health. Women, especially young mothers and pregnant women, sacrificed themselves to keep children clothed and fed as best they could. Clinics and other welfare services came, late on, in the second half of the 1930s but preventative measures were only just beginning amidst a chaotic and haphazard spread of vital services. Teeth were the quickest to go — almost a quarter of all south Welsh miners aged 25–34 had lost all their teeth. The young aged quickly in Wales between the Wars.

Contemporaries knew instinctively what we must reconstruct. The inter-war years were not the odd-men-out in Welsh history. They were the product of untramelled economic development and they funnelled a population through a conscious sense of themselves as a distinctive people which has lasted well into our own day. These years, as the essays and documents that follow illustrate, raise the most acute problems any practising historian could confront — from the hidden history of women to the interaction of politics and culture, from the control of an economy to the depiction of a society in literature and historiography, from the impact of generational change on communal activity to the gender roles of men and women within a society whose traditional family structures were, one way or the other, under attack. Were there turning points? blind alleys? selected exits? Inter-war Wales, like the eighteenth century that began in 1660, was a 'long' period that began, perhaps, in 1917 and only ended in 1947 with the nationalization of the coal industry. It has not ended yet in our minds, in our interest and in our ongoing history.

1   See, for example, J. Stevenson and C. Cook, *The Slump* (1974).
2   As in Peter Stead's interesting and combative review article 'And Every Valley Shall be Exalted', *Morgannwg*, XXIV, 1980: 'Those were the bad years . . . but . . . remain an aberration as far as the general history is concerned [for] it is the consensus of late Victorian and Edwardian days and social improvement since 1945 that have been the most significant forces shaping contemporary Wales.'
3   Gwyn A. Williams, *When Was Wales?*, 1985, p.253.
4   Kenneth O. Morgan, *Rebirth of a Nation: Wales 1880–1980*, 1981, p.230.
5   See Geraint Jenkins, *Life and Tradition in Rural Wales*, 1976, pp.103–5.
6   L. J. Williams, 'The Climacteric of the 1890s' in *Modern South Wales: Essays in Economic History*, Colin Baber and L. J. Williams (eds.), 1986.
7   Hywel Francis, *Miners Against Fascism*, 1985.
8   Hywel Francis and David Smith, *The Fed: A History of the South Wales Miners in the 20th Century*, 1980.
9   See John Stevenson, *British Society 1914–45*, 1984, p.478.
10   See Dai Smith, 'A Novel History' in *Wales: The Imagined Nation*, Tony Curtis (ed.), 1986.
11   Quoted in D. Smith, 'Alun Lewis: A Case of Divided Sensibility', *Llafur*, 1981.
12   For this, and what follows, consult Charles Webster, 'Health, Welfare and Unemployment During the Depression', *Past and Present*, November, 1985.

Economic Decline

DENNIS THOMAS

The experience of the coalfield area of south Wales reflects the characteristics of the inter-war Depression to the full — both in its causes and in its effects. It is also this experience which truly fits the description of 'economic decline' — from a position of boom which was enjoyed at the beginning of the twentieth century.

[The region's overspecialization in a narrow range of heavy industries which were crucially dependent on the export market made it especially vulnerable to events.] The area was subjected to the coincidence of a downturn in the business cycle and a decline in the primary metal and coalmining industries. These industries also suffered from an overvalued currency with Britain's return to the *Gold Standard* in 1925. After 1930 they were to receive the full brunt of a worldwide Depression and a dwindling international trade which was part cause and part effect of a growing economic nationalism that expressed itself in a general policy of *protection* and self-sufficiency.

[The heavy reliance upon coal, steel and tinplate and the considerable interdependence which existed between these industries and transport, commerce and the ports, meant that when they became continuously distressed, all other activities suffered in consequence (A.1). This resulted in high unemployment rates and the emergence of some acutely distressed areas.]

A.1

[The Government responded only slowly to the particular problems of south Wales and similar depressed regions in Great Britain. Seemingly, faith was placed on a general recovery of trade together with an enthusiastic pursuance of a policy of

Cardiff Docks, 1923. (*Source: County of South Glamorgan Libraries.*)

transferring persons from depressed to prosperous regions. When a general recovery after 1933 produced little relief for the country's 'black spots', specific Government action was introduced in the form of the politely named Special Areas' legislation. Half-hearted in intent and meagre in its results, this legislation was unable either to alter significantly the employment situation or to create a new industrial future for the depressed areas.

The economic decline of the south Wales industrial area is well-documented. The area was the subject of a series of investigations and surveys, as well as being chosen as one of the country's Special Areas. However, the fact that the area exhibited the classic features of Depression in an extreme and prolonged form should not distract from appreciating that those depressive forces were at work throughout Wales during the period.

Different areas had different problems, but common features may be identified — concentration on a few activities, several of which were declining simultaneously (A.2). There were favoured trades and favoured areas, but in general there was a relative absence of the new and growing industries (A.3), a factor which is of considerable importance in explaining the failure of the employment situation to respond to any significant degree to the general cyclical recovery.

A.2

A.3

Although it is inappropriate to treat Wales as a self-contained economic region, a recitation of the basic statistics indicate that Wales as a whole experienced what, by any test, was as severe a deterioration in economic circumstances as any part of Great Britain.

Wales was the only one of the Ministry of Labour's Divisions in which the number of *insured workers* aged 16–64 actually in employment was smaller in 1939 than in 1923 (A.4). The fall experienced was over 9 per cent, as compared with a rise of over 27 per cent in the country generally. The unemployment rate in Wales was consistently higher than for any other Division in Britain between 1928 and 1939, never below 20 per cent, and as high as 38 per cent (A.5). Unemployment averaged 10 per cent

A.4

A.5

above the national level between 1927 and 1931, and 16 per cent above it between 1931 and 1936.

Prolonged unemployment was more severe in Wales than in any other part of the country. With 4.5 per cent of the insured population of Great Britain, Wales contained 19 per cent of the workers unemployed for twelve months or more in December, 1936, and 16 per cent in February, 1938. In June, 1938, a quarter of all unemployed workers in Wales had been out of work for more than a year.

Unemployment was widespread as well as severe. There was no county in Wales in which unemployment between 1931 and 1936 was below the average for Great Britain, and in most cases far above it. In view of these circumstances, it is not surprising that Wales experienced very heavy out-migration during the inter-war period. Although it is impossible to give a compre-hensive figure for total migration, which consisted of a substantial amount of voluntary movement in addition to that assisted and recorded by the Ministry of Labour, it was estimated that some 440,000 people left Wales, on balance, A.6   between 1921 and 1938 (A.6). Over 85 per cent of the loss was accounted for by Glamorgan and Monmouthshire.

In the absence of a detailed excursion through the rural A.7   counties of Wales (A.7), the geographical diversity of Depres-sion during the inter-war period can be indicated by recording that Anglesey displayed unemployment rates of over 40 per cent and that Montgomeryshire lost an estimated 8,470 of its population between 1921 and 1938. In the extreme south west, Pembroke Dock displayed an acute and particular distress as a direct consequence of State policy, which involved the closure of the naval dockyard in 1926. Between 1921 and 1931, some 3,500 persons, amounting to a quarter of the population of the borough, migrated, and in 1937 more than half the insured population was unemployed.

The mixed blessings enjoyed by the iron and steel industry in north-east Wales were cushioned by the existence of a diversi-fied industrial sector in Flint. In fact, progressive industrial development in the county saw a significant influx of popu-lation, estimated at nearly 10,000 persons, between 1921 and

Dowlais iron and steel works in 1912, on the occasion of a visit by King George V and Queen Mary. *(Source: Welsh Industrial and Maritime Museum.)*

1938. The economic circumstances of the coal-mining areas around Wrexham were appreciably worse. Unemployment in the Wrexham district stood at nearly 40 per cent in 1931, and remained around 30 per cent up until 1936. Although coalfield output fell considerably in relative terms, however, the industrial development of the area was on a smaller scale than that of south Wales. As such, the circumstances of the north-east coalfield were dwarfed by those prevailing in the south.

When studying the situation in the south Wales industrial area during the inter-war period, it is again necessary to appreciate that it would be misleading to regard the region as a homogeneous entity. Within the region itself there were clear variations in its economic structure and experience. It is not merely a matter of distinguishing between the coastal strip and the coalfield area, but also of distinguishing between different districts within the coalfield.

The boom conditions enjoyed in the south Wales industrial area on the eve of the First World War were not a sham but they were nonetheless insecure. Certain potentially damaging trends had already begun to appear but the artificial prosperity of wartime, which persisted into the early post-war years, concealed the underlying deterioration of the area's economic base. During the 1920s, however, all three of the area's primary employers were to suffer from changing conditions.

In the case of coal, problems arose due to declining demand, to a large extent due to the emergence of substitutes, in particular oil for steam coal in shipping. In the case of steel and tinplate, difficulties were encountered because of changing production techniques, such as the development of continuous strip-mill production in the USA, which placed the plant of south Wales at a disadvantage with foreign competitors. Technical improvements in combustion led to substantial economies in fuel consumption, and these had a dual consequence for south Wales. A lessened demand for coal was accompanied by locational changes in the steel industry, which completed the movement away from the northern and eastern parts of the coalfield.

All three industries suffered from relative inefficiency, falling

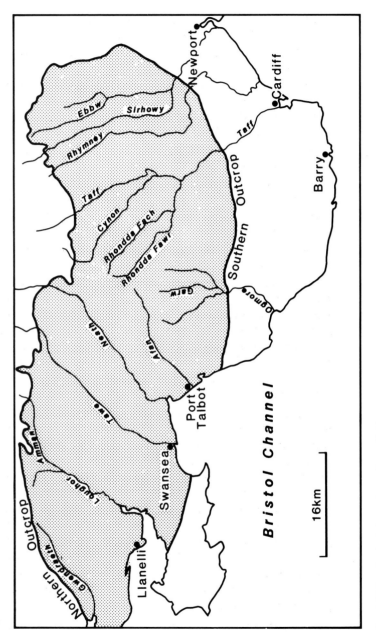

South Wales: the shaded area shows the coalfield.

exports and excess capacity. Although their responses varied in the particular, each indulged in amalgamation and concentration. The end result was the closure of mines and works and declining employment. The true plight of the steel and tinplate trades did not fully manifest itself until after 1930 but

A.8
A.9
A.10
A.11

that of coal-mining became marked from 1923 onwards (A.8, A.9, A.10, A.11). The employment decline in the latter industry became particularly exacerbated by increasing mechanization during the period. Between 1920 and 1939 the labour force fell from 272,000 to 136,000. The fact that coal-mining was by far the area's dominant employer, accounting for some 52 per cent of the total insured labour force in 1923, compared with 10 per cent in the other two industries, meant that unemployment in coal-mining was of greater absolute consequence for the area as a whole.

It is the differing weights and combinations of the contraction of the coal and primary metal industries, both spatially and over time, which largely explain the variations in unemployment in the industrial region. In the south west of the coalfield, for example, the unemployment rate was comparatively low, at 8 per cent in 1930, compared with 32 per cent for the industrial area as a whole. This low figure was explained to a large extent by the relative stability of the trade in anthracite, but also by the more balanced industrial structure in the Swansea district. This diversity of experience within the coalfield was also reflected in the economic circumstances of the

A.12

Bristol Channel ports (A.12, A.13).

A.13

The incidence of unemployment was greatest in those areas which were narrowly dependent upon steam coal or in those areas in the north east which experienced a decline in the iron and steel industry. The extremes of unemployment suffered by some of these heavily specialized localities were to a large extent due to factors which were inherent and inevitable. Many of these districts had outlived their usefulness as coal and steel producers, and a general revival in the fortunes of these industries would have had little effect on their circumstances.

A particularly melancholy line of semi-derelict communities could be found along the Merthyr to Abergavenny road at the

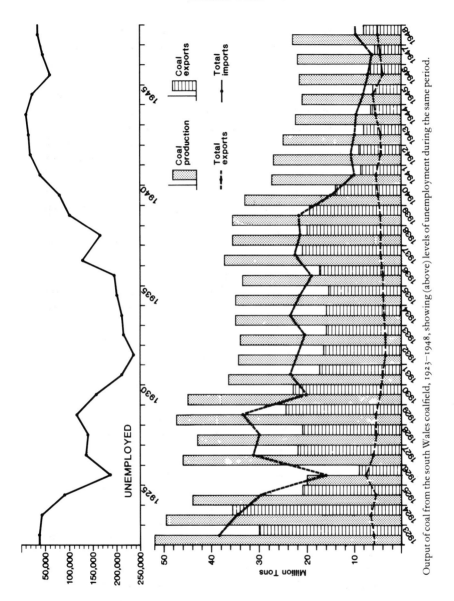

Output of coal from the south Wales coalfield, 1923–1948, showing (above) levels of unemployment during the same period.

heads of the valleys — comprising Merthyr Tydfil, Dowlais, Pontlottyn, Rhymney, Blaina, Nantyglo and Brynmawr. As the demand for dry coals declined, many towns and villages in this part of the coalfield were left without an economic base, with their inhabitants having to seek work elsewhere. The problem was greatest higher up the valleys, where the coal measures lay close to the surface and, consequently, were the first to be worked. As a result, many communities lost their status as parts of the coalfield and towns like Brynmawr became mere dormitories whose populations travelled many miles to find work. In 1921, 63 per cent of the total occupied residents of Brynmawr, almost all coalminers, worked outside the Urban District. In 1934, 74 per cent of the insured population were unemployed. Blaina, similarly, had 72 per cent unemployment. Such districts were pockets of acute unemployment throughout the inter-war years.

A similar intensity of unemployment was experienced by districts which had owed their existence to the coincidence of coal and iron ore in their vicinity. As iron supplies became exhausted, the industry had gradually moved down towards the coast. This movement continued in the 1920s, reaching a climax in 1931, with the closure of Dowlais following that of Cyfarthfa in 1921. The developments at East Moors in Cardiff, and at Port Talbot during this period, cannot detract from the distress caused in the older centres, even allowing for the siting of a new works at Ebbw Vale at the end of the 1930s. In September, 1936, Merthyr Tydfil recorded 60.6 per cent of its insured population out of work.

In addition to these extreme examples of economic distress, high rates of unemployment were displayed throughout the central and eastern region after 1930. As late as 1937, Pontypridd experienced an unemployment rate of 40 per cent, and Maesteg one of nearly 35 per cent. Even Cardiff, Newport, Swansea and Bridgend recorded unemployment rates exceeding 20 per cent.

The unemployment situation also worsened considerably in the western part of the industrial area during the 1930s. Unemployment in 1934 was recorded as 28.6 per cent of the insured population. The region also contained its own 'black spots', as exemplified by the rate of 57.5 per cent recorded in the Garnant employment exchange area in March 1937.

It is clear from the above account that the problem of unemployment was widespread, and any diversity in experience was basically 'a variation on a theme'. The scale of intensity of unemployment was matched by the length of time that A.14 individuals found themselves out of work (A.14, A.15), while A.15 the deteriorating economic situation was also highlighted by A.16 the problem of juvenile unemployment (A.16).

The result of the heavy and prolonged unemployment was economic distress, at both an individual and corporate level. For the individual, prolonged unemployment resulted in the exhaustion of personal savings and family resources, growing A.17 indebtedness, and a diminished standard of living (A.17, A.18). A.18 The problem was accentuated because in most cases men were the only wage earners due to the fact that employment opportunities for women in the area were traditionally and A.19 particularly low (A.19).

This individual impoverishment was accompanied by corporate decline, both public and private. Local authorities were faced with the problem of heavy expenditure in large part due to the increased call for public assistance. The position was made more difficult by the need to meet high interest rates payable by various local authorities for loans incurred since 1920 on housing and other schemes. To meet the increasing burdens, rates climbed higher and higher. At the same time, assessments and the ability of commercial undertakings and of A.20 the people generally to pay the rates fell (A.20). It was a vicious circle. The reduced earning power of the local authorities saw a reduction in the standard of services, many of which had always been inadequate. Financial stringency made it impossible to proceed with necessary schemes of sewerage, drainage, housing A.21 and social services generally (A.21).

The decrease in the area's purchasing power at the individual and corporate level had repercussions for all the region's A.22 activities — both economic and social (A.22). The retail trade was particularly hit, while increasing difficulties were experienced by traditional social institutions such as chapels and A.23 sports clubs (A.23, A.24).

A.24   An obvious escape from the distress was migration, not only from the present, but also from an obscure future. Although not without its positive aspects, out-migration produced a number

A.25   of perverse consequences (A.25). The basic problem was that migration was a selective process. It involved an undesirable modification in the age- and skill-structure of the population. The transferees were mostly young; for example, 66 per cent of the net outward balance of migrants from south Wales between 1921 and 1931 were under 30. It was also the most active and adaptable element of the population, as well as the most skilled or potentially skilled, who tended to migrate. Whilst draining the labour surplus to some extent, the migration process contributed more to the dilution of the average quality of the

A.26   labour force (A.26). There were also consequences for the maintenance and vitality of social and community life.

         In general, migration further contributed to a diminution in
A.27   local purchasing power (A.27). It also aggravated the problems of revenue loss from rates and Government grants. Furthermore, any economies to be gained by local authorities were only realized slowly, if at all. Streets required lighting, draining and policing, even if half the houses were empty.

         For many of the unemployed who remained in the area, life was supported by the numerous unemployed clubs and centres which sprang up during the period. There were many experiments, undertaken on a voluntary basis, to try to adapt to what was euphemistically called the 'New Leisure' or 'Time to Spare'. To many, these were positive attempts at relief and rehabilitation, to others they were merely a 'smoke-screen' for the lack of more positive action by the State and private enterprise — 'an opportunity for charity, well-wishing and distant encourage-
A.28   ment' (A.28, A.29).

A.29   Apart from these voluntary attempts at coping with unemployment, there were local initiatives to encourage the area's revitalization. Some of the principal authorities in south Wales combined to form the National Industrial Development Council for Wales and Monmouthshire. Its work formed a major part of continuous agitation shown by public-spirited bodies and individuals in south Wales during the 1930s. This

COUNTY POPULATIONS. WALES 1911–1951

	1911	1921	1931	1939	1951
Anglesey	50,928	51,744	49,029	46,500	50,660
Caernarfonshire	125,043	130,975	120,829	118,950	124,140
Cardiganshire	59,879	60,881	55,184	51,650	53,278
Denbighshire	144,783	154,842	157,648	156,920	170,726
Flintshire	92,705	106,617	112,889	121,900	145,279
Merioneth	45,565	45,087	43,201	39,860	41,465
Monmouthshire	395,719	450,794	434,958	399,640	425,115
Montgomeryshire	53,146	51,263	48,473	44,830	45,990
Pembrokeshire	89,960	91,978	87,206	83,270	90,906
Radnorshire	23,590	23,517	21,323	19,520	19,993
Glamorgan	1,120,910	1,252,481	1,225,717	1,157,640	1,202,581
Breconshire	59,287	61,222	57,775	52,540	56,508
Carmarthenshire	160,406	175,073	179,100	171,980	172,034

(*Source: Based on statistics in L. John Williams (ed), Digest of Welsh Historical Statistics, Vol. 1, 1985, pp.8–24.*)

manifested itself in deputations and memoranda, diagnosis and prescription, but little positive action. The basic need of the area, as identified by successive surveys and investigations, was an industrial restructuring involving the introduction of new A.30 and growing industries (A.30). But the ability to self-generate such a solution was limited. There were a number of inherent disadvantages in locating industry in south Wales. These were now added to, and aggravated by, the circumstances of the Depression years, which were themselves a major factor in repulsing the remedy. Fact and fiction now intermingled to produce among entrepreneurs 'an indifference bordering on hostility' to a south Wales location.

The high unemployment and a heavy age- and skill-skewed migration flow produced a deterioration in the potential of the area to attract and service new industries. The decline in human capital was accompanied by the depreciation of the area's material equipment, as services, social capital and amenities, which had always been deficient, also deteriorated. The region's internal market potential, always low, suffered from the reduction in income, while the area remained cut off from the major markets of Great Britain. Transport difficulties made location costly, a fact not eased by the failure of the region to offer particularly cheap fuel and by the high rates which existed in many parts.

The tradition of heavy industry in the area was not well suited to the specialist requirements of the new and expanding light industries. The labour force tended to be male-oriented and skill-specific, while the female pool was virtually untapped. In addition, the area saw higher-than-average rates paid in many A.31 trades (A.31). The logistics of the transportation network in south Wales also bore the imprint of the development of heavy industry. The need was for more efficient road transport, and a major requirement in this respect was the construction of a road bridge across the Severn estuary. The industrial economy also suffered from a relative absence of business services. This was due, to a large extent, to the nature and behaviour of the characteristically large firms in the area which tended to incorporate many of the required services within their own organization.

Even if industry could be induced to come to south Wales, there remained the issue of where to locate. Valley locations had severe physical constraints. The configuration of the coalfield area meant that there was little flat land available for development. It was the coastal region which provided the major opportunities for new industrial settlement, and there existed 'an invisible line running across mid-Glamorgan beyond which the industrialist is most reluctant to go'. In addition to these physical aspects, the economic disadvantages of the south Wales industrial area were also augmented by a number of social and psychological factors — such as the absence of local amenities and 'middle-class' company (A.32), and the apprehension over the strong traditions of trade unionism and the reputation for left-wing labour.

A.32

The south Wales coalfield region appeared remote, inaccessible, incommodious and unsuitable for new industry. In all senses it seemed 'out on a limb' (A.33).

A.33

The general paucity of new industrial development in the area can be seen in the figures recorded in the Board of Trade's 'Surveys of Industrial Development' for the years 1932–8. During that period, 42 new factories, employing 25 or more people, were opened in south Wales, only 24 of which were within the Special Area boundaries, including 13 at the recently established trading estate at Treforest.

The impact of the Special Area policy on south Wales was particularly limited. Apart from the general limitations inherent in its operation, developments in the area were specifically hampered by the ill-advised amputation involved in the delineation of the Special Area boundary (A.34, A.35, A.36). The only real contribution of note was that made by the trading estate movement at Treforest and related sites. Its success in attracting a range of new light industries to the area, however, was largely due to an accident of history — the arrival and settling of refugee industrialists fleeing the persecutions in central Europe, which preceded a more general evacuation of industry during the war. Even then these developments were largely inappropriate, both in scale and nature, to meet the area's basic problem of hard core male unemployment. Women

A.34
A.35
A.36

and children were paid less than men and the involuntary motto was 'women and children first'. In June 1939, 2,196 persons were employed at Treforest: and only 914 were men.

In addition to the meagre impact of direct State action in alleviating distress and reconstructing the area's economy, the south Wales industrial area benefited but little from the rearmament boom at the end of the 1930s. Some Government factories, especially the Royal Ordnance Factories, were located in various districts, but the full impetus of war-related developments was yet to come. Government defence contracts were not as influential in stimulating activity in south Wales as elsewhere, because the area was lacking in those industries, such as engineering, which were the main beneficiaries.

In sum, the various developments during the second half of the 1930s produced little change in the south Wales industrial area. The industrial structure remained an anachronism, with over one-third of the insured population still attached to the coal-mining industry. Much labour was still surplus and its absorption 'postulated more than general recovery, rearmaments and good wishes'. In July 1938, over 70,000 men aged between 18 and 64 were wholly unemployed, and 17,000 had been unemployed for three years or more. It was estimated that as many as 20,000 persons had left the area during 1937. On the eve of the Second World War, the Special Area remained 'special'.

Sources

A.1   So large a proportion of the population do the coal and iron and steel industries employ directly and so great a part of the remaining commercial activity of the region consists in importing and exporting their raw materials and their products, that when they become depressed every other industry and service must languish too; . . . railway transport and the docks, and the business of exporting, ship repairing, and building have suffered. The business of shopkeepers, printers, amusement caterers, bus-proprietors, and even the salaries and fees of local government officials, teachers and professional men depend ultimately, in such a region, upon the spending power of miners and steel-workers and the profitability of mining and of steel-making to the owners of these enterprises.

(*An Industrial Survey of South Wales*, Board of Trade, 1932, H.M.S.O. Made for the Board of Trade by the University College of South Wales and Monmouthshire, pp. 11–12.)

A.2   See Page 30.

A.3   CHANGES IN THE ESTIMATED NUMBERS OF INSURED WORKERS EMPLOYED IN THE EXPANDING AND DECLINING INDUSTRIES IN JUNE EACH YEAR.

Area	Decrease in Declining Industries	Increase in Expanding Industries	Net Change	Employed in 1934 (1924 = 100)
United Kingdom	1,210,242	1,722,310	+ 412,068	104.0
London Division	37,937	427,511	+ 389,634	121.1
South-Eastern Division	12,005	241,826	+ 229,821	131.2
Midlands Division	151,327	250,632	+ 93,305	106.3
Lancashire Industrial Area	212,137	116,373	− 97,764	92.4
North East Coast Area	153,319	50,452	− 102,867	83.2
Wales Division *	199,686	24,053	− 175,633	73.2

* June 1924 to June 1933

(United Kingdom and Six Areas 1924–36, in Dennison, S.R., *The Location of Industry and the Depressed Areas*, London, 1939.)

A.2   PERCENTAGE DISTRIBUTION OF OCCUPIED PERSONS BETWEEN MAIN INDUSTRIAL GROUPS—WALES, 1931 CENSUS

Sub-Region	Fishing	Agriculture	Mines and Quarries	Building and Contracting	Manufactures	Transport	Gas, Water, Electricity	Distributive Trades, Banks, Insurance	Local and Central Government	Miscellaneous Personal Services	Total in Work aged 14 and upwards
	%	%	%	%	%	%	%	%	%	%	%
North Coast and Mountains	0.1	20.0	12.0	4.9	9.2	7.0	0.7	13.8	7.5	*24.9*	100
Industrial Denbighshire	0.0	6.9	*34.5*	4.0	14.7	5.3	0.8	12.8	7.0	13.8	100
Flintshire	0.1	12.0	7.8	5.4	*27.9*	5.7	0.6	14.1	8.0	18.5	100
Severn Valley Lowlands	0.0	*24.7*	1.5	3.4	14.7	5.6	0.4	18.6	8.8	22.3	100
West Coast and Central Moorlands	0.1	*38.0*	6.5	4.0	7.8	4.5	0.5	9.8	8.3	20.6	100
South West Wales	5.3	*28.4*	5.4	4.2	8.6	7.0	0.5	13.0	10.5	17.0	100
Western Anthracite	0.0	3.7	22.5	2.3	*35.7*	6.9	0.7	12.6	6.0	9.7	100
Swansea Valley	0.7	2.7	14.0	3.7	*29.7*	10.9	0.9	16.4	7.2	13.8	100
West Central Area	0.0	2.4	*40.1*	2.5	17.0	7.5	0.6	12.6	6.8	10.5	100
Merthyr Area	0.0	1.9	*43.6*	1.8	10.3	5.5	1.0	15.6	8.4	11.9	100
Pontypridd and Rhondda	0.0	0.9	*59.9*	1.5	4.8	4.2	0.8	11.8	7.6	8.6	100
Cardiff and Barry Area	0.3	2.5	1.7	4.1	21.8	17.4	1.2	*21.9*	9.6	19.5	100
Rhymney Valley and Tredegar	0.0	1.7	*60.7*	1.5	6.6	4.2	0.5	10.5	6.0	8.4	100
Eastern Valleys of Monmouthshire	0.0	3.9	*43.7*	1.5	15.8	5.8	0.6	11.7	6.7	10.3	100
Newport Area	0.0	3.7	0.9	3.9	*28.5*	18.0	1.4	18.2	8.1	17.3	100
Rural (East) Monmouthshire	0.0	*24.6*	2.0	5.8	8.6	11.3	0.8	12.2	10.1	24.4	100
ALL WALES	0.4	10.0	22.8	3.4	16.5	8.5	0.8	14.2	7.8	15.6	100

Largest group in each sub-region shown in italic

(Welsh Reconstruction Advisory Council. *First Interim Report. Office of the Minister of Reconstruction.* H.M.S.O. 1944. Table No.4, p.15.)

A.4   ESTIMATED NUMBER OF INSURED PERSONS AGED 16–64 IN EMPLOYMENT

Administrative Division	Index Numbers (June 1923 = 100)				
	June 1923	June 1929	June 1932	June 1938	June 1939
London	100.0	120.4	118.1	143.7	147.0
South-Eastern	100.0	126.9	127.1	159.6	164.5
South-Western	100.0	116.6	113.6	140.3	149.7
Midlands	100.0	110.7	101.0	127.9	135.9
North-Eastern	100.0	105.2	92.1	111.8	118.2
North-Western	100.0	108.7	95.5	103.5	112.2
Northern	100.0	98.6	77.3	101.2	105.9
Scotland	100.0	104.8	91.0	110.6	116.0
Wales	100.0	84.6	63.6	80.9	90.6
Northern Ireland	100.0	107.2	92.8	101.5	112.9
Great Britain and Northern Ireland	100.0	110.0	100.1	120.9	·127.5

(*The Ministry of Labour Gazette*, January 1940, p.10.)

A.5   UNEMPLOYMENT IN THE COUNTIES OF GREAT BRITAIN, 1927–38

Region and County	Percentage of insured workers unemployed: monthly average											
	1927	1928	1929	1930	1931	1932	1933	1934	1935	1936	1937	1938
GREAT BRITAIN	9.7	10.6	10.6	16.2	22.0	22.2	20.3	17.3	16.2	13.9	10.8	12.7
ENGLAND	9.0	9.8	9.8	15.3	20.7	20.6	18.6	15.4	14.3	12.0	9.6	11.8
WALES	19.8	21.9	20.0	26.5	33.5	37.5	35.4	33.5	33.1	31.4	22.3	24.8
SCOTLAND	10.5	11.4	12.3	18.6	25.4	28.0	27.2	24.6	23.2	20.5	16.0	16.4
South Wales												
Carmarthen	25.8	23.5	18.7	22.6	27.0	27.5	21.5	21.2	24.4	22.8	21.3	27.7
Monmouth	23.3	22.9	22.5	28.8	33.8	42.0	40.6	36.0	33.5	32.7	21.1	23.6
Glamorgan	21.1	21.5	21.3	28.1	36.7	40.4	37.9	36.9	36.4	34.9	23.7	26.4
Central and North Wales												
Anglesey	—	—	—	—	35.7	40.8	42.1	41.5	41.1	41.1	33.9	35.1
Brecknock	—	—	—	—	42.9	51.9	52.9	50.4	48.0	47.9	31.4	35.4
Cardigan	—	—	—	—	25.2	28.4	29.7	29.2	32.0	29.7	28.7	30.8
Caernarvon	—	—	—	—	18.9	22.5	21.5	18.3	19.4	17.6	15.2	15.0
Denbigh	9.9	10.9	11.6	16.2	21.8	28.0	28.9	26.5	28.2	23.9	19.0	19.6
Flint	—	—	—	—	33.8	28.7	25.7	19.8	19.2	15.8	14.5	24.1
Merioneth	—	—	—	—	20.9	26.2	21.9	20.7	19.6	17.9	14.8	11.8
Montgomery	—	—	—	—	21.6	24.2	30.8	27.5	29.5	25.1	23.8	21.9
Pembroke	—	17.7	20.8	21.0	27.4	31.8	31.9	31.9	33.4	32.1	28.2	23.5
Radnor	—	—	—	—	18.2	18.7	21.3	16.9	19.2	19.1	10.3	12.2
Rest of Wales	11.4	12.1	14.4	22.1	—	—	—	—	—	—	—	—

(Extracted from Table 8, M. P. Fogarty, *Prospects of the Industrial Areas of Great Britain*, London, 1945.)

A.6   ESTIMATED NET LOSS OF POPULATION BY MIGRATION — CENSUS 1921 TO MID-1938

	Brecon	Carmarthen	Glamorgan	Monmouthshire
Inter-Censal loss of resident population due to migration	7,329	8,902	154,965	65,574
Estimated Net Loss Census 1931 to Mid 1938	5,005	9,660	107,095	50,870
Grand Total	12,334	18,562	262,060	116,444

	Anglesey	Caernarvon	Cardigan	Denbigh	Flintshire
Inter-Censal loss of resident population due to migration	3,320	286	1,373	5,166	3,650 gain
Estimated Net Loss Census 1931 to Mid 1938	1,730	1,120 gain	1,060	2,000	6,225 gain
Grand Total	5,050	834 gain	2,433	7,166	9,875 gain

	Merioneth	Montgomery	Pembrokeshire	Radnorshire
Inter-Censal loss of resident population due to migration	319 gain	4,920	9,235	1,663
Estimated Net Loss Census 1931 to Mid 1938	1,980	3,550	3,687	1,605
Grand Total	1,661	8,470	12,922	3,268

(Welsh Reconstruction Advisory Council. *First Interim Report. Office of the Minister of Reconstruction.* H.M.S.O. 1944. Appendix I, p. 123.)

A.7   In North and Central Wales the slate quarrying industry underwent a painful process of contraction, enforced by the successful competition of cheap imported slates, the vagaries of building policy and the use of substitute tiles and other roofing materials competitive with slate.

     . . . Hopes of market stability raised by the Coal Production Act, 1917, and the Agriculture Act, 1920, were rudely dashed by the early repeal of that legislation. Welsh farmers who had purchased their properties with borrowed monies were increasingly embarrassed by every fall in prices. In common with the prices of primary products throughout the world, the proceeds of Welsh sheep, cattle and crop sales fell steadily and with disastrous results.

     . . . From the countryside the drift of population went on at a rate proportionately very nearly equal to that from the towns. Farm buildings were neglected through poverty, improvements went unmade, the land itself was sadly neglected; and although the family farm, which predominates in Wales offers considerable resistance to unfavourable economic conditions, it does so only by the acceptance of standards which elsewhere connote acknowledged bankruptcy.

(Welsh Reconstruction Advisory Council. *First Interim Report. Office of the Minister of Reconstruction.* H.M.S.O. 1944. pp.6–7, Paras. 6–10.)

A.8   . . . .in the year 1913 the output of the South Wales coalfield (56,830,000 tons) reached a peak unattained before or since, . . . in 1923 . . . exports reached their maximum (30,119,942 tons)

     . . . From the end of 1923 there began a decline in prices and profits, and a consequent contraction in the numbers employed, the formidable extent of which has been the chief reason for making this survey . . .

     . . . During 1927, output recovered to a higher level than that of 1925, but declined again to a new low level of 43,312,000 tons . . . in 1928. The year 1929 . . . saw an expansion of output by five million tons . . .

     . . . During 1930, however, the world slump further

intensified competition and restricted demand; and South Wales output fell again by nearly two and a half million tons.

(*An Industrial Survey of South Wales.* Board of Trade 1932. Made for the Board of Trade by University College of South Wales and Monmouthshire. H.M.S.O. 1932, pp.28–9.)

Exports have dropped every year since 1929, from 29.9 million tons to 19.1 million tons in 1935; and the position has worsened not only absolutely but relatively to the rest of the country . . .

The products of the industry, which on the 1929 ascertainment were less than half the average for the country, have turned to a loss in the last three years.

(*The Second Industrial Survey of South Wales.* Published on Behalf of the National Industrial Development Council of Wales and Monmouthshire. University Press Board. Cardiff, 1937, Vol.I, pp.37–38.)

A.9   THE SECOND INDUSTRIAL SURVEY OF SOUTH WALES

Year	Output of the South Wales Coalfield	Output of the United Kingdom	Percentage of the South Wales Output to Total
	Tons	*Tons*	
1929	48,149,613	257,906,802	18.7
1930	45,107,912	243,881,824	18.6
1931	37,084,852	219,458,951	16.9
1932	34,874,302	208,733,140	16.7
1933	34,354,884	207,112,243	16.6
1934	35,173,317	220,726,298	16.0
1935	35,117,700	222,940,300	15.8

(*The Second Industrial Survey of South Wales.* Published on Behalf of the National Industrial Development Council of Wales and Monmouthshire 1937. University Press Board. Vol.I, Cardiff, 1937.)

A.10   APPROXIMATE NUMBERS EMPLOYED IN IRON AND STEEL INDUSTRY IN THE
       INDUSTRIAL REGION OF SOUTH WALES IN JUNE OF EACH YEAR

Year	Estimated Total Numbers Insured (July)	Numbers 'in Employment' (June) Excluding Temporarily Stopped	Including Temporarily Stopped
1923	27,940	26,000	26,005
1924	28,440	25,931	25,931
1927	28,400	24,016	26,323
1929	26,440	20,779	24,922
1930	26,090	14,322	22,328
1931	24,120	12,368	19,226
1932	24,270	10,686	18,433
1933	24,940	13,051	19,151
1934	25,030	17,418	21,042
1935	23,510	15,615	19,990

(*The Second Industrial Survey of South Wales.* Published on Behalf
of the National Industrial Development Council of Wales and
Monmouthshire. University Press Board. Vol.I. Cardiff, 1937,
p.98.)

A.11   THE EXPORTS OF TINPLATE OF VARIOUS COUNTRIES, 1929–35 (APPROXIMATE
       FIGURES)

	1929		1930		1931		1932		1933		1934		1935	
	1,000 Tons	Per cent	1,000 Tons	Per cent	1,000 Tons	Per cent	1,000 Tons	Per cent	1,000 Tons	Per cent	1,000 Tons	Per cent	1,000 Tons	Per cent
Great Britain	610	65.6	530	70.0	412	72.0	487	74.9	476	63.4	417	49.6	345	50.9
America	259	27.9	159	21.0	80	14.0	40	6.2	91	12.1	194	23.0	134	19.7
Germany	30	5.2	36	4.2	44	7.7	80	12.3	126	16.8	140	16.6	125	18.5
France	31	3.3	32	4.8	33	5.8	35	5.4	37	4.9	63	7.5	40	5.9
Italy	—	—	—	—	3	.5	8	1.2	20	2.8	28	3.3	34	5.0
Totals	930	100.0	757	100.0	572	100.0	650	100.0	750	100.0	842	100.0	678	100.0

(*The Second Industrial Survey of South Wales.* Published on Behalf
of the National Industrial Development Council of Wales and
Monmouthshire. University Press Board. Vol.I. Cardiff, 1937,
p.106.)

A.12 The trade of the ports is so largely concerned with the export of coal that our account of the mining industry will already have made it clear that a considerable shrinkage of activity at the ports has taken place since the boom year of 1923. At Cardiff, for example, exports of coal and coke which totalled 10,576,506 tons in 1913, were only 8,540,167 tons in 1923, and in the 'good' year of 1929, were 7,211,609 tons. During 1930 they fell to 6,358,004 tons, a figure lower than any recorded (some during years of war or industrial dispute) since 1882.

The port returns . . . tend to confirm the conclusions concerning the incidence of the trade depression upon different parts of the coalfield . . . The peak of Cardiff's prosperity was reached when the demand for steam coals was at its maximum. Unemployment in the steam coal valleys has been paralleled by depression at Cardiff . . .

. . . The western ports have benefitted from the maintenance of the demands for and output of anthracite; and at the same time have had the inestimable advantage conferred by a more diversified industrial hinterland than surrounds Cardiff, Barry, and Penarth.

(*An Industrial Survey of South Wales*. Board of Trade 1932. Made for the Board of Trade by University College of South Wales and Monmouthshire. H.M.S.O. 1932, p.89.)

A.13 SUMMARY OF TRADE OF SOUTH WALES PORTS (CARDIFF, SWANSEA, NEWPORT, BARRY, PORT TALBOT, AND PENARTH)

TONS

Commodity	1929	1930	1931	1932	1933	1934	1935
Coal and Coke	29,802,482	27,386,050	21,747,474	20,385,131	19,596,356	19,767,408	19,420,965
Patent Fuel	1,095,094	886,504	727,081	769,462	760,748	657,514	590,299
Iron and Steel Rails and Iron Work	586,712	378,089	279,716	252,304	268,654	303,658	327,355
Tinplates	599,502	521,845	433,148	503,685	480,376	423,623	376,874

(Extracted from *The Second Industrial Survey of South Wales*. Published on behalf of the National Industrial Development Council of Wales and Monmouthshire. University Press Board. Cardiff, 1937, Table 2, p.454.)

A.14   If we compare the risk of being unemployed for a long period run by the worker in Wales with that in the South, we find that it is fifty three times as high for the very young worker (18–24), forty three times for the young (25–34), twenty one times for the middle-aged (35–44), sixteen times for the elderly and only six times for the old.

... The average long unemployed man in the Rhondda has faced no less than fifty six months (of continuous unemployment), nearly a full five years.

(Pilgrim Trust, *Men Without Work*, Cambridge, 1938, pp.37 and 43.)

A.15   ANALYSIS ACCORDING TO THE LENGTH OF THEIR LAST SPELL OF REGISTERED UNEMPLOYMENT OF WHOLLY UNEMPLOYED MEN (AGED 18–64) APPLYING FOR INSURANCE BENEFIT OR UNEMPLOYMENT ALLOWANCES WHO WERE ON THE REGISTERS OF EMPLOYMENT EXCHANGES SERVING THE SPECIAL AREAS (ENGLAND AND WALES) AT 20TH JULY 1936, AND 22ND JULY, 1935

Date	Claimants and Applicants (Men aged 18–64) who have been on the Register for:-										
	Less than 3 months	3 months but less than 6 months	6 months but less than 9 months	9 months but less than 12 months	1 year but less than 2 years	2 years but less than 3 years	3 years but less than 4 years	4 years but less than 5 years	5 years or more	Total	12 months or more
South Wales Men											
20th July, 1936	19,403	10,761	7,242	7,445	16,525	10,076	7,641	7,582	12,324	98,999	54,148
22nd July, 1935	19,104	10,994	10,143	7,942	16,777	11,744	10,897	10,282	6,654	104,537	56,354
Increase (+) or Decrease (−) during the year	+299	−233	−2,901	−497	−252	−1,668	−3,256	−2,700	+5,670	−5,538	−2,206

(Third Report of the Commissioner for the Special Areas (England and Wales) November 1936. H.M.S.O. Cmd. 5303, 1936. Extracted from Appendix VIII.)

A.16   In the South Wales Special Area, no less than 5,884 young men between 18 and 20, and 14,114 between 21 and 24, a total of 19,998, were unemployed in May, 1936.

... On September 21, 1936, there were no fewer than 12,578

Unemployed men clearing dumps in south Wales.

juveniles under 18 years of age registered as wholly unemployed; while during the first eight months of 1936 alone
3,529 boys and girls were transferred under official schemes to
other parts of England and Wales.

*(South Wales. Report of the Labour Party's Commission of Enquiry
into the Distressed Areas.* The Labour Publications Department,
May, 1937, p.28.)

A.17   The district is living on its savings. The extent to which this is
happening was brought home to us in various ways. (a) The
share capital of the Co-operative Society which was some
£250,000 in 1920 has now fallen to £80,000. Further withdrawals are now prohibited. (b) A great proportion of the
houses formerly owned by miners have either been sold or
heavily mortgaged.

    The district has become indebted. Thus it was estimated that
there was owing to the Council from the 16,000 inhabitants in
all sorts of debts no less than £120,000, of which part took the
form of rent on the Council Houses averaging no less than £43
per house. In addition some £50,000 or £60,000 is owed to
private traders; some £15,000 further in arrears of rent to
landlords. The Council and Guardians are in turn indebted to
the Ministry of Health.

('The Distress in South Wales'. *Report of the Labour Committee
of Inquiry.* The Parliamentary Labour Party, 1928, pp.6–7.
Referring to situation in Blaina and Nantyglo.)

A.18   . . . in Glamorgan and Monmouth 694 and 610 persons,
respectively per 10,000 of the population were in receipt of Poor
Relief in April of this year, only the County of Durham (with
734 per 10,000) being higher than the two Welsh counties.
Merthyr Tydfil had 1,149 per 10,000, being second to Sheffield,
amongst the County Boroughs, with 1,152 per 10,000 of the
population.

*(Report of Investigations into the Industrial Conditions in Certain
Depressed Areas.* Ministry of Labour. Cmd. 4728. 1934.
H.M.S.O. III — South Wales and Monmouthshire. Report by
Sir Wyndham Portal. p.167.)

A.19   INSURED FEMALES PER 1,000 INSURED MALES

Area	1923	1924	1927	1929	1930
United Kingdom	348	353	354	376	384
South Wales	82	84	89	99.9	100
	1931	**1932**	**1933**	**1934**	**1935**
United Kingdom	391	377	379	374	370
South Wales	105	101	105	104	106

(*Second Industrial Survey of South Wales*. Published on behalf of the National Industrial Development Council of Wales and Monmouthshire. Vol.II, p.80. Cardiff, 1937.)

A.20   We are losing our population, and the resources which would enable us to meet our community responsibilities. Take, for example, the town of Merthyr. Its rates are on a very much reduced assessable value. Its property is losing in value every day. It is assessed at a lower level, and the rates rise in proportion or the assessable value falls. The rates stand at 28s. in the pound, of which 16s. in the pound is accounted for poor rate. The resources of local authorities have been depleted. They have been reduced, and if the depression continues, there will have to be further reduction still. We have public debts of no less than £40,000,000. The interest rate is from 6 1/2 per cent to 3 1/4 per cent. The capital debt has been considerably increased and the aggregate amount of rates is 200 per cent higher than in 1914 . . .

In Aberdare, in 1913–14 the rates were 9s.8d. in the pound, and 1934–5 20s.; in Pontypridd, in 1913–14, 10s.10d. in the pound, and in 1934–5 21s.2d; in Rhondda in 1913–14, the figure was 7s.9d. in the pound, and in 1934–5, 22s.9d.; and in Gelligaer in 1913–14 it was 11s., and in 1934–5, 24s.3d. In all the Urban Districts the county demand for public assistance is greater than the total amount of rates in 1914.

(Mr D. Grenfell. *Parliamentary Debates*. Commons. Vol.3/4. Col.2091. 15 July 1936.)

A.21 The Rhondda Urban District Council, amongst other Authorities, presented me with a list of sewerage and other works which I understand, from enquiries that I have made, are quite desirable from the point of view of public health or public convenience, but the Council has been unable to proceed with them ... In regard to certain services connected with the Maternity and Child Welfare Act and School Clinics, I am informed that these are not carried out in some districts as well as they should be owing to financial restrictions ... Further, in this same locality, I have gathered that the training and equipment of midwives, and the provision of medical and nursing staffs are not satisfactory, though I believe that both the Authorities and their staff do all that they can, within their limitations.

(*Reports of Investigations into the Industrial Conditions in Certain Depressed Areas.* Ministry of Labour. Cmd. 4728. 1934. H.M.S.O. III — South Wales and Monmouthshire. Report by Sir Wyndham Portal, p.169.)

A.22 The growing volume of unemployment in the building industry undoubtedly reflects the general industrial situation of the South Wales coalfield. It also coincides with the decline in the number of houses erected ... These factors, working together, largely account for the rapid increase in the unemployment percentages, denoting a decline in employment far more steep than in the United Kingdom ...

(*An Industrial Survey of South Wales.* Board of Trade, 1932. Made for the Board of Trade by University College of South Wales and Monmouthshire. H.M.S.O. 1932. pp.106–7.)

A.23 The Co–operative Society covering Ferndale, Maerdy and Pontygwaith showed a great falling off in sales, the figures for 1927 being £139,000 against £204,000 in 1912, £585,000 in 1920, and £203,000 in 1925 ... The debts of this society have risen from £37,000 in 1925 to £49,000 in 1927.
   ... for Aberygwynfi share capital was £14,000 in 1920, £4,000 in 1927, sales £36,000 in 1920, £13,000 in 1927, while

the debts of its members rose from £1,800 to £4,600 in the same period.

('The Distress in South Wales'. *Report of the Labour Committee of Inquiry*. The Parliamentary Labour Party. 1928. p.13, p.15.)

A.24   Hospitals and churches were graphic illustrations of the withdrawal of support in service and subscription. The hospital in Mountain Ash had a contributory list of nearly 7,000; today this number was reduced to approximately 1,400.

The erection of church buildings during the period of prosperity to meet the expanding social and spiritual needs of the community incurred debts which under normal conditions would have presented no difficulties. Today these debts were a crushing burden.

(Extract from Memorandum submitted by the United Committee of the Churches in Wales to the Prime Minister on Thursday, 22 July 1937. Quoted in *Western Mail*, Friday, 23 July 1937.)

A.25   In the continuing discussion one member said that he did not want to prevent young men and women bettering themselves by securing employment outside Merthyr Tydfil, but what they did object to was the resultant effect on the rates and Social Services generally and the continuous depopulation of these parts . . . The Commissioner suggested . . . we could not get over economic facts and, rightly or wrongly, industry was moving away from these areas and it would seem that Merthyr was 'off the map' in relation to present day Industrial Development. In these circumstances he thought it best that Merthyr Tydfil men should have the opportunity of getting work in other parts of the country.

(Minutes of report — Meeting of the Commissioner for the Special Areas (England and Wales) with the Mayor and Special Sub-Committee of County Borough of Merthyr. 20 March 1935. PRO.Lab. 23/75.)

A.26   If prosperity does not return very quickly it will return to find two kinds of men — old men, too old to work, and thousands of young men who have never in their lives done a day's work . . . the best hope for a Welsh collier nowadays is to develop into an hotel worker on the promenade in Brighton.

(Revd John Roberts (Cardiff) at the South Wales and Monmouthshire Conference convened to form a petition to the Prime Minister — at Cardiff, March 10, 1936. Quoted in *Western Mail*, Wednesday, 11 March 1936.)

A.27 . . . if transfer is to continue at this recent rapid rate, a further contraction must inevitably take place among the trades and industries which cater for the needs of those formerly engaged in basic production. Some of the region's equipment in docks and railways, warehouses, shops, hotels, and houses, must either become definitely redundant or be wasted because of partial utilization.

(*An Industrial Survey of South Wales*. Board of Trade, 1932. H.M.S.O. Made for the Board of Trade by the University College of South Wales and Monmouthshire. pp.152–3.)

A.28 We heard a little too much about depressed Wales, and not quite enough of what the unconquerable spirit of Wales had helped to achieve in bringing about her own recovery . . . Wales had never yet suffered defeat, and I join with you, as we look for the dawn which is bound to come, in saluting the unconquerable spirit of the Welsh nation.

(Sir Thomas Inskip, Minister of Defence, Guest of Honour at the annual dinner of the Honourable Society of Cymmrodorion at the Mayfair Hotel, Park Lane, London. Replying to the toast of 'Our Guests'. 24 November 1936. As quoted in *The Times*, 25 November 1936.)

A.29 So many remedies have been tried in vain. South Wales has become a bore. It is like a crying babe in the hands of an ignorant mother. It is smacked by one department and kissed by another. Why won't it go to sleep like Dorsetshire? The philanthropists are trying a bromide mixture. The Commissioner has turned himself into a Red Cross Ambulance . . . The Carnegie Trust and the Pilgrim Trust and the Society of Friends, garbed in various disguises, scatter libraries, and settlements, and allotments up and down the area . . .

('What's Wrong with Wales' — a pamphlet published *The New Statesman and Nation,* 1935. First published as a Special Supplement, 27 July 1935, pp.14–15.)

A.30   The conclusion seems to emerge . . . that a deliberate attempt to secure the introduction of new industries into the region is not only desirable on sentimental or compassionate grounds but it is justifiable as a sound measure of public economy. A policy of transfer of population unaccompanied by any provision for the man and woman who cannot be transferred save at great expense will permit a deterioration to continue which is economically wasteful of manpower and resources.

(*An Industrial Survey of South Wales.* Board of Trade. 1932. H.M.S.O. Made for the Board of Trade by the University College of South Wales and Monmouthshire, p.153.)

A.31   Wages in the smaller towns in South Wales were fixed by national agreements after the War at a rather high (comparative) level, because, at the time, the coal industry was prosperous and miners' wages were high.

    . . . e.g. Rates in Southampton are lower than in Ystalyfera, a small town in the Swansea Valley [referring to the printing trade].

(*The Second Industrial Survey of South Wales.* Published on behalf of the National Industrial Development Council of Wales and Monmouthshire. Vol.I. p.327. University Press Board, Cardiff, 1937.)

A.32   No expert adviser of an expanding business will voluntarily recommend a site in South Wales. Where are the managerial staffs to live? Where are they to play? Where to hunt? . . . Porthcawl is not Deauville . . . The Pentyrch hunt is not the

Pytchley, and the Chepstow Races . . . are neither Newmarket nor Goodwood.

(Extract from 'What's Wrong with Wales' — a pamphlet published by *The New Statesman and Nation*, 1935. First published as a Special Supplement, 27 July 1935, p.17.)

A.33   Up to about 1926 both firms made cake in bulk for the South Wales market . . . in the main their customers were the family grocers, local multiple stores and some of the bakers' shops of the mining valleys . . .

The mining valleys are still an important market for both firms, but the demand has fallen very considerably. Their most important customers — the independent grocers — have been bankrupted or crippled by an accumulation of bad debts. The total demand for cake, because of unemployment and the reduced family incomes of the men in work, has diminished and changed for better qualities.

The Dowlais firm has difficulty with rail transport because of its situation . . . but if it were in Cardiff, it could use the express goods service . . .

The Dowlais firm uses coke and gas firing, but they find the price they have to pay for the latter makes it very expensive.

The Dowlais firm suffers a disadvantage as compared with the Cardiff firm in the high rate it has to pay for electricity for heating . . .

The Cardiff firm is very well situated in regard to raw materials . . .

The Dowlais firm, on the other hand, has to pay 10/- per ton freight on its raw materials from Cardiff.

(The experience of two firms. The only ones in the area manufacturing cake on a large scale and selling wholesale quantities to retailers.)

(*The Second Industrial Survey of South Wales.* Published on behalf of the National Industrial Development Council of Wales and Monmouthshire. University Press Board, Cardiff, 1937, pp.357–61.)

A.34   In Wales . . . the exclusion of important cities and towns, such as Cardiff, Newport and Swansea, has created an artificial boundary . . . it is impossible, in my view, to determine the prospects of the mining valleys irrespective of their relation to large industrial centres nearby.

(*First Report of the Commissioners for the Special Areas (England and Wales)* July 1935. H.M.S.O. Cmd. 4957. 1935. p.8. Para. 6(8).)

A.35   . . . the whole thing is an idle and empty farce, never intended to do anything. The Government are mocking the distressed areas with a proposition of this kind . . . the Commissioners are so restricted under the proposals of the Bill that there is very little, in any case, that they will be able to do, except perhaps to initiate a bit of colour-washing of colliers' cottages to make them look pretty enough to attract new industries to the depressed mining areas . . .

(Mr Aneurin Bevan, *Parliamentary Debates. Commons.* Vol.295. Cols. 1305–1310. 3 December 1934.)

A.36   . . . it has to be admitted that no appreciable reduction of the number of those unemployed has been effected. This, however, was not to be looked for, seeing that the Special Areas Act makes no direct provision for this purpose. Such increased employment as is likely to result from the operation of the many schemes initiated will prove altogether insufficient, in the absence of a spontaneous growth of new industries and expansion of existing industries.

(*Third Report of the Commissioners for the Special Areas (England and Wales)*, November 1936. H.M.S.O. Cmd. 5303. p.3. Para.9.)

Debating the Evidence

Professor David Smith's introductory essay, *Wales between the Wars*, reminds us of the diversity of sources available to the historian of the twentieth century. Of course there has always been pictorial as well as documentary evidence to utilize and evaluate. But never has there been such a profusion of material — newsreels, television recordings, photographs, let alone the volume of novels, poetry and plays — available. Each poses its own problems of interpretation. And the homing in on the 1930s particularly, is at once a strength and a confusion. Amongst this mass of material the historian has to be more than usually selective. The act of selection is itself subjective. It informs us about the historian as well as the topic under investigation. This is even true in the case of such a mainstream historical topic as the Welsh economy. Dr Dennis Thomas has a wealth of conventional primary material at his disposal, including government reports and newspaper accounts.

Source A.1
Paradoxically we start with a source which, though treating economic matters, is essentially literary. It is necessary here to bear in mind that the historian does not only use this term in the conventional way. Certainly she/he uses such literary sources as novels and poetry. But he also uses diaries, biographies, autobiographies and personal interpretations of events to be found in such official sources as this. Essentially this extract is a personal, though informed and expert, analysis of the inter-relationship between primary industries and service industries. Such sources normally contain a blend of factual information and assertion. Distinguishing between these categories in the extract are you convinced by the argument? Does your verdict affect your view of the essay author's argument in any way?

Source A.2
Here is the kind of indispensible statistical material which underlies any analysis of economic activity in modern society. It is an official record, a government record which is highly reliable in the raw statistics on which it is based. There has never been any question of the statistics presented here having been manipulated or 'massaged'. However, there are still significant limitations in these statistics. What additional information might be helpful to the historian here?

Source A.3
Documents A.2 and A.3 would seem to complement each other, indeed Dr Thomas uses them to strengthen his argument that the traditional industries on which Welsh wealth was based were declining and

industries generating wealth elsewhere were absent. Do you agree that the documents complement each other, and what problems of interpretation do they pose?

Sources A.4 and A.5
Again we have no reason to doubt the accuracy of these statistics. What is their most obvious limitation, however?

Source A.6
It is made clear in the essay that 'it is impossible to give a comprehensive figure for total migration'. Also, in the document, the figures for migration, 1921–38, are estimates. What kinds of reasons are there for this, when government statistics in the twentieth century are sophisticated, or at least capable of being so? What use are the figures if they are 'estimates'?

Source A.7
The date of this document and the name of the body under whose aegis it was brought into existence are highly significant. In what way might both have a marked bearing on the message, or witting testimony, of the document?

Sources A.8, A.9, A.10, A.11
What, if anything, does the existence of these documents tell us about the government of the day and its attitude to Wales? In what ways does the message conveyed in Documents A.8 and A.9 differ from that conveyed in the sources A.10 and A.11? Which are the more useful sources?

Source A.12
You can see from the attribution at the foot of this document that it was produced for the Board of Trade by academics in the University College of South Wales and Monmouthshire, the former name of University College, Cardiff. Does this information have any impact on the way in which you regard this document?

Sources A.14, A.15, A.16
The information here is culled from three very different bodies. What more would you like to know about them before making generalizations

based on the documents? Is there any moral to be drawn from the fact that the information in all three is mutually reinforcing?

Sources A.17, A.18, A.20
Dr Thomas writes in his essay: 'For the individual, prolonged unemployment resulted in the exhaustion of personal earnings and family resources, growing indebtedness and a diminished standard of living.' On the evidence of these three sources, is this a statement which is easier or more difficult to handle than those he has made about industrial decline and scale of unemployment? Why?

Sources A.21, A.22, A.23, A.24
Is the variety of sources of information cited here a strength or a weakness for a historian?

Source A.25, A.26, A.27
What issues other than strictly economic ones are raised in these sources? What attitudes are displayed to these issues?

Sources A.28, A.29
What do these documents reveal about their authors?

Source A.32
What information is it important to have about this source before it can be dealt with constructively? Do you take the source seriously? What does it tell us about contemporary attitudes — and contemporary journalism?

Sources A.34, A.35, A.36
What significance would you attach to the general agreement in these disparate sources that Special Area status had been ineffective in the valleys of south Wales?

Discussion

We have already encountered a wide range of the sources available to the historian of the twentieth century. These sources can lead to an infinite range of interpretations, some of which become history textbook truisms and are passed on from generation to generation. This is certainly the case with the 1930s. The residual image of the 1930s for many, even students reading history, is of a Britain devastated by the impact of the American Wall Street crash, wracked by unemployment, driven to *hunger marches* by a series of governments rooted to the spot by conservative fiscal orthodoxy. It still comes as a revelation to many students of history to be reminded that the row upon row of suburban houses so evident in the home counties, the expansion in the radio and other electrical industries, was indicative of a considerable increase in economic activity in the years after 1934, especially, and brought prosperity as well as much greater domestic comfort to many parts of the south and the midlands. It was a prosperity underpinned by an absence of monetary inflation. Indeed there was an increase in the value of money during the period.

In some ways this makes the situation in the north east of England or in south Wales yet more unjust, though the documents indicate that there were marked disparities in rates of unemployment here, too. Document A.12, for example, reminds us that the western region of the south Wales coalfield which produced anthracite coal was far less drastically affected than the steam coal areas. However, the documents certainly bear out the author's claims about the devastating effect on Wales of the recession in primary industry (A.3, A.4), the relative permanence of this compared with England and Scotland (A.5) and the impact in terms of loss of population (A.6).

One of the reasons why the author is able to make his generalizations so confidently is that he has such a range of official sources at his disposal, both literary and statistical. The existence of these sources themselves tells us something very important about the period. We have, for example, many extracts from *An Industrial Survey of South Wales*; *The Second Industrial Survey of South Wales*, published on behalf of the National Industrial Development Council of Wales and Monmouthshire, and *The Third Report of the Commissioner for the Special Areas*, which, by their very existence, unwittingly, tell us of official concern at what was happening in Wales. We do not know from these sources if anything was being done about the situation, but we are certainly aware that the government, willingly or unwillingly, was sponsoring a quest for information and canvassing opinion on the causes of the problem. The intentional record of such material is invaluable. We must still ask about the way in which the statistics were collected — for example, who were the *insured workers* as opposed to the uninsured — but within narrow limits and certainly in relative terms, these statistics will be accurate.

Judgements on them, of course, provide new challenges of inter-pretation. The irony of the pamphlet *What's Wrong with Wales* (A.29) is not lost on us. It is an acid comment and prompts us therefore to be rather suspicious. We need to treat assertions about 'bromide mixtures' of philanthropists rather cautiously. In the absence of official action they showed concern and provided some money and some amenities. In this light we need to take the statistical information supplied by the Pilgrim Trust (A.14) as seriously as that being collected for the government. Similarly, there is no reason to doubt the statistical information provided by the Labour Party (A.16) or that of individual Labour MPs (A.20). Such statistics could then, and can now, be easily checked against others so that it would be easy to destroy a case built up on fundamental statistical inaccuracies. It is part of the strength of Dr Thomas's case that he can draw on a wide range of mutually reinforcing primary evidence.

Social Reactions to Economic Change

DEIAN HOPKIN

The enduring image of Wales in the inter-war years is one of unremitting depression, unemployment, decline and misery, a hollow-eyed nation in permanent procession to the Soup Kitchen. It is an image reinforced by the most effective literature of the period and by the carefully nurtured nostalgia of politicians. It is also an image perpetuated by historians who readily march side by side with the hungry.

It is difficult to avoid this compelling imagery, even though our historical common-sense tells us that it cannot have been like that all the time, for everyone, and everywhere. At face value, the statistics are a litany of suffering — the levels of unemployment, the condition of housing, the state of the nation's health. Between 1920 and 1938 expenditure on clothing and footwear, among the most basic human needs, fell by almost 40 per cent, representing a decline of 15 per cent in the quantity of such items purchased after allowing for falling prices. This is a more graphic indication of destitution than any rhetoric. On the other hand, there were more wireless sets in Cardiff per head of population than in Slough and more cars than in Luton in the late 1930s and a casual examination of the local press in the period suggests that for some people at least these may not have been bad times at all. Where, then, does the truth lie?

In one major field, demography, the evidence is incontrovertible. After a century of unremitting growth, the upward climb of the Welsh population suddenly ground to a B.1 halt and then went into reverse (B.1). After an intercensal rise of 13 per cent over the previous half century, there was a 2 per cent decline in the total population in the 1920s and 4 per cent in the 1930s. From a peak of 2.7 millions in 1924, the Welsh population declined steadily year by year to 2.4 millions in 1939. The variation between the counties was considerable, however. The greatest decline was in Monmouthshire and parts of rural mid-Wales, while Flintshire and Denbighshire were alone in experiencing a population increase. The impact, of course, was manifest in individual communities, both urban and rural; Nantyglo, Mynydd Islwyn, Rhymney shared the decline of Brecon, Newtown and Haverfordwest. By contrast, Colwyn Bay and Conway, if not flourishing, were maintaining their recent growth.

Another indication of demographic change is revealed by the statistics for the Welsh language. The proportion of monoglot Welsh speakers dropped dramatically from 155,000 in 1921 to 97,000 by 1931, and probably to no more than 60,000 by 1939
B.2   (B.2). But it was the decline in Welsh speakers as a whole that was most serious. While the statistics for 1921 show an increase of around 5 per cent over 1911, by 1931 the downward trend had begun and accelerated throughout the period.

Much of the decline arose because a substantial sector of the population was fleeing. This was a process which the country-side had witnessed for the best part of half a century, but the experience was new to the latterly booming industrial areas
B.3   (B.3). A combination of structural decline and cyclical depression, with its concomitants of astonishingly high unemployment levels and a general sense of pessimism about the future, forced the young, the able-bodied and the adventurous to depart in their thousands for the alluring prospects of Slough, Sussex and even New South Wales, 430,000 of them between 1921 and 1940. In the 1930s, Wales was a point of origin, not a destination, but even that came into doubt with the decline in the birth rate which accelerated in the inter-war years. In 1926 the crude rate dropped below 20 for the first time since the eighteenth century and reached its lowest point of 15.0 in 1937. The declining marriage rate was only partly responsible for this, although the variation from pre-war levels was not noticeable. There was a marriage boom, inevitably, in the immediate post-war years with the rate per 1,000 of the population reaching 19.4

in 1920, the highest level since the advent of civil marriage registers. Thereafter, there was a sharp drop to an average of around 14.5 for the remainder of the 1920s, rising slightly in the 1930s to an average of 16.0.

Even if one only half-accepts a *Malthusian* explanation of rates of marriage and procreation, the economic condition of Wales must be seen to be partly responsible for the demographic crisis. Two features of the economy bore directly on people's lives; the nature of work, and the level of real wages.

Important changes took place in a number of occupations. The gradual decline of agriculture as a major employer of labour continued, especially among women. In Carmarthenshire, the reduction in the female agricultural labour force, which had been the largest in Wales, was five times as rapid as among men between 1911 and 1931; to a lesser degree, the same is true of every other Welsh county. In the economy as a whole there was a shift away from domestic service and an increase in the clerical

B.4   work force (B.4). There was a substantial increase in the number of labourers and professional workers, and a reduction in the number of textile and clothing workers. Generally speaking, however, the inter-war years did not create new trends in employment, apart from the trend towards unemployment.

In one section of the community, however, there was a hopeful new trend. The break-up of the great agricultural estates proclaimed a new dawn for small farmers; by 1941, 37 per cent of all farms in Wales were owner-occupied compared with only 10.5 per cent in 1909. Many of these were below 20 acres, barely enough for subsistence, but for many former tenant farmers, subject to the vicissitudes of absentee landlords as well as the uncertain climate, there was at least the prospect of a new beginning and for the most enterprising the chance to prosper.

In the second place, the rapid rise in real wages which most people had experienced during and immediately after the war was followed, in the inter-war years, by much more insecure times. Even before the unexpected collapse of the international banking system, there were harbingers of misery. The folly of the Allies' reparations arrangement produced a haemorrhage, the consequences of which were felt throughout south Wales.

The average earnings of coalminers, which had trebled to 16*s*. a shift between 1914 and 1920 spiralled rapidly downwards to 8*s*. in 1921 and remained at roughly that level throughout the rest of the period. The average weekly rates of agricultural workers witnessed a similar decline from 50*s*. in 1920 to 31*s*. by 1933. For those on the dole, the level of earnings was pitiful, a mere 23*s*. a week for a couple plus 2*s*. per child.

On the other hand, although *Geddes' Axe* and the other dreadful instruments of economic surgery cast long shadows over the lives of professional Welsh families, there is no doubt that what affluence there was in the inter-war years came the way of the middle classes. If the salaries of public servants, teachers and administrators declined by around 20 per cent, prices fell even further so that their real wages actually rose.

But what could such wages and salaries buy? For those who were in work and also able to keep abreast or even ahead of falling prices it was possible to maintain a very reasonable standard of living. The range of goods on offer increased with technical advance and improvement. The main semi-official source for consumption of durable goods in the inter-war years was the 1937 Marketing Survey of the United Kingdom. Somewhat surprisingly it revealed that the purchasing power of the major south Wales towns, judged according to a formula which included wage rates and rents as well as the value and quantities of the goods consumed, compared favourably with most towns in Britain. Indeed, Cardiff was regarded as an above average market (B.5), only a little behind Greater London, while Swansea and Newport were comparable markets to cities such as Coventry, Manchester and Derby. On the other hand, these were clearly the most favoured areas of south Wales. Elsewhere the picture was bleaker. Merthyr Tydfil had a purchasing power rating of 107 against a national average of 126 while Rhondda, with 104.6, was the fourth-lowest-rated market in the United Kingdom. More specifically, there were 932 telephone subscribers in the Rhondda, one for every fifty households, while in Abercarn, the figure was one in a hundred. By contrast, in Newport, the figure was one in nine, and in Cardiff one in six. An even more telling index of differential patterns of consumption was the figures for wireless receivers,

B.5

Queen Street, Cardiff, *c.* 1939. (*Source: BBC Hulton Picture Library.*)

which were to the 1930s what the video recorder is to the 1980s. There were 56,970 wireless licences issued in Cardiff in 1937, approximately one per household; there were half as many per family in Merthyr Tydfil. Much the same picture emerges from examining figures for houses which were wired or private car registrations; generally the depressed coalfield area of south Wales lagged behind the commercial, coastal towns. In north Wales, patterns of consumption were comparable to the most prosperous areas of south Wales. In Bangor, unemployment was well below 10 per cent, virtually all the houses were wired and there was one telephone per nine households. A similar picture emerges in Wrexham, Deeside and other industrial areas, while the coastal resorts of Llandudno and Rhyl in the north and Pembrokeshire in the south were booming (B.6, B.7).

B.6
B.7

Indeed, the expansion of the holiday resorts is a reflection of a growth in tourism and holiday-making in the inter-war years. Again, the experience was class-specific though there is much evidence of working-class outings in the apocryphal charabanc to the seaside. The Edwardian love of rambling and country-walking continued, but foreign travel began to extend to less affluent classes than hitherto. Nor should we forget that it was the experience of a wet day in Barry Island in 1935 that persuaded the young Billy Butlin to inaugurate the first holiday camp in Britain, in Skegness.

There were greater opportunities for travel than ever before. Above all, the great expansion of the motor car and motor bike (often with a sidecar attached) opened up new horizons for thousands. By 1938 there were 55,000 private cars licensed in south Wales, and 21,000 in north Wales. Cardiff, with 8,300 private cars, had the largest concentration, followed by Swansea with 5,000. Yet this greatly exceeded the number of families earning more than £10 a week, which suggests that car-ownership was extending down to quite modest middle class families by the end of the 1930s.

For the remainder, public transport expanded as never before. The number of people using public trams in Wales reached 100,000 in 1919 and remained at around that level throughout the 1920s. 1921 was the peak year in terms of the miles of available track, but from 1929 onwards both mileages and passengers declined. Indeed, the decline was extremely sharp in the last two years before the Second World War, with the number of passengers falling to 35 per cent of the peak year which, ironically enough, was 1926. On the other hand, this was largely due to the vast expansion of bus services which occurred at this time.

For those who could only dream about holidays or travel, there was always the Irish Sweepstake, which began in 1930, and the new Football Pools to fuel their fantasies. Their real world, however, was dismal enough. In economically depressed communities, people were denied access to the facilities which only the more prosperous communities, with their higher yields from the rates, could afford. This is not to say that the depressed communities did not make strenuous efforts to compensate for these deficiencies. The minutes of communities such as Rhos-llannerchrugog, Brynmawr, Llanelli and Bargoed, echo with the vigorous demands of local councillors for better facilities. Parks were cultivated, public film screenings were organized, and recreations were encouraged, but they were often im-provised and short-term. In the end, employment was the only real solution.

The economic contrasts and contradictions of Wales in this period are clearly revealed in the housing market. There is plenty of contemporary qualitative evidence for the decline of housing stock, with large numbers of houses unfit for human habitation. More seriously, however, the rate of housing replacement declined over the period. In the first flush of Lloyd George's promise of 'homes fit for heroes' ambitious plans were laid. Largely through the work of *Christopher Addison*, some 28,000 houses were constructed by private enterprise and local authorities between 1919 and 1925, and a further 34,000 were built in just three years to 1928, but this was the end of the boom. Thereafter, the number of authorizations and com-pletions fell dramatically. Over the next five years, a little over 21,000 houses were built, relatively few of them by local authorities. Indeed, almost three times more houses were built in the 1930s by private builders compared to local authorities, nearly all for the middle classes. It is the private estates of bow-fronted semi-detached houses in the Uplands in Swansea,

Garden Village in Wrexham and Cyncoed and Roath in Cardiff which are the legacies of the 1930s. The working classes would have to wait for a post-war Labour government before their needs were attended to.

For the needy, of course, there were alternative ways of acquiring goods, if not property. The official returns for indictable offences known to the police reveal substantial increases from 1920 onwards; compared to an average of 6,200 in the ten years up to 1914, the post-war average from 1920 onwards was just under 10,000. The number of non-indictable prosecutions remained at roughly the pre-war level while the number of convictions showed an actual decline.

For those who could neither earn nor steal their daily bread, there was, however, only one resource. It is difficult nowadays to imagine what terrors the idea of 'public relief' held for the indigent poor. The spectre of the workhouse had only been partially alleviated by the Report of the *Poor Law Commissioners* in 1909. Poverty was still held as a sign of moral failing and personal incompetence. In the early 1920s some courageous local authorities sought to lay the ghosts of the Victorian moralists by undertaking substantially greater commitments to poor relief than the official guidelines permitted. The most celebrated of these authorities in Wales were the *Bedwellty Guardians*. Taking their cue from the *Popular Guardians* of a few years earlier, they managed to spend half a million pounds a year on a wide range of public and personal services before the government brought its crushing weight of authority to bear in 1927 and dissolved it. Other local authorities adopted a less confrontationist policy, providing discreet but real subsidies for education and other social services. Nevertheless, the Bedwellty case forced the government to re-examine its social obligations and to replace the old poor law authorities with public
B.8   assistance committees (B.8).

All of this was scant consolation for those who were in receipt of public relief. For the unemployed these were harsh
B.9   times (B.9, B.10). The daily struggle for subsistence was
B.10   compounded by the humiliating rituals to which the unemployed were continually exposed; the probing enquiries of the *Means Test* official, the threat of a loss or reduction of

benefit, the despair which came with every new rejection. The world of the unemployed was a world of rumour, false dawns and eternal twilights, alleviated only by sharing the experience of misery with others. Great energy and enterprise was devoted to providing some form of organized support for the unemployed, ranging from recreational and occupational clubs, evening educational classes and tutorials, to full scale co-operative ventures, such as the Brynmawr and Maes-yr-haf schemes (B.11, B.12). There is no doubt that these contributed in no small measure to sustaining the community infra-structures which were mortally endangered by the economic holocausts of the 1930s.

B.11
B.12

In general, however, successive inter-war governments chose to ignore the evidence of economic deprivation, preferring to regard the unemployed as unfortunate but necessary casualties of a brutal economic reality. No government, however, could safely ignore the irrefutable evidence of the medical officers of health and the specialized committees of enquiry into infectious diseases. Despite the work of the *Welsh National Memorial Association* in fighting *tuberculosis*, the Welsh statistics remained grim. Seventeen sanitoria were opened, the death rate fell by 38 per cent but in a report in 1939 it was revealed that Wales supplied the seven counties which headed the list for the whole of England and Wales for this disease. Other diseases, too, were rife, including diphtheria and scarlet fever, and expert opinion was virtually unanimous in attributing many of these to the high level of malnutrition (B.13). While the steps which were taken in the 1930s to combat this scourge were largely ineffective, there is no doubt that the statistics culled from this mass of human suffering, and the chastening experience of those who had to deal with it, laid the foundation for the revolution in public health which came in the 1940s.

B.13

In the midst of economic adversity, moreover, there were some rays of hope for the future. The inter-war years saw bolder steps towards an adequate system of public education, at all levels, than ever before. Expenditure on elementary education rose by 44 per cent, while university income rose by 91 per cent and expenditure by 74 per cent. A fourth university college was opened in Swansea, while in Harlech a bold new experiment in

Coleg Harlech, 1939.

adult education was successfully launched. Perhaps the most important advances were made in secondary education, with 37 new schools being opened between 1919 and 1938, an increase of over 30 per cent; the number of pupils rose by almost 80 per cent. Many of these, of course, were pupils who had hitherto remained in the elementary schools as pupil teachers; indeed the total number of children in elementary schools declined by 24 per cent but this in turn was in large measure due to the substantial decline in the birth rate. In general, there is no doubt that educational provision and standards improved in the inter-war years.

On the other hand, if education was on the increase, religiosity as measured by church attendance was, on the whole, on the wane. Attendance at Sunday schools, for example, fell sharply in these years. By 1939 there were 27 per cent fewer *Congregational* pupils attending Sunday school, 30 per cent fewer *Baptists*, 31 per cent fewer Anglicans and 40 per cent fewer *Calvinistic Methodists*. This reflects a general fall in attendance

B.14 and affiliation in all the major nonconformist chapels (B.14). Even the Church in Wales suffered. In the wake of disestablishment, the number of Easter communicants increased, but the number of baptisms fell by 30 per cent. Indeed, the only major church to show any expansion were the Roman Catholics, with an almost 50 per cent increase in membership and a 66 per cent increase in the number of marriages solemnized. In the long term this helps to explain the boom in the number of pupils attending Roman Catholic schools in Wales in the post-war

B.15 years (B.15).

One explanation for this change, much favoured by an older generation of chapel-goers, is the rise of the cinema and dance-hall which offered an irresistible lure to a generation struggling to forget the horrors of the First World War. The 1920s and 1930s were an age of celluloid heroes and heroines, when the Hollywood stars lit up every coal-dark valley. It was also an age of gramophone records and popular music, and of the wireless

B.16 (B.16).

Sport, too, offered a release from the harsh real world, even though it was touched all too often by the turns and eddies of the economic current. The inter-war years were golden years of

Association Football in Wales with six Welsh teams in the Football League. In 1926 Swansea Town enjoyed a record income of over £33,000 but by the early 1930s the general depression in south Wales was badly affecting gates and in 1935 the club launched an appeal entitled 'Save the Club from Decline'. Not for the last time, the members rallied around and ensured the continuation of the club. Rugby, too, felt the pinch, with gross revenues of clubs like Cardiff plummeting to half the pre-war level. In rugby, moreover, the situation was complicated by the competition between the professional and amateur codes. During the inter-war years, 48 Welsh international players accepted professional terms and 'went north', often for substantial sums of money. Many more lesser-known men followed in their train. That they did so is hardly surprising. To an unemployed man, the prospect of an immediate cash sum, perhaps the equivalent of two years' earnings, together with the prospect of generous match bonuses, was often too much to resist, even in the face of the life-time ban from Rugby Union which invariably followed. In the 1920s, however, the North began to encroach on the South. Major matches were staged in Pontypridd and Cardiff, watched by thousands of spectators, and although the professional game was never established in Wales, the enthusiastic rugby follower B.17 was spoilt for choice in these years (B.17).

In other sports, too, these were good years. Glamorgan entered the first-class championship and in the 1930s Maurice Turnbull's excellent teams regaled crowds as never before, and in some people's view, never since, with players of the calibre of Dai Davies, Spencer, Sullivan, Able and, of course, the wonderful opening partnership of Emrys Davies and Arnold Dyson. To cap it all, in 1937 Emrys Davies achieved the unique Glamorgan record of 2,000 runs and 100 wickets in one season. In the altogether more individual sport of boxing, too, there were bouts to remember, with the emergence of Tommy Farr, immortalized in Wales as 'the man who nearly beat Joe Louis'.

If organized sport or the Saturday night hop helped to channel latent social violence into an ordered form, there were times when nothing could prevent the frustration and anger of the underprivileged from spilling over into the streets. In

Emrys Davies and Arnold Dyson, inter-war Glamorgan batsmen.

retrospect it is difficult to explain why Wales and the north of England did not follow the European path towards the twin poles of communism and fascism which, after all, flourished in similar conditions of economic deprivation and political bankruptcy. But there were confrontations and even pitched battles, usually between police and unemployed workers. Strikes were often accompanied by some violence, as in Ammanford in 1925, though there was nothing on the scale of pre-war battles such as Tonypandy or Llanelli. Social violence, however, was not confined to the industrial sphere. In Cardiff there was continuing racial tension throughout the inter-war years (B.18).

B.18

The enduring symbols of working-class resistance to economic illogic were the stay-down strikes of the 1930s. In the wake of the débâcle of 1926, organized unions were forced into political retreat and this was greatly compounded by the international financial collapse after 1929. Seizing their advantage, the coalowners attempted to organize the more pliable workers into 'company unions' by a combination of inducement and threat; the Welsh version of the *Spencer Union* in north and south Wales attracted as many as 50,000 members. Many more resisted, most dramatically in Nine Mile Point colliery near Bedwas, where a stay-down strike of a fortnight's duration helped to galvanize support for the *South Wales Miners' Federation*. By the end of 1935, the company unions were all but defeated.

There were few real victories or victors in the inter-war years. The struggle for peace floundered with the rise of European fascism, the struggle for better standards of living faltered in the face of profound economic obstacles. If the image of a destitute Wales persists, it is perhaps because that was the commonly experienced truth. Yet, for the lucky few, there were good times. High society continued its relentless search for new extravagances; the prophets of fashion were lionized as ever. The young found their compensations, the salary-earners their material satisfaction. But for far too many, the inter-war years were bleak years, in which the nightmare of French battlefields of the recent past was compounded by the hopelessness of the present. In the inter-war years, the future looked very distant.

Sources

B.1   POPULATION 1. TOTAL POPULATION AND INTERCENSAL CHANGES BY SEX, WALES 1801–1971

| Date of Census | POPULATION | | | INTERCENSAL CHANGE | | | | | |
| | Males | Females | Total | AMOUNT | | | PER CENT | | |
				Males	Females	Total	Males	Females	Total
1801 March 9/10	279,407	307,838	587,245						
1811 May 26/27	322,371	310,969	673,340	42,964	43,131	86,105	15.38	14.01	14.66
1821 May 27/28	390,735	403,419	794,154	68,364	52,450	120,714	21.21	14.94	17.93
1831 May 29/30	445,702	458,698	904,400	54,967	55,279	110,246	14.07	13.70	13.88
1841 June 6/7	518,372	527,701	1,046,073	72,670	69,003	141,673	16.30	15.04	15.66
1851 March 30/31	581,840	581,299	1,163,139	63,468	53,598	117,066	12.24	10.16	11.19
1861 April 7/8	641,652	644,761	1,280,413	59,812	63,462	123,274	10.28	10.92	10.60
1871 April 2/3	706,048	706,535	1,412,583	64,396	61,774	126,170	10.04	9.58	9.81
1881 April 3/4 (1)	786,322	785,458	1,571,780	80,274	78,923	159,157	11.37	11.17	11.27
1891 April 5/6 (a)	892,256	879,195	1,771,451	105,934	93,737	199,671	13.47	11.93	12.70
1891 (b)	892,256	879,195	1,771,451						
1901 March 31/Ap. 1	1,011,458	1,001,418	2,012,876 (2)	119,202	122,223	241,425	13.36	13.90	13.63
1911 April 2/3	1,231,739	1,189,182	2,420,921	220,281	187,764	408,045	21.78	18.75	20.27
1921 June 19/20	1,329,994	1,326,480	2,656,474	98,255	137,298	235,553	7.98	11.55	9.73

1931 April 26/27	1,293,805	1,299,527	2,593,332	−36,189	−26,953	−63,142	−2.72	−2.03	−2.38
1939 Mid-year	1,228,000	1,259,000	2,487,000	−65,805	−40,527	−106,332	−5.09	−3.12	−4.10
1951 April 8/9	1,270,103	1,328,572	2,598,675	42,103	69,572	111,675	3.43	5.53	4.49
1961 April 23/24	1,291,764	1,352,259	2,644,023	21,661	23,687	45,348	1.71	1.78	1.75
1971 April 25/26	1,327,507	1,403,697	2,731,204	35,743	51,438	87,181	2.77	3.80	3.30

1) 1891 (a) Ancient County
         (b) Administrative County
      All figures 1801-81 for Ancient Counties
      All figures 1901-71 for Administrative Counties

2) Boundary change 1891/1901:-
    Sum of counties in 1891, for areas as constituted 1901, is 1,771,430

The source for all figures for Table 1 is the *Census Returns* 1801-1971.

(L. John Williams, *Digest of Welsh Historical Statistics*, Volume I, Cardiff, 1985, p.7.)

B.2   POPULATION AND LANGUAGE. NUMBER OF WELSH-SPEAKERS BY SEX IN WALES, 1891-1971.

	Population aged 3 yrs & over			Welsh-speaking			Speaking both English & Welsh			Total Welsh Speakers		
	Persons	Males	Females	Persons	Males	Females	Persons	Males	Females	Persons	Males	Females
1891[1]	1,685,614			508,036			402,253			910,289[2]		
1901	1,864,696	937,236	927,460	280,905	137,333	143,572	648,919	324,539	324,380	929,824[2]	461,872	467,912
1911	2,247,927	1,144,694	1,105,233	190,292	92,757	97,555	787,074	395,907	391,167	977,366[2]	488,644	488,722
1921	2,486,740	1,243,768	1,242,972	155,989	76,591	79,389	766,103	381,966	384,137	922,092[2]	458,557	463,535
1931	2,472,378	1,232,580	1,239,798	97,932	48,629	49,303	811,329	407,428	403,901	909,261	456,017	453,204
1951[3]	2,472,429	1,205,506	1,266,923	41,155	19,528	21,627	673,531	328,033	345,498	714,686	347,561	367,125
1961	2,518,711	1,227,512	1,291,199	26,223	13,542	12,681	629,799	301,747	328,032	656,002	315,289	340,713
1971[4]	2,602,915	1,261,705	1,341,255	32,725	15,865	16,860	509,700	239,925	269,775	542,425	255,790	286,630

(L. John Williams, *Digest of Welsh Historical Statistics*, Volume I, Cardiff, 1985, p.78.)

Tommy Farr. (*Source: BBC Hulton Picture Library.*)

B.3   The other general consideration is that Wales is primarily a national, not an economic, unit, and that economic policies should be framed in the light of this fact. There are many issues, including particularly the question of communications, which need to be judged in the light of Welsh national feeling; but undoubtedly the most important is the problem of controlling the location of industry. It is inconsistent with the preservation of the Welsh culture and traditions that a solution to the economic difficulties of Wales should again be found, as it was before the war, in extensive migration to other parts of Great Britain, or even in large-scale movements of population over long distances within Wales itself. Movements of these kinds occurred before the war, and they may well recur afterwards; but there is no essential reason for them. It is clear from an examination of the problems of the Eastern valleys of South Wales or of the depressed Western valleys of the anthracite belt that some movement of population will be needed; but this movement need not be so great as to involve losing touch with the areas from which migrants come, and in most cases it should be possible to establish new industries within daily reach of workers living in their existing homes, even where they cannot be found work actually in their own home districts. Substantial measures of re-housing and general redevelopments will be needed throughout Wales after the war; it should be possible to plan these measures so as to bring population and new industries very much closer together than in the past, without in any way encouraging the break-up of the life of Welsh communities.

(Michael Fogarty, *Prospects of the Industrial Areas of Great Britain*, Chapter 3: Wales and Monmouthshire. London, 1945. Nuffield College Social Reconstruction survey.)

B.4   LABOUR 1. OCCUPATIONS, WALES, 1801–1971
C. 1911–71

	Males						Females					
	1911[1]	1921	1931	1951	1961	1971	1911[1]	1921	1931	1951	1961	1971
1 Fishing	1,282	1,879	2,379	1,334	730	470	68	35	18	3	—	20
2 Agriculture	102,371	95,480	92,510	79,457	61,230	45,130	20,192	11,355	8,606	10,267	6,470	7,620
3 Gas, Coke and Chemicals	1,342	5,011	3,489	9,408	11,440	12,090	229	102	81	1,348	1,420	1,020
4 Metal Manufacturing and Engineering	94,436	98,558	81,449	112,430	142,370	160,120	3,859	4,527	1,627	7,345	13,910	19,550
5 Mining and Quarrying	256,250	274,682	234,554	110,000	79,470	36,500	268	146	32	32	20	60
6 Woodworkers (+ Cork and Cane)	23,325	20,575	17,770	19,667	17,580	17,330	493	170	72	225	300	470
7 Leather Workers, Fur Dressers	9,057	5,544	4,897	3,325	2,130	1,620	1,007	211	132	1,011	800	1,390
8 Textile Workers	6,856	1,876	1,291	1,892	1,530	2,850	7,358	1,629	2,237	2,106	2,050	2,120
9 Clothing Workers	8,030	6,342	4,718	3,131	1,930	2,220	32,464	19,436	10,447	13,116	11,710	13,130
10 Food, Drink and Tobacco	8,549	8,824	8,878	7,534	10,930	9,170	1,976	2,609	1,912	2,831	3,150	3,690
11 Paper and Printing	4,966	3,824	3,768	3,170	3,940	4,850	1,933	1,272	1,120	1,291	1,700	2,410
12 Building and Contracting	35,928	38,735	43,227	63,098	30,690	31,900	20	100	42	81	20	80
13 Makers of Other Products (Rubber, Plastics etc.)	50	5,671	3,833	2,695	6,450	9,950	10	216	160	1,395	3,940	5,240
14 Painters and Decorators	6,652	8,019	8,503	12,113	12,410	11,820	2	82	85	397	540	480
15 Stationary Engine and Crane Drivers	14,826	20,203	20,965	22,472	26,990	25,970			23	150	130	170
16 Labourers (n.e.c.)	23,145	39,264	42,371	67,736	77,120	72,350	77	446	131	17,988	5,260	6,150

17 Transport and Communication	89,720	88,674	94,774	86,167	74,660	64,080	2,679	2,920	2,597	5,353	4,800	5,830
18 Warehousemen, Store-keepers, Packers, Bottlers etc.	212	5,727	6,880	12,972	18,190	19,870	6	1,294	1,552	4,416	6,470	8,480
19 Clerical Workers	16,695	21,746	25,986	36,715	45,320	41,300	2,763	12,303	13,179	45,393	63,600	85,420
20 Sales Workers	49,683	59,026	77,211	60,996	58,440	50,780	15,995	32,191	34,165	42,219	52,180	54,050
21 Services, Sport and Recreation (inc. Personal Service)	20,393	21,730	25,877	31,960	34,680	39,510	106,719	94,827	98,234	67,059	67,590	95,230
22 Administrators and Managers	—	9,578	4,510	15,681	21,480	28,680	—	3,323	198	1,357	1,190	2,410
23 Professional, Technical Workers, Artists	21,282	22,117	23,829	37,326	56,720	66,140	16,854	22,536	23,580	30,334	39,350	48,850
24 Armed Forces	3,000	4,933	2,746	20,776	11,640	7,450	—	—	—	641	230	290
25 Inadequately Described Occupations	4,448	9,349	34,187	8,567	18,390	16,200	245	936	5,763	2,465	7,980	22,480
26 Glass, Ceramics, Cement	5,096	3,040	2,070	2,901	2,580	2,040	484	483	146	498	560	509
TOTAL OCCUPIED	807,594	880,407	872,672	833,523	829,040	780,390	215,681	213,149	206,139	259,361	295,550	387,230
27 Retired and Unoccupied	144,895	123,643	95,533	135,455	154,470	215,095	696,687	792,497	773,655	779,844	759,050	701,430

[1] The Figures for 1911 represent an attempt to redistribute the information from the 1911 Census on the same basis as that used for 1921–1971.

(L. John Williams, *Digest of Welsh Historical Statistics*, Volume I, Cardiff, 1985, p.97.)

B.5

Cardiff

MARKETING SURVEY'S PURCHASING POWER INDEX (1938) 130.7 (1937) 129.7

Population

Estimated total (1937)	220,200
Total insured persons (1938)	70,970
Employed (% insured) (June 1938)	82.7
On Poor Relief (1938)	8,627
Total Census	223,589

Males: 107,309 Females: 116,280

Under 14: 53,158	Occupied, 14 and over 100,322	
Out of work	Males 14,586;	Female 2,600
Unoccupied, retired	Males 8,069;	Female 62,040

Towns and Villages within 5 miles

Barry, Caerphilly, Penarth, Michaelston-le-Pit, Rumney, Whitchurch.
Total: 92,386

Standard of Living Factors (1938)

Telephone subscribers (1937) 7,789;	(1938)	8,288	
Private cars licensed (1937) 7,612;	(1938)	8,290	
Commercial vehicles licensed (1937) 2,072;	(1938)	2,153	
Wireless licences		56,970	
New houses built (1936) 1,400	(1937)	1,251	
No. of dwellings at diff. rateable values (1938)		47,542	

Industries: Docks — engineering — chemicals — smelting — iron and tin plate, etc. — (exports coal, machinery, etc.).

Private Families

Estimates (1937) 55,050	Total (1931) 54,820
Class A (£1,500 a year and over)	3,250
Class B (over £5 and under £10 per week)	7,650
Class C (over £2 10s. and under £5 per week)	32,700
Class D (£2 10s. a week and under)	11,450

Public Services Data (1938)

Amount of rates in £ (1938)	12s. 6d.
Amount of rates in £ (1937)	12s. 1d.
Amount of rates in £ (1936)	12s. 1d.
Total rateable value (1937) £1,851,963;	(1938) £1,824,815
Average per head of population	£8 9s.
No. of schools	Elem. 54; Sec. 4
No. of scholars	Elem. 30,291; Sec. 3,208
No. of houses in area	47,542

Electricity Supply:
Cardiff Corporation Electricity Dept.
Charges L. 3d.; H. 1d. –¾d.; P. 1d. per unit
Voltage A.C. 200/230 v.
Houses wired 47,351; A.C. 45,535; D.C.

£35 and over 4,096
Under £35 and over £13 33,902
£13 and under 9,544
Dog licences 9,936
Cinemas 15; Seats 20,965
Cinemas 6; Seats unascertainable

Gas Supply:
Cardiff Gas Light & Coke Co.
Charges .... 9.3d sliding to 6.5d. per therm
Town Clerk: D. KENVYN REES
M.O.H.: J.G.G.WILSON, M.D, M.R.C.P.

Retail Outlets

Outlet	No.	Outlet	No.	Outlet	No.
Bakers, pastrycooks	116	Fruit, greengrocers	312	Men's outfitters	65
Bicycle dealers	61	Grocers, prov. dealers	817	Women's outfitters	40
Boot, shoe dealers	198	Men's hairdressers	154	Stationers, newsagents	231
Butchers, pork butchers	261	Women's hairdressers, beauty shops	58	Sports stores	12
Chemists	88	Ironmongers	59	Tobacconists	289
Confectioners	400	Jewellers	33	Tailors	106
Dairies	175	Laundries	18	Transport contractors	42
Drapers	163	Milk Bars	9	Wireless dealers	53
Fishmongers	101	Off licences	81	Co-op. stores & branches	18
Fried fish dealers	85	Public houses	221	Department stores	5
Furniture dealers	73			Fixed price stores	4
Garages	98				

Employment Analysis

Industry	Male	Female
Fishing	334	
Agriculture	481	38
Mining, quarrying	476	43
Non-metalliferous products	414	9
Bricks, pottery, glass	137	1
Wood furniture (inc. basket ware)	1,241	93
Paper goods, stationery requisites	408	176
Printing, bookbinding, photography	1,195	446
Building, decorating, contracting	3,473	34
Rubber mftrs. (exc. clothing, belting)	48	15

	Male	Female
Chemical, dyes, explosives, paint, oils	377	72
Metal mftrs. (exc. electrical apparatus, precious metals, plate)	5,567	491
Elec. apparatus, cables, install.	577	96
Prec. metals, jewellery (+ watches, etc)	60	8
Textile mftrs. (inc. cellulose, but not dress, except knitted goods)	159	135
Skins, leather, leather substitutes (not clothing, footwear)	83	45
Clothing mftrs. (inc. boots, shoes other than rubber, but no knitted goods)	1,009	1,734
Food, drink, tobacco	2,860	1,761
Musical instruments	90	13
Other manufacturing industries	201	137
Gas, water, electricity	1,046	48
Transport, communications	13,667	338
Commerce, finance, insurance	13,554	6,113
Public administration, defence	5,460	2,316
Professions	1,840	1,731
Entertainments, sport	673	426
Personal service (inc. hotels, catering)	2,378	8,733
Other industries	228	48
TOTAL IN INDUSTRIES	58,036	25,100

Professional Occupations

	Male	Female
Clergymen (Anglican Church)	57	
Roman Catholic priests, monks, nuns	14	25
Ministers of other religious bodies	118	1
Judges, stip. magistrates, barristers	16	1
Solicitors	89	1
Physicians, surgeons, etc.	171	20
Dental practitioners	71	7
Veterinary surgeons, practitioners	10	
Teachers (not music)	544	1,098
Professional Engineers:		
Civ. 120, Mech. 62, Min. 18. Total	199	1
Architects	45	
Ship designers, surveyors, etc.	18	
Chartered, incorp. accountants	115	1
Authors, editors, journalists	100	9
Other professional occupations	631	1,104

Media and Services

(a) Press Media pub. from Cardiff:-

Press Facilities

Mornings: WESTERN MAIL & SOUTH WALES NEWS, St. Mary's Street, Cardiff: 7000.

Evenings: SOUTH WALES ECHO & EVENING EXPRESS, Cardiff: 7000.

Weeklies: SOUTH WALES FOOTBALL ECHO & EXPRESS, Cardiff: 7000; pub. Sat.

WEEKLY MAIL & CARDIFF TIMES, St. Mary Street, Cardiff: 7000; pub. Fri. & Sat.

(b) The National Newspaper, Magazine and Periodical Press (see p. 59).

Poster Services

CARDIFF & GLAMORGAN ADVERTISING CO., LTD. 59-63, Penarth Rd., Cardiff: 522.

CENTRAL RHONDDA & DISTRICT BILLPOSTING CO., 117, St. Mary Street, Cardiff: 3404.

GRIFFITHS & MILLINGTON, LTD., 6/7, St. John's Sq., Cardiff: 6381.

PERRY PUBLICITY, 102, Broadway, Cardiff: 7403.

Sampling and House-to-House Distribution

PERRY PUBLICITY, 102, Broadway, Cardiff: 7403.

Railway Services

G.W.

Airport

PENGAM MOORS

Factory Sites

GEO H. WHITAKER, City Engineer and Surveyor, Development Section, City Hall, Cardiff.

(*Marketing Survey of the United Kingdom*. London, 1937.)

B.6

North Wales

Distribution of Population

	Urban	Rural	Total
Population (mid-1937)			535,130
Sep. families (mid-1937)			135,475
Population (census)			531,069
Separate families	55,414	78,953	134,367
Children under 14	46,071	73,100	119,171

	Urban	Rural	Total
Domestics per family			.17
Families in 8-rm. dwellings	6,758	7,017	13,775
Percentage of whole	12.2	8.9	10.3
Total insured persons			105,940
Unemployment (June, 1938)			18.6

Standard of Living Factors

Private cars licensed (1938)	21,175
Commercial cars licensed (1938)	5,350
Wireless licences (1938)	79,122

Telephone subscribers (1937)	14,785
Rateable value (exc. County Boros., 1938)	£2,478,718
Rates per head (exc. County Boros., 1938)	£4 12s. od.

Professional Occupations

	Male	Female
Clergymen (Anglican Church)	503	105
Roman Catholic priests, monks, nuns	74	2
Ministers of other religious bodies	672	
Judges, stip. magistrates, barristers	20	
Solicitors	229	4
Physicians, surgeons, etc.	382	30
Dental practitioners	156	5
Veterinary surgeons, practitioners	72	1

	Male	Female
Teachers (not music)	1,518	2,996
Professional Engineers:		
Civ. 299, Mech. 100, Min. 41. Total	439	1
Architects	105	
Ship designers, surveyors, etc.	5	
Chartered, incorp. accountants	84	1
Authors, editors, journalists	148	16
Other professional occupations	1,105	2,398

(*Marketing Survey of the United Kingdom*, London, 1923.)

B.7   The changing scene in Pembrokeshire:

Outwardly the new era is mostly evident on the coast — the usual rash of newly built bungalows on the dunes and on the cliff. And need the affront have been so obvious? Might not the rest of the tiles have been grey-green, instead of that florid red, to harmonize with the quiet sad colours of the dune land? And there is the danger, growing greater yearly, that you and I who love this grand coast may be barred from the cliffs and the shore where the land has been bought to be 'developed' . . . There is in progress — and it has been proceeding for a quarter of a century and more — a steady 'suburbanization' of the life of the country districts . . .

(Dr E. Roland Williams, *Tenby Observer*, 11 November 1938.)

B.8   Co-operative Society.

The Co-operative movement in South Wales has been very flourishing in the mining towns, much more than in Cardiff, Newport and Swansea. The Blaina Industrial and Provident Society is the biggest in South Wales. It has branches in nine towns. I have gone into the finances and working of the Society thoroughly, and have the balance-sheets and reports for two half-yearly trading periods. The justification for the somewhat extended treatment that follows is that the Society is virtually the food-depot or Food Ministry for the people of Blaina.

There is no doubt that the Society is, next to the Ministry of Labour and the Poor Law Union, the most important agent in feeding the Blaina population. The Society has suffered heavily, as the details following show, but, supported by the immense resources built up in the past years, the Co-operative Wholesale Society, and the spirit of co-operation, it is facing the present conditions in a manner not possible to a private trading concern.

In comparing the two periods ended January 17, 1921, and June 26, 1922, period must always be read to consist of twenty-nine weeks. This difference of six weeks does not, in so great a contrast as the two periods show, affect the conclusions to be drawn.

SHARE CAPITAL ACCOUNTS

Total share capital—January 17, 1921 .... £249,210
    (Blaina, £61,229)
    (Abertillery, £50,179)
Total share capital—June 26, 1922 .... £111,542
    (Blaina, £19,041)
    (Abertillery, £25,479)
Contributions to share capital—January 17, 1921 .... £36,694
    (Blaina, £10,986)
    (Abertillery, £8,730)
Contributions to share capital—June 26, 1922 .... £2,951
    (Blaina, £989)
    (Abertillery, £699)
Withdrawals of share capital—January 17, 1921 .... £51,568
    (Blaina, £18,314)
    (Abertillery, £10,240)
Withdrawals of share capital—June 26, 1922 .... £4,226
    (Blaina, £820)
    (Abertillery, £1,537)

N.B.—The Society stopped withdrawals early this year, save as against goods supplied.

PENNY BANK DEPOSITS

Depositors' Balances—January 17, 1921 .... £59,346
    (Blaina, £13,031)
    (Abertillery, £9,905)
Depositors' Balances—June 26, 1922 .... £25,202
    (Blaina, £3,450)
    (Abertillery, £4,092)
Half-yearly Deposits—January 17, 1921 .... £18,581
    (Blaina, £4,490)
    (Abertillery, £3,353)
Half-yearly Deposits—June 26, 1922 .... £2,097
    (Blaina, £204)
    (Abertillery, £463)
Half-yearly Withdrawals from January 17, 1921 .... £21,664
    (Blaina, £5,369)
    (Abertillery, £4,878)
Half-yearly Withdrawals—June 26, 1922 .... £8,707

TRADING ACCOUNTS

Sales for year 1920 .... £800,641 or £15,396 per week
Sales for year 1921 .... £495,511 or £9,529 per week
Sales for 23 weeks, 1922 .... £156,163 or £6,790 per week

This is a reduction of 55.9 per cent. from 1920 and 28.7 per cent. from 1921.

(The Third Winter of Unemployment. The Report of an Enquiry undertaken in the Autumn of 1922, London, 1924, pp.181–3.)

B.9   Example 1.

Mr E. P. of Aberdare, Glamorgan. Number in family, man, wife, and four children, aged two, four, six, and nine years. Income per week from unemployment allowance is 38*s*. Conditions in the home are that all cooking has to be done on an open fire; there is no gas-stove. There are no decent cupboards or meat safes. By way of utensils the family have one kettle with a broken spout, three saucepans, one frying-pan, and one pot. There are two bowls with holes stopped up with pieces of rag. No dinner-plates, no bread-knife. Only four cups and two saucers for six in the family, two knives and two spoons, three forks and four small plates. The floor of the kitchen in which they live is bare stone, with no lino or carpet covering. There is only one blanket in the family, no sheets, no pillow-cases. Articles of clothes such as old coats are mostly used for bed-covering. A rent of 8*s*. 6*d*. a week is paid, 1*s*. 3*d*. insurance, 3*s*. 4*d*. coal, 1*s*. 6*d*. light, and an average of 2*s*. for boot repairs, etc., leaving £1 1*s*. 5*d*. for food, clothes, and miscellaneous expenditure for six people. There are only three chairs for six people. Two spring mattresses in the bedroom are broken, and the room has no furniture in it besides the bed, not even a table on which to place a candle. There is electric light in two out of the four rooms, but one is completely empty.

Mrs E. M. W. of Pontypool, Monmouth. There are nine in the family, the ages of the children being fourteen, thirteen, eleven, seven, five, three, and two. The income from all sources is £2 7*s*. a week. Living-conditions in the home are that all food has to be cooked on the open fire — there is no gas-stove or oven. There is only one small cupboard for food and no meat safe. In regard to cooking utensils, the family has only one kettle, one small frying-pan, two small saucepans. Utensils for preparing food consist of only one bowl, which is used for making puddings and to wash up in. They have only seven cups and saucers between nine persons, two knives, six small spoons, six forks, and eight plates. The family live in three rooms, one living-kitchen and two small bedrooms. The kitchen has a stone floor and the bedrooms have bare boards; no lino. There are two full-size beds and one small bed. In bedclothes the family have only two flannelette blankets on each bed, one quilt and one sheet, three pillow-cases. All bed-clothing is very thread-bare and has little warmth. The small bed does not belong to them; they have it only on loan. Four boys sleep in one bed and two boys sleep in the small bed. Husband and wife and child two years of age sleep in the other bed. The springs in one of the beds are badly broken and there is no money to get a new mattress. The house is old and very damp and cold. In a statement appended by the signatory who verifies the correct-ness of the above, he says: 'I have known the family for a number of years. Both parents are very sober and industrious persons and the mother strives very hard to keep her children clean and respectable. The family endeavoured to get a special grant from the U.A.B. [Unemployment Assistance Board] in order that they could make good the deficiency in household goods, but this was refused. The mother is now suffering from a skin disease which is considered to have been brought on by poor quality food and nervous tension.'

(From Wal Hannington, *The Problem of the Distressed Areas*, 1937, pp.65–6, 67.)

B.10   A casual visitor to Rhondda, walking through one of its shopping-centres, might not notice many visible signs of a depressed area. As is frequently remarked, the people of the valley cling tenaciously to their standards. If, however, we should accompany a housewife on her weekly shopping expedition and observe how careful she must be not to deviate from the routine of expenditure which the limitations of her unemployment income dictate, we shall begin to realize something of the monotony and anxiety of her life. The following budgets show the expenditure of two unemployed families as actually spent during the current week.

MRS A. — EXPENDITURE OF FAMILY OF FOUR
(HUSBAND, WIFE AND TWO CHILDREN)

Income—£1 10 6

	s.	d.	£	s.	d.
Rent				7	o
Food—	*s.*	*d.*			
Milk and bread	4	o			
14 lbs potatoes	1	3			
2 lbs butter	2	2			
½ lb margarine (for cakes)		3½			
½ lb cheese		4½			
2 packets flour		5			
4 lbs sugar		9			
½ lb tea		8			
1 lb currants		5½			
Meat for weekend	2	o			
Meat for Wednesday and Thursday	1	o			
Cabbage for weekend		4			
				13	8½
Other household expenditure—					
Coal	2	6			
Electric light	1	o			
2 boxes matches		2			
1 lb soap		5			
1 packet washing powder		3			
Polish (floor, boot, metal etc. according to need)		6			
				4	10
Insurances				1	1
Boot and clothing clubs				3	o
Doctor and Hospital					4
Sunday paper and sundries					6½
			£1	10	6

MRS B. — EXPENDITURE OF FAMILY OF FIVE
(HUSBAND, WIFE AND THREE CHILDREN)

Income—£1 13 6

			£	s.	d.
Rent				8	6
Food—	*s.*	*d.*			
Bread	4	0			
2 tins condensed milk		3			
Potatoes	1	6			
2½ lbs butter	2	6			
½ lb margarine		2			
½ lb lard		4			
1 lb cheese		8			
4 lbs flour		7			
4 lbs sugar		9			
1 lb tea		8			
½ lb currants		3			
2 lb pot jam		10½			
Cocoa		2			
Salt		1			
1 lb bacon		10			
1 lb peas		2½			
Meat for Sunday	1	0			
				14	10
Other household expenditure—					
Coal and coke	1	8½			
Light and matches	1	0			
2 lbs soap and Persil		7½			
Polishes		4½			
			3	8½	
Insurances				1	3
Boot and clothing clubs				4	0
Doctor and hospital					4
			£1	12	9½

(*The Geographical Magazine*, March 1936.)

B.11   The Maes-yr-haf Settlement is in the centre of the valleys, a section of the 'derelict area' of South Wales, where a very high percentage of the workers are unemployed. In attempting to meet the educational needs of people in this position, it is facing a new situation; constantly presenting great difficulties and problems. But these very problems bring opportunity for experiment, the breaking of fresh ground. The keynote of the work of Maes-yr-haf has been continued adaptation to the needs of a society struggling to make the best of the unexpected collapse of its means of livelihood.

Maes-yr-haf was actually opened as a centre for educational and cultural activities in the spring of 1927. An Adult School, which had been started in 1926, was moved to the Settlement, and additional schools for women and young people were opened. These schools, with four others outside the Settlement, united to form a Sub-Union of the National Adult School Union. In the winter of 1927 two Oxford graduates came into residence at the Settlement, and regular classes were held. Philosophy was a popular subject, and brought to light an interesting problem. It was found that the men's minds were keen enough, but were prevented from functioning fully and freely by an obsession derived from the doctrine of economic determinism on which they had been nourished. It was decided that a different form of mental discipline was needed as a training for philosophic studies. Accordingly classes were planned, with this idea in mind, on 'Man's Place in the Universe' — looking at mankind against a biological background rather than a specifically political one; and English Literature was also offered as a subject of study.

These schools and classes were maintained and developed, but, during the first three years of the Settlement's life, distress was so great that the organization of relief was necessarily very much to the fore. It was a temptation 'to sink all other interests in the attempt to meet purely physical needs.' However, in the cobblers' groups, which were reorganized and extended, and the sewing and mending groups for women, the principle of self-help was kept constantly before the people, and 'every opportunity sought of promoting constructive and educational activities and interests.'

(From *Education Yearbook*, 1935, pp.684–93.)

B.12   When the (1926) strike was over and we had settled down sufficiently to gain a detached view, we were able to regard it as only a preliminary skirmish which should prepare us for further and greater struggles ahead. This conception, we felt, was due entirely to the work of our evening classes in economics where students had been persistently taught that industrial action was the sure and only means of winning industrial salvation. And what I was trying to teach in my valley was taught by others in other valleys.

These classes were a great success, and by the end of 1927 they were larger than they had ever been. Every student had Marx controlling his mind and 'Das Kapital' on his bookshelf. Thus we had an army of class-conscious students capable, we believed, of spreading a gospel of revolutionary ideas throughout the coal-field. Our students had been trained to understand the nature of capitalism, how it developed and, we believed, how it would disappear. Disciplined to act when the opportunity came, they would nurture the revolutionary forces and speak for them. A minority, it is true; but revolutions depend on minorities. But even in our wildest moments we never considered violence as necessary. The revolution would be bloodless, a democratic triumph.

It was an overall picture that gladdened our hearts; we were succeeding in accomplishing what we had set out to do and, as I thought of it, I was proud of the part I had played in bringing it about. There appeared, however, a nigger in our wood-pile; he was at first only a baby nigger in our enlightened eyes, like the one on the old-fashioned money-box and one which we felt we could soon send back to the dark forest of useless ideas.

But the little nigger grew in stature in the period following the strike and he was apparently received with approbation in the valleys, where he loudly proclaimed that the cure for all his ills in the coal-fields was nationalization. We had been teaching that the control of the industry should be from the bottom, by the workers. The new idea, first brought to the valley by Keir Hardie and left to sleep for a long time, was that the industry should be controlled from the top, from Whitehall.

When it became clear in time that nationalization might push our enlightened ideas into the background we decided to act. A meeting was called of the more advanced economic students to decide on a plan of campaign. Convinced of our greater wisdom, we decided to preach our gospel from the house-tops, actually at Sunday night meetings and, in addition, to preach at organized week-end schools. At all costs we must succeed in persuading the miner and his wife that Post Office socialism would not cure their ills, that a change of ownership, from the mine-owners to the state, would not end exploitation.

The result of this was that during the few years that followed a choice of two meetings was offered to the people of the valleys, sometimes in the same street, always on the same Sunday evening, where state socialism was expounded at one with great eloquence and the Russian brand at the other. As it happened, the Russian brand lost popular appeal steadily and, I have to confess, the materialistic philosophy I had been teaching and preaching began to lose its appeal and meaning for me. And while I could never renounce my carefully-studied philosophy, that inner reserve of strength and faith which a crusader must have was no longer mine.

And thus I left the two ideologies to fight it out without me, not then certain which would dominate my valley's future.

(W. J. Edwards, *From the Valley I Came*, London, 1956, pp.260-1.)

B.13   The district has again had a continued epidemic of scarlet fever during the year, the majority of the cases being of severe type and complications were common. The general want of resistance to attack and the severity of the symptoms were, in my opinion, due to general malnutrition among the children, the result of the unfortunate economic conditions prevalent in South Wales.

(Report of Dr J. H. Rankin, Medical Officer of Health for the Gelligaer Urban District Council, 1933, in Wal Hannington, *The Problem of the Distressed Areas*, London, 1937, pp.53-4.)

B.14   In all denominations . . . the congregations have shrunk a great deal in size and the older folk are in the majority. In 1936 a survey was made of the effects of migration on the churches in the Rhondda Valley. It was found that 8867 members of the Nonconformist chapels of the Rhondda had moved away between 1925 and 1935. If we also take into account the Episcopal Church, the total loss of members due to migration cannot be less than 10,000 . . . By their very constitution and voluntary character, the Free Churches cannot protect their material resources by appealing to the state or to the public purse.

(Discussion between Revd Alban Davies and Revd Maurice Charles. Brinley Thomas, 'The changing face of south Wales', *The Listener*, 20 March 1938. The substance of ten broadcasts from Wales by Dr Brinley Thomas.)

B.15   For some years now men who have believed themselves to be feeling the pulse of our national life have been telling us that religion in Wales is not what it once was and is far from what it ought to be. They point to the growing predominance of secular interests, the decaying allegiance to spiritual leaders, the decreasing membership in the various Churches, the growing prevalence of what our forefathers regarded as heinous sin, namely, Sabbath desecration, betting and gambling, an increasing levity concerning morals, together with countless other tendencies all moving in the same direction. Where religion is showing some feeble signs of life is in what is becoming known as the Catholic Movement. In the Church in Wales those who call themselves Anglo-Catholics are becoming increasingly active and are undoubtedly making themselves felt as a powerful religious force. Among Roman Catholics there is manifesting itself a deepened sense of national sentiment which is engendering in the minds of many Welshmen the feeling that they need not lose any whit of their nationality by being members of that communion. The gibe that the Roman Catholicism in our midst is merely an Irish and an Italian mission is rapidly becoming untrue. Even among chapel folk there seems to be a turning to certain Catholic points of view; there is among them an increasing demand for a more artistic manner of worship, even if such a worship should mean a dallying with the things strictly forbidden to a past generation; sacramentalism too, on account of a growing dissatisfaction with the old-fashioned extempore prayer and the long drawn

out sermons full of literary inconsequences, logical incon-
sistencies, crude metaphysics and an emotional fervour foreign
to our colder modern attitude to life, is asking to have its place
recognized both in thought and worship. Nor are men so bitter
towards Catholicism as they were even a few decades ago; they
are content to let it pursue its own way, and if it can claim men's
allegiance they are willing to wish it well.

('Wales and Catholicism', Revd Dr E. E. Thomas, *Welsh
Outlook*, Volume XIX, Number II, February 1932, p.47.)

B.16   Expressions of dissatisfaction with the inadequate provision
        made by the B.B.C. to meet the special needs and conditions
        prevalent in Wales have been persistent since the establishment
        of the Cardiff Station in February, 1923. Time and again has the
        matter been discussed and made the subject of representations
        by various public bodies in Wales. Much appreciated features
        such as the monthly broadcast of a religious service in Welsh
        through Daventry have found a secure place in the B.B.C.
        programme as a result of such representations. But the tendency
        of the British Broadcasting Corporation to overlook the claims
        of Wales as a living and progressive national entity continues to
        manifest itself to a degree that has become most disquieting.
        The Court of the University of Wales, at its meeting held in
        Cardiff on July 19th, viewed the situation with grave concern.
        Fully realizing the immense influence which 'wireless' is
        destined to exercise in every sphere of national life, it resolved
        to urge upon the B.B.C. directly specific claims on behalf of
        Wales and to call upon all bodies and individuals interested in
        the maintenance of our national traditions to support these
        claims . . .
            Wales has never been treated as a separate entity in the
        broadcasting system in the same sense as Scotland and Northern
        Ireland. The Cardiff Station, established in 1923, was not
        designed to provide a broadcast service that would 'cover the
        whole Principality'. It was intended to serve the teeming valleys
        of Glamorgan and Monmouth and the populous Bristol area
        across the Severn. Today it is officially the West Regional
        Station. Every claim made for more programmes designed 'to

keep alive the memory of historical associations' has been countered, quite properly in the circumstances, by the reminder that the West of England has at least an equal claim upon the services of the Cardiff Station. The establishment of a relay station in Swansea in 1924 extended for a time the opportunities for broadcasting Welsh programmes and interludes conducted in the Welsh language. But 'Welsh' Wales, where the Welsh language is largely the speech medium of home and school, of office and workshop, was completely out of hearing of Cardiff and Swansea. The only service that could be relied upon in 'Welsh' Wales was that provided by Daventry.

In the autumn of 1928 I was making a brief sojourn in a Welsh village in Pembrokeshire. As a programme which I particularly desired to hear was due to be broadcast from Daventry during the period of my stay, I sought to arrange an opportunity to listen in. The hostelry in which I was a guest and the homes of two or three of my acquaintances in the village were furnished with wireless sets, but in all cases they were out of commission and had been in that state for varying periods. The explanation given was invariable: they could not 'get' Cardiff and Swansea, while the London programmes broadcast from Daventry contained too little that interested them to warrant the trouble and expense of keeping the sets going. I suspect that such cases are numerous. What Wales should demand is no more than the B.B.C. is presumably prepared to concede once it is convinced of the reality of the demand, — no more than it has already granted to Scotland and Northern Ireland.

('Wales and the British Broadcasting Corporation', Professor E. Ernest Hughes, *Welsh Outlook*, Volume XVI, Number VIII, August 1929, p.230.)

B.17 It is my considered opinion that Welsh rugby has made definite progress during the past few seasons, and particularly during this present one. There can be small room for doubt that since 1922 we have had our very lean years. Primarily that has been due to the nature of our forward play. It has always been an anomaly to me that Welshmen, who have rugby football ingrained in them, and who have so often been the teachers of the game, should so lag behind the other countries in the matter of forward play. Rugby football has altered considerably since the war, and nowhere to such a degree as forward.

Speaking generally, rugby football is in a decidedly healthy state all through South Wales, in spite of the fearfully depressing state of our trade. At Bridgend, Abertillery, Neath, Aberavon, and a host of other places enthusiasm is greater than ever. All that Wales needs now is for the game to spread with equal zeal into North Wales. We hear from time to time that the game is rapidly gathering strength there. I hear efforts are being made by certain clubs to seek membership with the Welsh Rugby Union. We want North Wales in the fold. It would be quite refreshing to be witnessing an encounter between England and Wales, say, at Rhyl, Colwyn Bay, or Wrexham.

The question of a national rugby ground for Wales was hotly debated in our borders at the beginning of the present season. This controversy followed the purchase by the W.R.U. [Welsh Rugby Union] of the Brewery field, Bridgend.

Whatever side you take in this debate, all are agreed that the present accommodation at either Cardiff or Swansea does not satisfy. If the accommodation were adequate and guaranteed, you could house double and perhaps treble the people who attend at present. But even present conditions are not what they could easily be made. I have recollections of my press seat in the game at Swansea between ourselves and France. The weather was bitterly cold, it snowed, and I felt I ought to apologise to all the English press visitors amongst whom I sat. Spectators near us had paid 10*s.* for a grand stand ticket. Really they were accommodated in a temporary stand in front of the permanent structure. I should have felt very aggrieved if such had been my ten shillings' worth.

Personally I am all for one central commodious ground at Bridgend. For goodness sake do not condemn the idea because the crowd could not be catered for — the demand always ensures the supply. Neither view the actual position concerning approaches and exits as it is now. Just use your imagination in a normal way and the rest is easy. I can quite understand vested interests in Cardiff and Swansea using powerful weapons to pour ridicule on the scheme. For my part I have a shrewd idea that the Welsh Rugby Union will refuse to be panicked into a surrender. We want a ground comparable with a Wembley or a Murrayfield. Time will bring it — and probably at Bridgend.

('Welsh Rugby Review' by Clem Lewis, *Welsh Outlook*, Volume XVIII, Number IV, April 1931, p.108.)

B.18   Thirty-five extreme cases were selected and thoroughly studied to expose the wilful misapplication of the Alien Registration Act of Great Britain in the case of Coloured British subjects residing and and working out of Cardiff as Seamen.

a) Eight persons who rightly claim British Nationality. And who have been and are to-day classified by the Cardiff Police as Aliens are in lawful and regular possession of British Passports. When summoned by the police for Alien Registration, each of the Coloured British Subjects displayed the certificates of Nationality to the said Public officials. Two of these men had birth certificates which they also presented. Even this indisputable proof, accompanied by avowed assertions of their British Status, and firm protests against being classified as Foreigners, did not deter the Police from forcing Alien cards on the men.

b) Seven persons who rightly claim British Nationality, and who have been and are to-day classified by the Cardiff Police as Aliens, were in lawful and regular possession of British Passports when they were so classified. These documents are not now with their rightful owners! Some were forcibly withheld by the Cardiff Police when displayed for inspection as a protest against Alien Classification and no receipts were given for them. The other Passports were mailed to the Home Office in London for renewal, and were acknowledged by letters now held by the persons concerned. Correctly considered by these world-travellers as high and fixed proof of Nationality (irrespective of the date of expiration) when supported by continued and honourable residence in the country, their Passports were never lightly treated or released.

c) Thirteen persons who rightly claim British Nationality, and who have been and are to-day classified by the Cardiff Police as

Aliens, were in regular and lawful possession of British Mercantile Marine Identification Certificates, at the time of this classification. These documents clearly certify the Nationality of each holder as 'BRITISH', and are only issued above the signature and office of a responsible servant of His Majesty's Service. three of these thirteen possess British Certificates, three possess Passports, and two held Passports which were surrendered during the Alien Registration drive among the Coloured Seamen.

d) Fifteen persons who rightly claim British Nationality, and who have been and are to-day classified by the Cardiff Police as Aliens, have honourable records for Military Service for King and Country. One was at the memorable battle of Jutland; one served for three years in Mesopotamia; one carried the British colours against the 'BOERS'; Two joined in the British West Indies, and served the British Empire in its military conquest of Africa; Eight fought in the Great War; and Two hold good conduct and long service Medals. One held a letter of gratitude and the thanks from H.M. George V for military service during the War of 1914–1918. Serving either in the military ranks at sea or on land, or in the Merchant Marine, some of these men were injured. Three now classed as Aliens were torpedoed during the Great War, and subsequently received compensation awards from His Majesty's Government of £42, £42 and £29 respectively. Three men bear scars from severe injuries.

e) Nineteen persons who rightly claim British Nationality, and who have been and are to-day classified by the Cardiff Police as Aliens, have lived in Great Britain longer than ten years. Of these nineteen, three have resided in this country thirty years or more; twelve from twenty to twenty-nine years; and four have lived here between ten and twenty years. As these men are seamen, employment records at various seaports in Great Britain reveal the fact of their residence. One of these men is sixty years of age, of which thirty-seven were spent in England. Fifteen of the thirty-five, originally selected, are married, with from one to seven dependents. In a few cases men, unable to secure employment because of an apparent discrimination against coloured British seamen in favour of non-coloured

British seamen, have been out of work and on the dole for four years.

Thirty-five persons whose rightful claims to British Nationality have been forcefully disregarded by the Cardiff Police are now in possession of the Seamen's Continuous Certificate of Discharge — wherein either the Nationality is recorded as British or the place of birth clearly appears. Some fifteen hundred are now forced to carry Alien Cards where the Nationality is unintelligently stated as 'SEAMAN' and the place of birth is purposely left unanswered.

SUMMARY AND RECOMMENDATIONS

If it is criminal and anti-social to tax out of existence a worthwhile enterprise, or ruthlessly to exterminate a helpless community in war; how shall a purposeful policy to drive some 3000 wage-earners out of their sole industry, be characterized? As this report goes to print, CARDIFF is doing 'just that'!

Thus a new monument to economic ignorance and racial animosity rises in England. Fresh, vigorous and dynamic, abundantly nourished by the poisons of the depressions, this tower threatens all intelligent attitudes, and submerges the vital problems still unsettled among shipping labourers. Envious brutality is ever that way. It has recruited as fellow-artisans in this hostile construction, some strange bed-fellows. The Trade Union, the Police and the Shipowners appear to co-operate smoothly in barring Coloured Colonial Seamen from signing on ships in Cardiff. The legislative history of this policy has been traced chronologically, and due emphasis placed upon the stipulation to carry only British Seamen which accompanied the two million pound grant to hard hit shipping industry. These plans and methods were never unknown to the coloured seamen nor did they pass unchallenged by them. Tenseness increased tenseness until on April 16th, 1935, a riot broke out at the Cardiff Docks over the flagrant discriminatory actions of a labour delegate in refusing the Chief Engineer of the *S.S. Ethel Radcliffe* the right to repick his coloured crew for a voyage.

This hostile labour attitude towards coloured seamen respects neither kith nor kin, creed or colour. For these coloured men have their homes in this country. Their wives are products of the soil, and their children are ENGLISH. Many of them have given of their youth and labour to the industrial and military services of this great nation, and they suffer, keenly in their deep sensitive souls, this unmerited assault. One feels it in the frank sincerity of their conversations; one knows it by the unassailable records they possess. True these men are coloured, so are five out of every seven persons in the British Empire! Without people of colour there would be neither Cardiff nor an Empire. For numerically and territorially this is over-whelmingly a coloured Empire, not a white one. It is true these 'yellow', 'red', 'brown' and 'black' men are said to be out of place in this 'white' country, consorting with its native women. These same charges may well be laid at the door of white men in some 'yellow', 'red', 'brown' and 'black' countries. Clearly, therefore, charges and counter charges may mount and re-mount, proving conclusively that the basis of the present Cardiff seamen's trouble lies more deeply rooted.

('Investigation of Coloured Colonial Seamen in Cardiff. April 13th–20th, 1935', Geo. W. Brown, from *The Keys. The Official Organ of the League of Coloured Peoples.* October–November, 1935, p.21.)

Debating the Evidence

In an essay bearing this title we might expect a different dimension from the charting of economic decline. We expect more value judgements, for the author has every opportunity in dealing with such a topic to engage sympathetically with the people and communities under that devast-ating economic strain which has already been brought to light. We might expect, too, that the kinds of sources will reflect this, perhaps with scope for more literary, more subjective and more private testimony. Here, then, are some rather more pronounced problems of inter-pretation, especially if the literature of political statements referred to in the author's first paragraph is to find expression; more so if the author himself is one of those 'historians who readily march side by side with the hungry'.

Source B.1

As Deian Hopkin says, the evidence for population *trends* is incontrovertible. But is there anything you would need to know about these
census returns before accepting the actual figures as totally accurate?

Source B.2

The statistics of numbers of Welsh speakers are taken from the census
returns because in 1891, for the first time, this information was required.
What significance might there be in it being required in that year? What
difficulties of interpretation might there be in dealing with these
statistics?

Source B.3

What does the document tell us about its author? How far is the
document evidence for seeing economic theory as being far from
neutral?

Source B.4

In what ways might the material in this source be held to be impartial,
and in what ways biased? Given the author's immediate purpose in the
essay, how far do you regard this information as being wholly adequate
for his purpose?

Source B.5

The existence of a marketing survey is in itself significant, as is the fact
that the author calls it a 'semi-official source'. In what ways might the
motives of government and the motives of traders in seeking such
information differ? Do you see any significance in the categories of
information required?

Sources B.6 and B.7

Here we have two very different kinds of documents. The market
survey of north Wales, like that of Cardiff in Document B.5, is statistical,
carefully categorized. Dr Rowland Williams is presumably a columnist
in the *Tenby Observer* which certainly ran features of this kind regularly.
We might infer that he was an educated man and a local man. But it is
obvious that this kind of literary source is very different from statistical
information. Decide what the differences are in the use the historian
might make of the two different types of documents. Would it be

reasonable to class the former as 'objective' and the latter as 'subjective'?

Source B.9
How could the factual information provided here about Mr E.P. be made to show his circumstances in a far more favourable light?

Source B.10
This appears at first sight to be a rather different kind of document from B.9. One is more 'literary', the emphasis in B.10 is statistical. How far is this apparent discrepancy a real one? Despite the impressive appearance of the balance sheet what information do we need before being able to make informed judgements about the adequacy of the diets of unemployed Rhondda families? What significance is there in that this information appeared in the *Geographical Magazine*?

Source B.11
What information about the *Education Yearbook* would be useful to you in making use of this document?

Source B.12
Why might you regard the unwitting or unintentional record of this document as being of more significance than the intentional record, or witting testimony?

Source B.13
What significance, if any, would you attach to the fact that the Medical Officers of Health in this document were employees of local councils?

Sources B.14 and B.15
From reading these two documents would you be able to tell to which denominations or churches they belonged? Why might it be important information?

Source B.16
The author uses this document to illustrate his assertion that this 'was also an age of gramophone records and popular music, and of the wireless'. Yet nowhere in this document does such a statement occur. On what basis, therefore, is the author able to make this assertion? Is his evidence adequate? What other evidence would help to bolster his case?

What other judgements about radio broadcasting in Wales in the 1920s might you make on the basis of this document? Professor Ernest Hughes was a professor of history at University College of Swansea. Do you regard this information as significant?

Source B.17
This is the third successive document which the author has taken from the magazine, *Welsh Outlook*. What have we learned about *Welsh Outlook*?

Source B.18
In what ways do allegations of, and evidence for, racism tie in with other social reactions to the grim conditions of inter-war Wales? How far do they fit uneasily into the remainder of Dr Hopkin's analysis?

Discussion

Inevitably, an essay discussing social reactions to economic plight ranges more widely than one charting dimensions of economic decline. So, we make short forays into topics as diverse as religion and association football.

It is hardly surprising that the range of sources on which the conclusions are based is more catholic, though the early groundwork is established by means of the statistics contained in B.1, B.2 and B.4. These documents are based on an invaluable collection of statistics, published in 1986, (L. J. Williams, *Digest of Welsh Historical Statistics*) and many of the tables rely on material culled from census returns. But census returns, excellent as they are, need to be treated with caution. We know that the early census returns, especially that of 1801, are not as reliable as later ones. But even of the later ones we need to know, for example, whether the questions asked in successive censuses were the same and, if not, how this might distort the resulting information. And the table itself reminds us that administrative boundaries of counties can change so that if we needed exact county figures there would be particular difficulties. Fortunately, the author, as is the case with most historical problems, is seeking to establish trends, and here the statistics provide firm enough evidence. We would need to be rather more cautious with the statistical information provided in B.5 and B.6. A marketing survey might well want to concentrate on particular areas of the country, particular areas of the economy and ask questions related to the higher spending categories of the population. This would certainly appear to be true in these two documents and, if taken alone, provide a very distorted view of the economic structure of Cardiff and north Wales. It would certainly be misleading, therefore, to think of B.6 as objective and B.7, a literary source, as subjective. Both reflect the people who were responsible for bringing the sources into existence.

That subjectivity of language which is evident in B.7 is perhaps even more pronounced in B.9 which appears to be a straightforward account of living conditions for two families in the parts of south Wales most affected by the depression. Yet, at each stage, there are statements which might, in the absence of further evidence, be misleading. For example, the fact that Mr E.P. of Aberdare has no gas stove might indicate that this was a badge of great poverty, but a hundred years earlier the aristocracy would have been cooked for on open fires. A covering of lino for a bare stone floor was obviously considered in this document to be a mark of respectability. Nowadays lino is regarded as an inferior floor covering to carpet. Judgements here are relative — and the author has an axe to grind. He uses 'only' and 'but' at strategic intervals to point a moral. It would not be hard to find a mass of corroborative evidence for his general statements, but this should not blind us to the necessity for it. The problem is more subtly displayed in B.10, but here again we need to know what quantity of milk and bread 4*s.* could purchase for Mrs A.'s family, and how such balance sheets compared with those of people in employment at a variety of levels. At the same time it is significant to us that this information should be of importance to readers of the *Geographical Magazine* with its international readership. Reporters and readers must be reflecting that unemployed south Wales has become something of a by-word.

B.12, B.15, B.16 and B.17 are very different types of sources. Indeed an autobiography (B.12) raises a variety of questions about historical sources. W. J. Edwards writes from personal experience — he was there. But he writes thirty years afterwards. This source, like taped oral evidence, so useful to the historian of recent times, must probably be adjudged a primary source. Yet the gap in time is a yawning one and must pose questions about reliability. From extracts B.15, B.16 and B.17 we learn that *Welsh Outlook* was a publication which catered for a reading public interested in religion, broadcasting and rugby — that is unless the magazine was subsidized to such an extent that it did not have to bother about the concerns of its readers, but merely those of its editor! In such documents information about authors becomes crucial to the interpretation and reliability of the pieces they write. Since the Reverend Dr E. E. Thomas was not a Catholic, source B.15 is a highly significant indication of a more ecumenical outlook than might be expected in inter-war Wales. Professor E. Ernest Hughes's political affiliations would be of interest to us in assessing the importance of B.16 and certainly we would need to know if these views were typical not only of highly educated Welsh people but also of other sections of the Welsh community. Such questions are just as significant in relation to documents like B.18. We have here a clear necessity for an assessment of the bias inherent in a publication on coloured people by the League representing that group.

Welsh Politics 1918–1939

KENNETH O. MORGAN

At the conclusion of the First World War, the politics of Wales were on the verge of massive and dramatic changes. The ascendancy of the Liberal Party, the dominant feature of Welsh political history for two generations from the time of the 1868 general election down to the First World War, was to be shattered for ever. Yet this transformation was at first disguised by the existence of coalition government between 1918 and October 1922, and the interruption of traditional party politics that resulted from it. The prime minister was the greatest Welshman of the day and the outstanding Liberal of the century, David Lloyd George. The *'coupon' election* [this refers to the electoral arrangements between *Coalition Liberals* and Conservatives] he fought with his Conservative allies in December 1918 was seen by the contemporary press as a 'ceremony of congratulation' for 'the man who had won the war' (C.1). The result was a huge landslide for the coalition government with 526 of its supporters returned (333 Conservatives and 127 *Coalition Liberals*). In Wales, 25 supporters of the Coalition were elected (20 being *Coalition Liberal*) as against one *Asquithian Liberal* and ten Labour. Lloyd George himself easily retained his seat in Caernarfon Boroughs with over 85 per cent of the poll.

But the Lloyd George coalition was rotten at the foundations. By 1921–2 its essential instability was becoming very apparent. At home, its social reform programme had foundered amidst mass unemployment in the mining valleys of south Wales. Abroad, its foreign policies were largely unsuccessful, while the prime minister himself had become a remote

C.1

99

Aneurin Bevan and Jenny Lee on their wedding day. (*Source: BBC Hulton Picture Library.*)

and widely unpopular figure even in his own land of Wales. Two features of these changes became apparent in the later stages of the coalition government. The first was much division and erosion of morale within the ranks of Welsh Liberalism, with growing support for the opposition Liberals who followed Mr Asquith. One of Lloyd George's women supporters described in March 1921 how Welsh Liberalism was rapidly C.2 being undermined (C.2). In rural Wales, the government's belligerent policy in Ireland was losing votes, while in the south the miners and other industrial workers were deeply hostile to the prime minister. There were warning signs when the *Asquithian 'Independent Liberals'* polled strongly against the government Liberals in a famous by-election in Cardiganshire in February 1921. Beyond party politics, the young and the intelligentsia were no longer instinctively Liberal and deeply concerned at the status of Wales in the post-war years. One consequence was the remarkable election of a Christian pacifist, George Maitland Lloyd Davies, by the graduate electors of the University of Wales in the 1923 general election.

But the main challenge to the coalition came from the growing rise of Labour, which won several by-elections in south Wales in 1919–22. Fuelled by rising unemployment, and the class solidarity of the miners and other organized workers, Labour was becoming dominant in the industrial south from Llanelli to Pontypool. In the 1922 general election, this was drmatically illustrated when Labour won 18 out of the 36 seats in Wales, mainly in the coalfield, but with victories too in Wrexham and Caernarfonshire in the north where the quarrymen were rapidly turning to the socialist cause. Throughout the twenties the Labour ascendancy, local and national, developed apace. The victory of the medical doctor, J.H. Williams, in C.3 Llanelli, was but one milestone in this process (C.3). Labour won 20 Welsh seats in the 1923 election, 16 in 1924 and, finally, 25 out of the 36 in the general election of May 1929 which saw the return of *Ramsay MacDonald* as Labour prime minister for the second time, with a parliamentary majority behind him dependent on the Liberals. Labour's progress in south Wales seemed pre-ordained, a simple reflection of the dominant working-class character of the social structure of the coalfield, while victories in Wrexham and Carmarthen testified to growing success in rural Wales as well. By contrast, the Liberals in 1929 held on to 10 Welsh seats only, all in rural areas, and the Conservatives could claim a mere one, Monmouth on the English border. At the local level, Labour's success in capturing control of Glamorgan and Monmouthshire county councils, and most local councils also in industrial areas, was further testimony to Labour's immense strength at least in south Wales. The failure of industrial action, as shown in the defeat of the *General Strike* in May 1926, gave further impetus to mass support for the Labour Party as the main instrument of working-class advance (C.4). On the other hand, it was noticeable, too, that most of the new Labour MPs and councillors largely conformed to the pattern of the Liberal past. They were almost all local men, of nonconformist background, often Welsh in speech and intensely patriotic. Far from being class warriors, they were evidence of the enduring strength of the old pre-war radical and national values (C.5). Only one new MP in 1929, perhaps, embodied a different, more international ethic. This was the fiery young miner MP for Ebbw Vale, Aneurin Bevan.

C.4

C.5

The most intriguing feature of Welsh politics in the 1920s lay in whether the older Liberalism could stage some kind of revival. The Liberal heritage was still a force to be reckoned with: even in 1924 the Liberals could still claim ten Welsh seats, a quarter of their entire representation in parliament. The reunion of the Lloyd George and Asquithian wings in 1923–4 brought the shattered forces of Liberalism together, save only in Cardiganshire where bitter memories of the 1921 by-election still ran deep. When Lloyd George assumed leadership of the entire Liberal Party in 1926 and used it as a launch-pad of a new series of radical economic policies, new life seemed to flow through the ageing frame of the Welsh Liberal Party. The 'green book', *The Land and the Nation* (1925), proposed a dramatic revival of agriculture and caused much excitement in rural Wales, though it also cost the party Sir Alfred Mond who joined the Conservatives in protest. *Britain's Industrial Future* (1928) was another exciting document, while it led to 'the *orange book*', *We Can Conquer Unemployment* (1929) in which Lloyd

George and his old adversary, the economist, *J.M. Keynes*, collaborated to offer a new scheme for counter-cyclical government spending policies to combat the slump.

In the 1929 general election, Lloyd George and his Welsh followers made much of these new economic panaceas (C.6, C.7). They urged that road-building, house construction and other publicly-financed schemes would reverse the tide of depression and unemployment in Wales. By contrast, Labour spokesmen doubted the practicality of Lloyd George's elaborate proposals (C.8). Lloyd George had most of the glamour and the headlines in 1929. But Labour won most of the votes. The Liberals did make some progress at the polls, increasing their share of the Welsh vote from 30 per cent to 33.5 per cent; proportional representation would have improved their prospects still further, of course. But they improved their tally of Welsh seats only from ten to eleven. Two seats were won from the Conservatives (Pembrokeshire and Flintshire) but three others (Swansea West, Carmarthen and Wrexham) were lost to Labour. With 43.9 per cent of the Welsh vote, and 25 out of its 36 parliamentary seats, Labour's ascendancy was beyond question. Even the three Cardiff constituencies went Labour's way. After the polls, Liberal supporters and propagandists in Wales were despondent (C.9). The contest, in Wales as elsewhere, seemed to lie between Labour and the Conservatives, with Liberals, even under so charismatic a leader as Lloyd George, an increasingly marginalized and irrelevant third force.

This pattern of Welsh politics did not change fundamentally for the remainder of the inter-war period. The 1931 general election did, momentarily, seem to produce a transformation. The second Labour government fell from office ignominiously in August 1931, amidst a huge run on the pound and a tally of unemployment already over three and a half million. *Ramsay MacDonald*, Labour's premier, formed a 'National government', mainly with the Conservatives and most Liberals, and with a vast majority of the Labour Party hostile. In the October 1931 general election, amidst a mood of some hysteria in which Labour was branded as '*bolshevik*' and an obstacle to national recovery, Labour lost eight seats in all in Wales, five of them to

C.6
C.7

C.8

C.9

the Conservatives. Labour was left with only 16 seats, together with an *ILP* (*Independent Labour Party*) man returned for Merthyr Tydfil. But the 1931 election was an unreliable guide to the political temper of Wales. Indeed, it is testimony to Labour's residual strength there that it held on to so many of its Welsh constituencies, and actually improved its share of the poll, compared with 1929 (44.1 per cent as opposed to 43.9 per cent). In the early and mid-1930s, galvanized by the crusade against the *Means Test* and the mass unemployment that crucified the valleys, Labour retained its unique position as a vehicle of working-class protest. Aneurin Bevan in particular emerged as a socialist of national stature. In the 1935 election, Labour won 18 Welsh seats out of 36 and, by the outbreak of war in 1939, was making rapid headway in such rural fastnesses as Anglesey and Merioneth as well. It showed the capacity to enlist distinguished new recruits, notably James Griffiths, the president of the *South Wales Miners' Federation*, elected for Llanelli in a by-election in 1936. Another interesting new member was S.O. Davies, a *Marxist* Welsh home ruler, formerly active in the far left 'Minority movement' in the twenties. Although in the *Independent Labour Party*, he was elected for Merthyr as an official Labour candidate in 1934. Labour's ascendancy was most influential and significant at the level of local government, where its representatives, often much abused, laboured valiantly to rebuild or preserve community during the depression years, maintain local educational and social services, and introduce new industry.

The challenge of Liberalism further diminished in the 1930s. In the 1935 election, only seven *Independent Liberals* were elected in Wales, six in rural areas and the seventh in the University of Wales. Lloyd George made a final bid for power in 1935 with his 'new deal' schemes to regenerate the economy, on much the same lines as 1929. But he was a spent force now, living mostly in Surrey, holidaying abroad and making only rare forays back on ceremonial occasions to his own land. By the start of the Second World War, now in his mid-seventies, he was remote from the mainstream of Welsh politics, 'a sarcophagus not a symbol' as the young Gwyn Jones wrote in the *Welsh Review* in 1939. Liberalism, then, was only a challenger to Labour in rural areas of declining population. The Conservatives, although temporarily boosted in 1931 by the freak returns of that unusual year, had never struck deep roots in most parts of Wales, and only in border areas such as Monmouth and Breconshire, and the suburbs of Cardiff did they have much success.

An alternative challenge to Labour's ascendancy came from the far left. This was the Communist Party which claimed some colourful recruits in Wales including the minister-bard, Revd Thomas Nicholas, and some leading figures in the *South Wales Miners' Federation*. The most notable of these was *Arthur Horner*. In 1931, and again in a by-election in March 1933, he stood for the Communists against W.H. Mainwaring, an old far-left

C.10 associate of his, and part-author of the *Miners' Next Step* (C.10). In a bitter campaign, in which Mainwaring was supported by the official strength of the *Miners' Federation, Horner* was defeated by less than 3,000 votes. *Horner* and other Communists remained powerful figures in the mining union world; *Horner* was promptly elected agent for the anthracite district and in 1936 was to become the first Communist president of the *SWMF*. But the by-election was a watershed. Even in the radical heartland of the Rhondda, mainstream official Labour had been preferred by the working-class voters to the more extreme postures of the Communists. Never again did the Communist Party look like presenting a serious political challenge to Labour.

The other novelty of Welsh politics in this period was one of much greater importance. This was the emergence, at least at an intellectual level, of a new support for the idea of nationalism. A number of discontented young patriots, dismayed at the failure of Lloyd George and other politicians to pay political acknowledgement to the needs of Wales (a point made even by the *Welsh Outlook* in 1919 as shown in C.1 above), formed a new party, *Plaid Cymru*, at the Pwllheli eisteddfod in 1925. The dominant figure was the writer and intellectual, *Saunders Lewis*, who became *Plaid Cymru*'s president in 1926 and served as its major ideologue and inspiration. *Lewis* was much attracted to medieval Christian ideals of an organic community and shortly joined the Roman Catholic church. There were many who accused him also of undue sympathy for Mussolini's corporate

Lewis Valentine, Saunders Lewis (centre), and D.J. Williams. (*Source: National Library of Wales.*)

state and the anti-democratic ethos of Italian and German fascism, even perhaps anti-semitism as well, though *Lewis* hotly disputed this. *Lewis* poured immense scorn on the bogus 'nationalism' of the Liberals of pre-1914 days — the 'spare time hobby of corpulent men' (C.11). It was precisely this attempt to sever links with the radical and national ideals of the past which offended other patriots for whom the name of Lloyd George was still something to conjure with (C.12).

C.11

C.12

At first, *Plaid Cymru* was essentially a pressure-group with very few members (perhaps 500 in 1930), concerned mainly with preserving the Welsh language and culture. However, in 1929 the party did fight Caernarfon in the 1929 general election, when its candidate gained just one per cent of the vote, a humiliating result. In 1931 *Lewis* himself fought the University of Wales seat (C.13) but his poll of 914 votes was again disappointing, as was another attempt at Caernarfon.

C.13

Gradually the party became somewhat more political in its approach. In the early 1930s it committed itself formally to Welsh self-government, aspiring to the kind of dominion status enjoyed by Canada and Australia. However, it was small and intensely controversial. *Lewis's* own bizarre economic ideas, in which he proposed the break-up of mass industry, the deindustrialization of south Wales and the establishment of a small-scale, co-operative system for industry and agriculture, did not add to his party's appeal (C.14). In 1935 the party fought Caernarfon for a third time but once again a lost deposit was the only result. Then, quite unexpectedly, the party gained much-needed publicity and the aura of martyrdom. In September 1936, three senior members of the party, *Saunders Lewis*, Revd Lewis Valentine and D. J. Williams, set fire to an RAF bombing school at Pen-y-Berth aerodrome in the Llŷn peninsula in Caernarfonshire. They then gave themselves up to the authorities. They objected to the bombing school on cultural, environmentalist and, above all, nationalist grounds. There was immense local uproar when the Baldwin government then decided to transfer the case from a local Welsh court to the Old Bailey on the grounds that a Welsh jury might show undue bias. Lloyd George, no friend of *Plaid Cymru*, reacted angrily in writing to his daughter from Jamaica (C.15).

C.14

C.15

Eventually the 'three' were imprisoned for several months in Wormwood Scrubs; *Lewis* was, further, removed from his university lectureship at the University College of Swansea. The martyrdoms of the three nationalists — which is how it appeared to many at the time — gave the fledgling *Plaid Cymru* a much-needed boost. Writers and poets like *Kate Roberts* and R. Williams Parry, previously almost apolitical, now publicly declared their support for the nationalist cause. *Plaid Cymru* remained a small, deeply controversial movement; it was still far short of winning a seat in parliament. Most Welsh-speaking intellectuals remained true to the old Liberalism; the workers were Labour almost to a man and woman. The rise of fascism made *Plaid Cymru*'s ethos seem open to question, while rearmament and the threat to national security made *Plaid Cymru*'s neutralism and anti-militarism suddenly less fashionable in 1938-9. Nevertheless, the party was clearly established as a durable force in Welsh politics by 1939 while the enlistment of the support of young intellectuals and idealists like the youthful Gwynfor Evans was a portent of hope for the future.

In the inter-war years, Welsh politics were, therefore, totally recast. The older Liberalism went increasingly into decay, the product of social as much as political change. The old nonconformist radicalism of pre-1914, girding against the dominance of the parson and the squire, seemed out-dated. The ascendancy of Labour, at least in the mining valleys, seemed testimony to the new realities of the class struggle between capital and labour amidst an economy in near-collapse and ravaged by the scourge of mass unemployment. In north Wales, too, from Wrexham in the east to Holyhead in the west, Labour was making inroads. In the thirties, Labour's ascendancy was firmly established in much of Wales. It was able to beat off the rival appeal of the Communists and the Conservatives with much ease. On the other hand, Labour still held firm to the old values, too. New left-wing leaders like James Griffiths were as staunch in their commitment to the traditional Welsh culture and the values of community and kith-and-kin relationships as ever the pre-war Liberals had been. The other new theme to be announced, of course, was the emergence of *Plaid Cymru* and the new appeal of political nationalism and the urge for Welsh self-government; but this was a minority movement, mainly of interest to writers and intellectuals, in the years down to 1939. On the eve of the Second World War, with the old hero of the First, Lloyd George, a very old man, physically and emotionally remote from the life of his own Wales, Welsh politics presented a totally different face from that of twenty years earlier. Labour seemed the dominant, fresh force in Welsh political life, rooted in the old values but committed to sweeping future trans-formations of social and economic structures. There were a handful of intellectuals even in 1939 who speculated that perhaps Labour itself might in time become ossified and antiquated, as the Liberal ascendancy had been in the past. The inbred, unadventurous, even corrupt nature of Labour rule in local government was already noted. There were those, too, who speculated that Welsh national sentiment might prove a more significant force in the future than the puny membership of *Plaid Cymru* might immediately suggest. But these were distant portents, no larger than a man's hand it seemed. For the moment, Labour ruled, as the Liberals had done in former years, pointing confidently, even aggressively, forward to the challenges and conquests of the future.

Sources

C.1   The election was, in some ways, a very unique event for Wales; as one of the candidates aptly said, the great majority of Welshmen must have looked upon it as a great ceremony of congratulations; its central figure was their distinguished countryman who had served his political apprenticeship with them but had at last become a great European figure. Their pride and their affection naturally made them, if not Coalition-ists in the strict sense — for that they are not — at any rate devoted supporters of the Prime Minister. But what a glorious opportunity for developing and emphasizing importance of a real national policy was the moment when this son of Wales, whose sympathies we had every right to expect to be with our cause, had reached the full zenith of his power. Did we avail ourselves of the opportunity to any degree? We are fortunately in a position to give some answer to the question, and it is very disquieting.

We were surely not too sanguine in expecting specific references in most of the addresses to the peculiar aspects of the policy of reconstruction and particularly to such questions as must of necessity come up for treatment in the next Parliament if its existence is prolonged for anything like the normal period. The questions of Welsh Home Rule and all it involves, of Welsh Education, of Welsh Land Reform, of Welsh Housing, of a special Health Bill for Wales, of the regional treatment of such problems as transport development and town-planning, should have found a place in the addresses of a high percentage of the candidates. We have carefully examined over thirty of the addresses, and the overwhelming majority of them, consisting only of 'standard' paragraphs manufactured by the thousand in some dingy room in a central office, would be just as suitable for Norfolk or the Orkneys as they are for Wales. Of those we have read seventeen contain not even an allusion to the possibility of devolution and the grant of some form of self-government to Wales, and of those which contained some incidental reference to Welsh Home Rule, eleven were addresses of Labour Candidates.

When we sought for references to peculiarly Welsh issues in this Sahara of generalities, we could only find four addresses which contained the slightest indication that the candidate had realized that any of the problems of reconstruction presented any pecularities in Wales.

We looked forward with considerable expectation to Mr Herbert Lewis's first University address. The occasion, we thought, was somewhat inspiring, and Mr Lewis was a man who had been brought up in the idealist atmosphere of the Cymru Fydd Movement, and had spent many years of this life in intimate touch with all the educational affairs of Wales. We were also aware of the devoted service he had rendered to every deserving Welsh cause, and we confess that we expected some treatment of the urgent education questions of the moment in Wales — some reference to the results of the University Commission, some indication of Mr Lewis's attitude towards the questions of educational co-ordination; of the extension of adult education and the part the University might play in it; of the place of the University in connection with Schemes of Reconstruction, e.g., development of agriculture and afforestation — but we looked in vain and found little more than a promise to support the Coalition faithfully.

(*Welsh Outlook*, January 1919, 'Wales and the General Election', pp.6–7.)

C.2   Dear Prime Minister

I have spent most of my time since I returned here in seeing people of the inner political ring. I have heard a good deal of interest & am anxious to pass certain information to you.

Wee Frees

They are working as quietly as they can — have plenty of money and are appointing full time Agents who have orders to appear independant [*sic*] of Abingdon Street. They are approaching prominent Welsh Liberals as to their willingness to contest seats if funds are provided. They have invited Walter Jones to stand. Two Labour Agents last week stated that though *officially* Labour & Wee Frees will not ally themselves, yet in Wales negociations [*sic*] between them have been practically concluded providing for a tacit understanding as to which shall be left free by the others to contest each Welsh seat.

Walter Jones

I had a long interview with him last night. D.H. Williams, who lives with him, had refused to meet me owing to my action in moving the Resolution re supporting E. Evans at the London meeting in Feby.

   It seems the anti-Coalition element in the W. National Liberal Council regards me as the person chiefly responsable [*sic*] for 'leading the Council to destruction' — i.e. to the position of clearly 'Lloyd George Liberals', & are bitterly hostile to me — in good company!!

   Walter Jones position is that the Council must go back on its Cardiganshire decision, remain a home for Wee Free & *Coalition*

Liberal Liberals, sink everything in the one aim of 're-establishing the unity of the Liberal Party' & refuse to take sides as between Wee Frees & *Coalition Liberals.*

If the Council at Shrewsbury adopts a definitely pro Coalition position he & certain others will consider themselves to have been 'drummed out' of the Council. He stated that even if the Executive took up such a position a great effort would be made at the Annual Council meeting (which has to be held before July) to get the decision reversed, & he believed it would succeed unless you were present in person.

Professor Joseph Jones of Brecon had been with him recently, had told him the staffs of the Welsh Colleges almost to a man were opposed to you, & at least 80% of the students.

He told me D.H. Williams had decided to stand for Gower as 'a Liberal without qualifications', i.e. non-Lloyd George & non-Asquith. He is actively engaged in strengthening opposition to Coalition in every direction.

I am not clear whether he is coming up to Shrewsbury to make trouble, but Walter Jones is. D.H. Williams is Secretary of the Gower Liberal Association — which gives him a pull.

The Secretary of the Port Talbot & Aberavon Liberal Assn. is an ardent Asquithian. There is every likelihood of Runciman being up as a Free Liberal for *Swansea.* He spoke there recently to the Chamber of Commerce.

Welsh National Liberal Council

I have had a long talk with Mr Salathiel, though I am anxious Lord St David's should not know this as it might get Salathiel into trouble.

He is very keen to see regular spade work done & his view is that advisory bodies for N.S. & W. Wales (or Divisional Councils) will not achieve actual results unless paid agents are employed. He wants every two constituencies to have one paid Agent, that is his ration, in order to get

> Revision of Lists
> Political Meetings
> Coalition groups in each centre, including Villages
>   (Labour has such all over Wales).
> Resurrect Liberal Associations where dormant.

Form Coalition Associations where Liberal Associations have gone Asquithian.

Promote social meetings in Coalition interest. Salathiel is convinced you must have paid workers for this. The Conservatives now have 21 fully paid Agents in Wales.

The reason why the paid Agents of your present Coalition Organization (run from Old Green Street) have failed is because they had not status & were suspect to the existing Liberal Agents — & though about £6000 a year has been spent on Wales the results have been almost nil.

I am certain the W.N. Liberal Council can do the work under a carefully thought out scheme but it must declare itself 'pro Ll.G.' (Coalition is an unloved word in Wales) & it must be trusted to do the work.

Three Labour seats are capturable [*sic*] in Salathiel's eyes — Rhondda West, Caerphilly, & Gower.

The Liberal Agents in Wales are agitated over the Circular issued by their Society. The older men fear loss of Pension, towards which they have contributed. This deterred Crocker of Swansea from going into Cardiganshire, and the younger men coming into the work fear they will not be accepted as members. I enclose a copy of the circular in question.

I also enclose a letter from Mrs Price-White, your chief Woman Organizer for North Wales — a very shrewd worker. You see what Wee Frees are doing in your constituency — Certainly *Ireland* is being run for all it is worth against you — The Shrewsbury Meeting of the Executive takes place April 8th & it will be essential for you to see Lord St David's (after hearing Mr Evan R. Davies' scheme for reorganizing the work of the Council) before that.

I hesitate to send you this long in view of the coal strike but I thought you might find time to look through it during the week end.

Our miners are *very* surly: I have never known them more so. On the other hand public opinion has hardened dead against them, including the opinion of other workers, though they dare not say so. Public opinion down here will back the government in a firm attitude & is prepared for a big fight. Many of the pits in this area will never open again if flooded; small collieries

James Griffiths. (*Source: BBC Hulton Picture Library.*)

many of them. The calling out of the pumpmen has set everyone against the Federation. The only people I have met who look pleased are the extreme Communists!
Believe me,
Yours sincerely,
WINIFRED COOMBE TENNANT

(Mrs Winifred Coombe Tennant to David Lloyd George, 31 March 1921. Lloyd George Papers, F/96/1/15.)

C.3   When I returned from my two years' sojourn at the Labour college to work at the mine in 1921, I resumed my association with the Labour Party in the constituency. The splendid result we had achieved in the difficult circumstances of the 1918 election had encouraged us to hope that the next time victory would be ours. The party decided in 1922 to employ a full-time agent and I was appointed to the post. When I took up my new duties at the beginning of September 1922, the Lloyd George Coalition seemed to be firmly entrenched and likely to go its full five years' term. I estimated that I should have a full year in which to work at improving the organization, but no sooner had I installed myself in the rooms above a boot stores in the town's main shopping street than the famous Carlton Club meeting of the Tory Party, led by Bonar Law and Stanley Baldwin, threw Lloyd George overboard and plunged the country into a general election. Fortunately our candidate, Dr Williams, was ready to fight his fourth election campaign in eight years, and by this time his name was well known throughout the constituency.

From the moment we kicked off we sensed that the wind was in our favour. Our meetings — and we held a dozen every evening — were joyful rehearsals in preparation for the festival of the eve of the poll at the market hall in Llanelli. I have warm memories of those meetings in the market hall with its crowd of five thousand in serried ranks cheering us on to victory. The memory of the 1922 eve-of-poll meeting remains vivid in my recollections. We were living in the aftermath of the 1914–1918 war with the disappointed hopes of 'a world fit for heroes to live in'. There was a sickness to be cured and we had a doctor as our candidate. My brother, the bard 'Amanwy', came to our aid with a slogan, in Welsh, which I rendered into English as 'the doctor who cures man's ills will help to cure the world's ills'. And Wales and the world were ill in that year of 1922; the depression which was to engulf the valleys was already arousing fears, and the Graeco-Turkish War had revealed how precarious was the peace made at Versailles. These were the themes of that memorable eve-of-poll rally at the market hall. Tomorrow was to be a new day for Llanelli! When the result

> J.H. Williams (Lab.): 22,213
> G. Clark Williams (Lib.): 15,947
> *Majority*: 6,266

was declared from the balcony of the town hall the immense crowd that filled the square cried with joy: 'We've won!' The cry echoed through the town and re-echoed through the valleys on that memorable day in November of 1922.

(James Griffiths, *Pages from Memory*, 1969, pp.49–50.)

C.4   After 1926 I think the miners made up their minds that we cannot solve our problems by industrial action and looked afterwards to a Labour Government to do it . . . So after 1926 you see the big growth of the Labour Party in South Wales . . . in the coalfields generally, and thereafter looking for a political solution and not for an industrial solution.

(James Griffiths interview, 20 November 1972. South Wales
Miners' Library, Swansea.)

C.5   The majority of the Labour MPs and candidates were, and are, of the type better known as Lib-Lab, though they wear the Socialist ticket and always vote Labour. Respected trade union officials who had made themselves prominent and useful in local affairs, they would probably be elected whether they stood as Liberal or Labour. It is because Labour candidates in South Wales and Monmouthshire are local men of this character that they are so strong politically.

(*Manchester Guardian*, 20 May 1929.)

C.6   The Liberal party considered that the relief of able-bodied unemployed should be a charge on the National Exchequer, and not a part of the poor rate. Impoverished areas where there was excessive unemployment due to national and international, rather than local, causes, had been saddled with the expense of a large proportion of their unemployed. The burden should be more equitably distributed over the whole country. There were parts of the country today where only 5 or 6 per cent of the population were unemployed and they had not suffered anything like the depressed areas.

(Speech by D.L. Powell, Liberal candidate for Ogmore at Nantymoel, reported in the *Western Mail*, 21 May 1929.)

C.7   When you come to consider the criticism directed against my scheme because it involves the borrowing of £200,000,000 you should also consider that it is computed a workman on full time is of the value of £220 per annum to the nation . . . Total up the accumulation of loss to the nation through the unemployment of 1,000,000 people for five and a half years, which means during the time of the Conservative administration, this loss, this waste is tremendous, nearly £3,000,000 a year.

(Lloyd George speaking at Bangor drill hall, reported in the *Liverpool Daily Post*, 7 May 1929.)

C.8   Mr Lloyd George did not appear to realize that the great majority of the unemployed were totally unfit to undertake road-making work. There were a quarter of a million women unemployed, and even Mr Lloyd George had not the audacity to suggest that they should do road work. Then when all the different types of skilled labour were deducted, Mr Lloyd George had only some 300,000 of the unemployed who were physically fit and adapted to the manual toil of road making, land draining and so forth. The bulk of these were miners, and it was safe to say that 100,000 men were over 60 years of age and were not really capable of standing the strain of navvy work. Of the miners under 50 there was every prospect that most, if not all, would be quickly re- absorbed into the coal industry within the next twelve months if it continued to recover at its present rate of progress.

(Speech by T.I. Mardy Jones, Labour MP for Pontypridd, reported in the *Western Mail*, 21 May 1929.)

C.9 The battle for Liberalism has been fought and lost. The tragedy of the General Election is not the defeat of the Conservative Party because the Conservative Party will rise again. There will always be a swing of the political pendulum, because people have a habit of growing tired of governments . . . We who are Liberals should not hide our heads in the sand but should frankly recognize the position. The country no longer takes Liberalism into account. The only alternative to Conservatism is Labour. If we could not obtain 100 seats from the present campaign, with all the magnetism of its leader, its organization, its magnificent platforms, its ringing slogan, then what can we hope to win them by?

(*Rhondda Gazette*, 8 June 1929.)

C.10 In March 1933 came the by-election caused by the death of the sitting Labour member, Colonel D. Watts-Morgan. My opponent was W.H. Mainwaring who had been with us in the anti-war movement in the Rhondda during the First World War and who had been secretary of the Anti-Conscription Council. Mainwaring was a Labour College man, part author of *The Miners' Next Step*, and had been associated with me in many of the plans we had discussed for the reform of the Welsh coalfields and the mining industry. Naturally in the campaign — and I did not blame him — he made use of my quarrel with the Communist Party and quoted the criticisms I had made during the 'Hornerism' episode and the bitter things that had been said about me in the *Daily Worker* and in Communist Party circles. But I was at least able to retort with an account of the very fair hearing I had had and with counter-charges about the way the Labour Party leaders and some of the trade union leaders in South Wales were attempting to fetter the freedom of discussion of the militant rank and file.

It was a bitter election, fought against the background of the unemployment figure of more than three million and the mounting poverty right through the country. All the big guns from both the Labour Party and the trade unions came down to support Mainwaring, many of them personal friends of mine who had been with me for many years in the struggle.

The officials of the *South Wales Miners' Federation* issued an appeal for the support of Mainwaring, calling for his election in order to support a programme of a miners' minimum wage bill, adequate pensions, abolition of the *Means Test*, improved unemployment benefits, cuts in the miners' hours and improved compensation laws; all principles for which I had been fighting for all my life. Ebby Edwards, who had succeeded Arthur Cook as secretary of the *Miners' Federation*, sent an appeal on behalf of Mainwaring, also claiming that the improved conditions for miners depended on support for the official Labour candidate.

I fought the election as a Communist because I felt that the record of the Labour Party during the 1929–31 Government and the policy of class collaboration which was being carried out by both the trade unions and the Labour Party at the time had to be challenged. Mainwaring, in his election address, claimed that the Labour Government was brought down because it refused to cut the pay of the unemployed at the demand of the Liberals and Tories. That of course was true. But he failed to take account of the fact that this situation was reached only because the Labour Government had accepted the economics of capitalism, and had no alternative policy. I stood at the election for an alternative policy for the Labour Movement, based on militant working-class struggle. I did not win, but I believe I had the support of most of the miners even though some of them, because of loyalty to the Labour Party, did not vote for me when it came to the ballot box.

Incidentally, during the election all the newspapers blazoned the news abroad that Mr Mainwaring had secured a promise from the coal owners that they would reopen the pit which they had closed down when I was elected checkweighman. I retorted that everybody knew the company would reopen the pit as soon as they had a guarantee that the wage cuts they were determined to impose would be accepted by the men, and this proved a true forecast.

After the election I was given an opportunity to test how the miners, my own people, felt about me. I was nominated by a large number of lodges for the vacant post of agent for the anthracite pits.

(Arthur Horner, *Incorrigible Rebel*, 1960, pp.128–9.)

C.11   The deceased gentleman was also an ardent Welsh Nationalist, presided frequently on the platform of the National Eisteddfod, was a prominent figure in denominational assemblies, and attended regularly the annual dinner of the Honourable Society of Cymmrodorion.

(Saunders Lewis in *The Welsh Nationalist*, January 1932, p.1.)

C.12   I no longer consider myself a member of *Plaid Cymru*, and I do not believe at all in putting up such a candidate in Caernarfon-shire against a brother like Mr Goronwy Owen who is a true Welshman.

Isn't the spirit of *Plaid Cymru* very narrow and its conception of a patriot very limited? I know of no-one who has done more for Wales than Mr D. Lloyd George. Indeed, the wide world would know nothing of Wales were it not for Mr Lloyd George. I believe conscientiously that *Plaid Cymru* is doing great harm to Wales by bringing out a candidate. There is no more secure leader for Wales than Mr Lloyd George and great benefits have come to Wales through him. He has served his own nation by serving the world as every true patriot should. It is high time that we Welsh should be loyal to one another and to our best men instead of fighting amongst ourselves.

(J.R. Jones to H.R. Jones, ? 1929).

C.13   A Welsh Nationalist group in the House of Commons would:

(1)   Proclaim and maintain the right of Wales to be a self-governing Dominion in the British Common-wealth of Nations;

(2)   Defend with its utmost force the present national institutions of Wales as well as its cultural, agricultural, industrial and financial interests;

(3) Oppose all measures of excessive centralization and bureaucracy;

(4) Defend the legitimate rights of other minorities within the British Empire;

(5) Maintain such a standard of information on international affairs and so European — in opposition to Imperialist — a standpoint in matters pertaining to the organization of peace and the co-operation of peoples, that the entry of the Dominion of Wales into the League of Nations, when the moment for that crowning achievement arrived, would be gladly voted and acclaimed at Geneva;

(6) Finally in domestic affairs, it would work forthwith for the restoration of social order in Wales and would enlist the co-operation of all men of good will in the initiation of local enterprises and the fostering of a spirit of personal and social responsibility in every section of the community.

We believe that only under a Welsh Government responsible to the Welsh people can the Welsh co-operative state be established. We see no other solution for our industrial and agricultural problems. We shall resist strongly the present government's determination to use all its resources, its well-disciplined press, its wireless propagandists, its docile publicists and economists, its Orders in Council, in order to fasten on us permanently the dictatorship of the City of London.

If this dictatorship revolts you, electors of the University of Wales, I suggest that you can have in a Welsh National Party at Westminster the best immediate protest against it, and you will have in the establishment of the Dominion of Wales the only ultimately secure refuge from its degrading tyranny.

In addressing this electorate I may properly end with a note on education. From a Nationalist point of view the matter has peculiar importance. The whole development of modern Welsh nationalism is linked with the growth in Wales of a demand for an educated democracy. The safeguarding of the dignity of the teaching profession in all its categories, the importance of the search for truth, its value in elevating standards of conduct in public life, these are traditional principles that a Welsh Nationalist must constantly uphold.

I have, Ladies and Gentlemen, the honour to be,

Your obedient servant,

SAUNDERS LEWIS

(Saunders Lewis's election address, University of Wales, 1931.)

C.14   3. That industrial capitalism and economic competition free from the control of government (i.e. free trade) are a great evil and are completely contrary to the philosophy of cooperative nationalism.

4. That it is part of the task of a Welsh government to control money and conditions and credit institutions for the benefit of industry and social developments.

5. Trade unions, works committees, industrial boards, economic councils and a national economic council, co-operative societies of individuals and of local and administrative authorities, should have a prominent and controlling role in the economic organization of Welsh society.

6. The families of a nation should be free, secure, and as independent as possible. To enable that it is necessary to legislate and plan substantial distribution of ownership, because only a man with property can be a free man. Ownership should be distributed so widely among the families of the nation that neither state nor individual nor a collection of individuals can oppress the people economically.

7. Agriculture should be the chief industry of Wales and the basis of its civilization.

8. For the sake of the moral health of Wales and for the moral and physical welfare of its population, South Wales must be de-industrialized. All the natural resources of Wales are riches to be dealt with carefully for the benefit of the Welsh nation and for the benefit of its neighbours in other parts of the world.

9. No right or unqualified ownership will be recognized unless linked with social duties and responsibilities.

10. It will be part of the function of a Welsh government to cooperate with other governments with regard to the problems of provisions and industrial organization. Freedom and en-

couragement will be given to trade unions and Welsh industrial boards to cooperate and consult with equal and similar unions and boards in other countries or by means of the International Labour Office.

(From Saunders Lewis, 'Ten Points of Policy', *Y Ddraig Goch*, March 1934.)

C.15   Your joint telegram as to the action taken by the Government in reference to the bombing school incident gave me a great shock, and I immediately wired you my first impressions. I think it an unutterable piece of insolence, but very characteristic by the Government. They crumple up when tackled by Mussolini and Hitler, but they take it out of the smallest country in the realm which they are misgoverning. It is the way cowards try to show that they are strong by bullying. They run away from anyone powerful enough to stand up to them and they take it out of the weak. In the worst days of Irish coersion [*sic*], trials were never taken out of Ireland into the English Courts. They might be removed from Roscommon to Dublin, but they were never taken to the Old Bailey. I cannot recall a single instance in the past of its having been done in the case of Wales. Certainly not in a criminal case. This is the first Government that has tried Wales at the Old Bailey. I wish I were there, and I certainly wish I were 40 years younger. I should be prepared to risk a protest which would be a defiance. If I were *Saunders Lewis* I would not surrender at the Old Bailey; I would insist on their arresting me, and I am not sure that I would not make it difficult for them to do that. This Government will take no heed of protests which do not menace it. I hope the Welsh Members will make a scene, and an effective one, in the House. It is a supremely foolish thing to have done; the majority of the Jury were in favour of a verdict, and they might at any rate have had a second trial, or removed it to some other part of Wales, but to take it out of Wales altogether, and, above all, to the Old Bailey, is an outrage that makes my blood boil. It has nothing to do with my views as to the merits of the case. It will reinforce the pacifist movement in England.

(David Lloyd George to Megan Lloyd George, 1 December 1936.)

Debating the Evidence

Political history is probably based on more prolific quantities of sources than is any other category of human activity. In Britain we have central government records at the Public Record Office where, after a discreet thirty year interval, scholars may consult the papers of all the great departments of state as well as, say, records of discussions in Cabinet. Politicians can scarce forbear to write about themselves, so auto-biographies, diaries and letters are available in profusion, especially for the more recent past. Newspapers regard the reading public's appetite for political comment or, in some cases, comments on the public and private personae of politicians, as insatiable. The problem for the political historian of the twentieth century is plethora not paucity. 'Total' history can *still* not be written; it is perhaps made more difficult by the profusion of sources.

Source C.1
We have already encountered *Welsh Outlook*, with its articles on religion and sport. Does the fact that the magazine carries serious political comment change your view about the nature of this journal?

Source C.2
This is a substantial, detailed and specific document, but what would we need to know about its author, and those in the Liberal Party with whom she had contact, before deciding on its signficance? What does the document tell us about the position of women in society in 1921?

Source C.3
This is an extract from the autobiography of a famous Welshman who started life with all the disadvantages of someone born into the working class in a highly stratified society. His enormous talent took him through the ranks of miners' leaders to become a Labour MP and the first Secretary of State for Wales. He writes here of 1921/2 in the hindsight of experience and success. How far should the historian allow for these factors in using this document?

Sources C.4 and C.5
How far are these extracts mutually reinforcing?

Sources C.6, C.7 and C.8
The author's generalization, based on these three documents, is a very careful one — he says that Lloyd George and his followers 'made much of these new economic panaceas'. How might you follow up the ideas floated both in text and documents to arrive at a fuller picture of Liberal attitudes to economic policies in the late 1920s — and the Labour Party's opposition to them?

Source C.9
The message in this document, like that in C.6, C.7 and C.9, is of a decline of Liberalism — from a paper supporting the Liberals and, this time, after the election. In what ways does this information change our perspective on this document compared with the way in which we might evaluate C.8?

Source C.10
There are many references in this document which merit further research. What are these? How might we follow them up and why might the results of our enquiries influence our interpretation of the document?

Source C.11
In what way might this source illustrate the dangers inherent in interpreting historical documents?

Source C.12
The author has indicated here that the date of this letter is uncertain. Why is the absence of a firm date particularly important in this source?

Sources C.13 and C.14
How far do you think *Saunders Lewis*'s material here is influenced by the constituencies at which it is directed?

Source C.15
What does this document, and the author's comment on it in the text, tell us about Lloyd George and his 'Welshness'?

Discussion

The range of sources employed here is wide — magazine articles, autobiography, election addresses, newspapers, private letters and transcribed oral history. In dealing with magazine articles and newpaper pieces (C.1, C.5, C.9) we have to be particularly careful because in these instances we do not know the authors, nor, necessarily, the political affiliation or bias of the editors. Furthermore, we do not know the possible interference from some ideological base or other, of the proprietor concerned. As soon as newspapers go beyond reporting facts — and those, too, can often be far from accurate or neutral — we have to be particularly on guard in assessing the reliability and usefulness of the information. At the same time such attitudes are invaluable in allowing us to take the political temperature of the period and, indirectly, tell us something incontrovertible about the media of the time and their audiences.

Interpreting the significance of letters should be simpler, but they pose problems of their own. In C.2 Winifred Coombe Tennant, one of the most important organizers of the *coalition Liberals* in Wales, must be accounted a particularly significant authority because of the depressing picture she paints, though of course we still need to gauge whether or not she was exaggerating opposition to Lloyd George in order to prompt him into remedial action. So even here we have to take into account the 'audience', just as in far more significant fashion, we have to take the audience for political speeches into account (C.6, C.7, C.8). When such speeches occur at election time they differ little in purpose from election manifestos (C.13). In the case of C.6 it is hardly surprising that the Liberal candidate speaking in Nantymoel in 1924 should concentrate on unemployment and the relief of poverty. It is equally unsurprising that an election address to the *University of Wales constituency*, a separate representation long since disappeared, by *Saunders Lewis*, an academic himself, should concentrate on the importance of education in the life of the nation. We know that he genuinely believed in 'the dignity of the teaching profession in all its categories', but we are also conscious of the fact that large numbers of members of the University of Wales were teachers or potential teachers.

Another particularly interesting category of sources which Dr Morgan uses is autobiography — and it takes two forms in his selection. C.3 and C.10 are written autobiographies of the 1960s and the extracts concern events of the 1920s. C.4 is an extract from a taped interview which Jim Griffiths gave in 1972, again recalling events of 1926. There are both strengths and weaknesses in such sources. Here we have the comments of people at the heart of events of central significance in Welsh history. They were there, actively involved in and, in some degree, directing events. Their testimony is crucial. But time dims all our memories, not necessarily falsifying but certainly changing perspectives of what was important and what was not. Such discrimination of memory must be heightened or, at least, moulded, to some extent by subsequent successes. In Jim Griffiths's case, a career which embraced the Secretaryship for the Colonies and for Wales marked a signal personal achievement, made possible by the success of the moderate constitutional Labour Party he helped fashion in the 1920s. It is extremely difficult to assess the extent to which this would influence his assessment of the strength of his case in the 1920s, for example, but obviously we have to consult other, opposing personalities, in allowing for it.

Rachel Thomas as 'the Welsh Mam' in *Blue Scar*, 1948. (*Source: MacQuitty Collection.*)

Women between the Wars

DEIRDRE BEDDOE

The history of women in Wales remains to be written. Welsh historical studies have operated within a tradition of historical writing which simply omitted women — on the grounds that women's actions and lives were of no consequence to the great unfolding chronicle of History and anyway, women's lives were somehow always 'the same'. But this state of affairs has been challenged and Welsh feminist historians, writers and film makers, are engaged in an urgent rescue operation to salvage Welsh women's history. The main problem facing present day historians of Welsh women's history is not one of resolving conflicting well-researched and well-argued points of view: the task is simply presenting a history of women in Wales based on wide-ranging and thorough research in order to challenge received myths and oft-repeated platitudes. The 'mythological' view of Welsh women's history in the inter-war period — though so historically imprecise is it, that dates are of no particular consequence — would run along these lines: Welsh women were 'Welsh Mams' — the wives of miners and the mothers of miners; they had enormous power in what was predominantly a matriarchal society and, somewhat contra-dictorily, their horizons and interests did not expand beyond their own front door or, at most, the end of the street. The historical sources, oral, written, printed or visual, do not lend credence to this view. The sources of the history of women in Wales, though not as abundant or perhaps as obvious as those for the history of men, are nevertheless plentiful. There is much work yet to be done in collecting and analysing these, particularly with regard to the inter-war period. There are, however, two major weaknesses in the statistical evidence. First, most government collections of statistics lump Wales in with England and it is difficult to isolate information on Wales. Secondly, the census is a useful source for historians and although there are census reports for 1921 and 1931, no census was undertaken in 1941, because of the war, and consequently, we are deprived of information which would help us measure change in the 1930s.

It is important to stress one further point before setting out a framework for a study of women in Wales between the wars and before embarking on that study. It is integrally bound up with the history of women in Britain in that period and it is important to be cognizant of the main developments of British women's history in this era. The broad facts may be summarized as follows. The period before the First World War had been a tenacious and long drawn out struggle for the enfranchisement of women. It is important to note that the suffragette movement was not confined to London, or Manchester. There were active groups of the *Women's Social and Political Union* in north Wales, notably Bangor, and in the south Wales valleys, particularly in the Pontypool area, and there were cells of the constitutional branches of fighters for 'the Cause' in many major Welsh towns. In 1918 women over the age of 30 were 'given' the vote. But the struggle for the enfranchisement of women on equal terms with men continued, until this was eventually granted in 1928. Welsh women continued to be involved in this fight. There had been a lull in this particular campaign whilst the whole British nation was engaged in the greater struggle against Germany and Austro-Hungary in the First World War. During the Great War, in Wales as in the rest of Britain, women were called upon to work in munitions and to take over men's jobs in civilian walks of life: they drove trams, worked on the land and on the railways, cleaned chimneys or acted as clerks. When the war ended, the Restoration of Pre-War Practices Act, together with trade union pressure, ensured that men's jobs would be returned to men. The year 1919 therefore heralded a period of massive female unemployment. The wholesale sacking of women from jobs taken up during the war was accompanied by a national and media exposition of a re-vamped version of the domestic ideology, i.e. women's place is in the home. The media lighted upon the image of the housewife: it was to this role that women in Wales, as in the rest of Britain, were exhorted to conform. Meanwhile feminists, who had optimistically hoped to build on their war-time gains, were forced to rethink. British feminism in this period forked into two branches. 'Old feminism', as it was labelled, continued to fight for equal rights for women and 'new feminism' concentrated upon the rights of women in the home and particularly upon their rights as mothers. Lady Rhondda, who was without doubt the leading and most influential feminist of the inter-war period, represented 'old feminism' and concentrated on equal employment and education rights for girls and women. Eleanore Rathbone, who is identified as the prime advocate of child allowances, represented the 'new feminism' with its emphasis on improving the lot of mothers. Broadly speaking, this was a class division. Welsh women had gains to be made from the advocacy of both kinds of feminism, though the new mode of feminism had more to offer *most* Welsh women. In terms of women's rights a variety of legislation had improved their lot. The *Sex Disqualification (Removal) Act* of 1919 had in theory, but certainly not in practice, opened the doors to the professions. An equal divorce law of 1923, i.e. granting women divorce on the same terms as men, and an act giving equality between the sexes with regard to the guardianship of infants in 1925, improved the lot of married women. 1925 also saw the granting of widows' pensions. But Eleanore Rathbone's brainchild, child allowances, had to wait till the end of the Second World War. All in all the optimism of feminists in 1918, was to be proved to be grossly misfounded: they were thanked for their services to the nation (a term which seems to exclude women) and expected to disappear quietly back 'into the home'.

The history of women in Wales fits into this over-all British pattern. In this essay I should like to examine the history of Welsh women in the inter-war years. It is necessary to do so to make any valid comparison with the mythology of Welsh women in the same period. In order to do so I shall look at the waged work of women in Wales, women and the home and women's campaigns.

Late evening in the kitchen. Bill Brandt, 1936. (*Source: Copyright estate of Bill Brandt — courtesy of Noya Brandt.*)

Women's Waged Work

The waged employment of Welsh women demands attention. Several factors must be noted. Wales had a very low female economic activity rate. For women aged over 15 years the rates were 1911: 27.26 per cent, 1921: 23.0 per cent, 1931: 21.52 per cent, and 1951: 24.95 per cent. This was the result of limited job opportunities for women in Wales and the fact that traditionally women in many parts of Wales gave up paid employment on marriage. Nevertheless it is important to note that in the inter-war years some 17 per cent of women did not marry and therefore had to earn a living. The other vitally important point is that, given the lack of job opportunities in Wales, Welsh women migrated in large numbers to the more prosperous regions of England. They were an army of domestic servants and in 1931 there were *at least* 10,000 Welsh women domestic servants in London. Welsh women, like women throughout Britain, worked in a wide range of occupations during the First World War. They worked as clerks, postwomen, chimney sweeps, tram drivers and conductors; they worked in munitions factories (for example, Blaenavon and Caernarfon), on the land and in the docks (for example, Cardiff). At the end of the war they were dismissed: between November 1918 and October 1919 three-quarters of a million women in Britain were dismissed to make way for returning ex-servicemen. They were expected to disappear back into the home — their own or somebody else's (as domestic servants). Women ex-war workers were entitled to unemployment pay of 25/- per week for 13 weeks: this caused a public outcry (D.1). At this time there was a great shortage of servants (D.2), this was the most unpopular type of women's work and it was the only sector of the labour market to experience a *shortage* in the inter-war years.

D.1
D.2

Women were *coerced* into service. If a woman refused a job as a domestic servant she lost her unemployment benefit; if she accepted it, at very low wages, she became an *uninsured worker*, who was entitled to no further benefits. During the inter-war years, a time of very high unemployment, the *only* training schemes open to women were in domestic service. These were organized by the Central Committee for Women's Employment, under the auspices of the Ministry of Labour and the

Pencil-making in Port Penrhyn, *c.* 1940. (*Source: Gwynedd Archives Service.*)

'home training centres' were concentrated in the depressed areas. In Wales they operated in such places as Aberdare, Barry, Bridgend, Brynmawr, Caerphilly, Ebbw Vale, Maesteg, Merthyr Tydfil, Pontypool, Pontypridd, Wrexham and Ystrad Rhondda.

D.3   These unemployed Welsh women, trained in domestic management for 12 weeks, were mainly placed outside Wales (D.3). They went to work in private and, increasingly, in public institutions. This work was characterized by low pay, long hours, low status and no protective legislation. Conditions in

D.4   service varied but were frequently harsh (D.4). There are tales of bed-bugs and starvation. Such stories are not uncommon as the work of rescue organizations, such as the National Vigilance Association and the *London Welsh Girls Friendly Aid Society* show

D.5   (D.5).

    Domestic service was the main source of employment of young Welsh girls in these years. Only in a few areas did women do industrial work. In the Llanelli area women did heavy, and

D.6   often dangerous, work in the tin-plate industry (D.6). Light industrial factories did not come to Wales until the late 1930s. Treforest industrial estate was established in 1938 and Poly-koff's clothing factory was set up in the Rhondda in 1939. Professional women made some gains and suffered some losses in this period. Women entered teaching and the civil service in large numbers. The civil service, newly opened to women, operated a *marriage bar*. This *marriage bar* was also applied to teaching from the mid-1920s onwards.

Women in the Home

Seventeen per cent of Welsh women in the inter-war years came into the census category of 'never married': 83 per cent came into the category of 'ever married'. The large majority of Welsh adult women were married women and were classified as housewives. Since the dominant ideology of the times dictated that the housewife's place was in the home, housing was very important to her. Housing in Wales, as in the rest of Britain at this period, was characterized by shortages, appalling conditions

Cookery book cover, *c.* 1930

and high rents; it was a bad situation, further exacerbated by the fact that no new houses were built during the war. Investigations highlighted the problems of housing. Evidence given to the *Sankey Commission on coalmining* by Mrs Elizabeth Andrews, Labour Party Women's Organizer for Wales, stressed

D.7 high rents and poor conditions (D.7). The wartime government had recognized the important part played by housing in women's lives and had set up a Women's Committee on Housing in 1918. The centrality of housing to women's lives and the need for improvements and new houses was clearly stated by the Women's Co-op Guild at a conference in 1923

D.8 (D.8). Mrs Alwyn Lloyd in an article in *The Welsh Housing and Development Association Year Book*, 1921, listed the features she would like to see in an *ideal* home: hot running water was the

D.9 dream of the miner's wife! (D.9) This ideal can be compared with the worst reality — in the sort of home where *tuberculosis (y*

D.10 *dicai)* was rampant (D.10). Such housing as existed in Wales, whether in urban or rural areas, although often in a very poor condition, could be kept habitable by very hard work. Women worked very long and hard hours in this struggle against

D.11 poverty and grime (D.11). Many women fought constantly in the battle against poor housing and dirt. They took a pride in their task and ordered their work on strict weekly plans — for example, Monday — washing; Tuesday — ironing, bed-making; Wednesday — upstairs rooms; Thursday — mats beaten; Friday — parlour. It was a never-ending round. But times of great economic hardship in some cases eroded women's pride not only in their homes but in their own appearances, as

D.12 the Pilgrim Trust Investigators found (D.12).

The inter-war years saw some women in Wales breaking out from the limitations of the private sphere of the home into the public world of politics, commerce and the professions: nevertheless the home still remained the sole province of many Welsh housewives and the only place where they had any influence or authority. Some older-style historians have failed to recognize the limited sphere of the authority of the 'Welsh Mam' and consequently have written nonsensically about Wales being a matriarchal society. This myth is rooted in the practice of miners and dockers and other manual workers handing over their unopened wage packets to their wives. The practice was widespread but it is important to realize that the miner, etc., was handing over the responsibility of managing on what was often a very low wage. Industrialists did not hand over the annual profits to their wives and ask them to manage. But the picture of the 'Mam's' power because of this practice is enshrined in literature and folk memory (D.13). In reality she had to manage — to pay the rent, to buy food, fuel, light, insurances, household items and clothe husband, children and herself — from a fixed wage. When there was no wage, and in many parts of Wales this was frequently the case in the 1920s and 1930s, she still had to manage: weekly budgeting was an art. The Caerphilly woman whose weekly budget, together with her own personal diet, is included in the sources collection, chose to illustrate her budget in a week when her husband's wage was at its highest: even so, she was criticized by medical analysts at the time for not spending on fish and eggs (D.14). In hard times, women frequently cut expenditure by cutting down on their own food. This had severe repercussions on their health: the Caerphilly woman suffered from giddiness and palpitations. Many researchers, Sir John Orr, Seebohm Rowntree and the British Medical Association team, demonstrated the inadequacy of the working-class diet. People filled up on bread, and did not drink enough fresh milk; even in the country they drank tinned milk. Poor housing, poor diet and overwork, combined with a medical service that had to be paid for (mining areas were exceptional in that they had medical insurance schemes), made for a low standard of women's health. There was, among working-class women in Wales, almost an expectation that their health would be below par — and it often was. Apart from major diseases, there were simply the ailments they learned to live with (D.15). Tuberculosis was one of the most serious diseases of the period. It is a disease linked with poverty and poor housing and it was contracted by far more people in Wales than in England. Megan Lloyd George, making her maiden speech in Parliament in 1930 in response to a government initiative on housing, concentrated on the danger of *tuberculosis* to women in rural Anglesey (D.16). A major report of 1939 closely linked *tuberculosis* in Wales with housing.

D.13

D.14

D.15

D.16

The problems of childbearing also increased the dangers to women's health. The rate of maternal mortality in Britain was regarded as a scandal in the 1920s. In Wales the figures were consistently worse than those for England. Whereas the mortality rate of women in childbirth from all causes in England and Wales was 4.33 per 1000 in 1920, 3.91 in 1921 and 3.81 in 1922, in Wales alone the figures were 5.52 per 1000 in 1920,

D.17 5.35 in 1921 and 5.43 in 1922 (D.17). The child death rate (infant mortality rate) was also alarmingly high, though food parcels from outside actually brought that figure down in 1926. In Monmouthshire infant death rates per 1000 registered births fell from 83.8 in 1925 to 66.1 in 1926, only to rise again in 1927 to 87.3. In the 1930s, children in Pengam contracted rickets within their mother's womb. Successive pregnancies were debilitating to women's health, as the heart-rending collection of essays, *Maternity*, published in 1915 by the Women's Co-operative Guild had shown. The birth rate had in fact fallen from an average of 5.5 to 6 live births per couple in the middle of the nineteenth century to 2.2 live births in the years 1925–9. But despite the efforts of campaigners, birth control provision was still abysmal. Welsh women wrote pathetically to *Marie Stopes*

D.18 and other birth control campaigners (D.18). The campaigner Stella Browne, on a tour in South Wales and Monmouthshire in the 1920s, was struck by the eagerness with which audiences

D.19 listened to her (D.19).

But it was the exhausting effect of successive pregnancies which wore out many young women. In 1930 the government partially gave way to campaigners for birth control by conceding that existing Maternity and Child Welfare clinics (set up after the war to give advice on pregnancy and child care) could give birth control instruction to mothers whose health would be injured by further pregnancies. This government memorandum to local authorities merely allowed them to give birth control advice: there was no compunction to do so. Many Welsh counties were very slow: Monmouthshire was very bad. Cardiff saw many women die from illegal abortions before it

D.20 acted (D.20). Merthyr had an unusual, and quite different,
D.21 problem (D.21).

1934. Welsh hunger marchers resting. *(Source: Dora Cox.)*

Women's Campaigns

Women's employment prospects were bleak and home life and health left much to be desired. But it is important not merely to see Welsh women as victims in this period. Some of them began to enter public life and many of them became involved in women's or community campaigns. Welsh women continued to
D.22   fight for equal suffrage until this was granted in 1928 (D.22). They struggled for improved conditions in the community, too, by such campaigns as that for pit-head baths. Welsh women participated in the 1934 *Hunger March* to London: they marched at the head of the contingent the whole way in an effort to prevent further cuts in unemployment benefit and to demand
D.23   work (D.23). In 1935 women from the South Wales valleys launched an attack on the Unemployment Assistance Board's offices in Merthyr; the result was that the government backed down in its attempt to cut benefits. It was a triumph of popular protest.

Sources

D.1   In the case of women, however, the hope of meeting the demand for 'suitable' employment seems hopeless, chiefly because these women war workers, were prior to 1914, either employed in domestic service, to which they will not return at the wages offered to them, or were at home with their parents. During the war they have had artificially inflated high wages, and they have not a sufficient grasp of economic factors to appreciate that the country's post-war industries, now in a state of flux, cannot absorb them on the old abnormal wage terms. Human nature being what it is they decline to accept anything offered to them as 'suitable' and stick to the 25 shillings a week donation, on which they continue to enjoy their holiday . . . Thousands of young Welsh women from the south Wales areas went to the large munition districts. Now they have returned and claimed the donations, and unless new industries are established or old industries extended and developed these women cannot possibly be absorbed and the time is approaching when they must realize that domestic service, which they were originally engaged in, must again be their main source of livelihood, that is if they want to do anything at all. Seaside places and other holiday centres throughout the country are said to be now reaping a harvest from young women who are out for a good time on their savings as munition workers, and their donations.

(*Western Mail*, 20 January 1919.)

D.2   ... I have just advertised for a domestic help in a Cardiff evening paper for 6 days specifying any requirements as to expertise, etc., but with no response whatsoever. I find that I am by no means the only sufferer in this respect. Most women and girls can do some domestic work and there must be hundreds of Cardiff householders who would be glad to get unskilled help. It seems evident that most of the 2000 women in Cardiff now in receipt of the unemployment donation prefer to remain as they are.

(Letter from 'Constant Reader' in *Western Mail*, 29 March 1919.)

D.3   See Page 143.

D.4   At one place I was only there one night . . . it was alive with bugs . . . when I went to bed I lit the candle and oh my goodness I picked up the pillow like that and without a word of a lie they were there scattering . . . I had never seen them before. I couldn't sleep on the bed so I spent the night on the boards . . . When it came to daylight I went downstairs . . . and I told her. Oh she said, you must have brought them with you . . . I left that place and went to my brother's . . . I was all lumps, oh I was in a terrible state. I couldn't even look for another job until all these had cleared . . . but then I went from the frying pan into the fire . . . I was starved to death there. She (her employer) locked everything up and gave me 3 lumps of sugar for one day and I had a small pat of margarine . . . and for my dinner *every*

D.3   CENTRAL COMMITTEE ON WOMEN'S TRAINING AND EMPLOYMENT TRAINING IN HOMECRAFT AND ALLIED SUBJECTS:
RECORD OF EMPLOYMENT AFTER TRAINING
"The Hollies", Maindy Crescent, Ystrad Rhondda
12 week course—End 14/6/1929

Name	Address	Age	Previous Employment	Employment Secured	Remarks
Edith T.	Treherbert	17	Nil	Housemaid £22 p.a.	Royal Northern Hospital, N.7.
Margaret T.	Treorchy	19	Nil	Laundress 10/- per week plus tips	Mr Ashley, Ashley's Cafe, Aberystwyth
Rebecca W.	Treherbert	16	Nil	General 7/6 per week	Mrs N. Cox, 21 Cornwell Gardens, Brighton
Mabel M.	Treorchy	16	Nil	General £20 p.a.	Mrs Fuller, Clifton, Bristol
Mary M.	Treorchy	17	General	Unsatisfactory Report	Not Yet Placed
Mary D.	Pentre	19	Nil	General £2/10 per month	Mrs Powell, 87 Sunny Gardens, Hendon

(P.R.O. Ministry of Labour, Lab/2/1365.)

day I had half a bag of potato crisps for 3 weeks . . . and yet I was cooking for them but being what-do-you-call being slow, I suppose in those days I wouldn't think of taking anything. That's one thing that was always drummed into us . . . don't you ever take anything that doesn't belong to you . . . She said her daughter was dieting . . . and she wouldn't diet if I ate . . .

(Oral interview. Mrs E.D., Rhondda, 1983.)

D.5   We have repeatedly drawn attention in the columns of the VIGILANCE RECORD to the very significant and disturbing migration, which has been in process for some years past, of Welsh girls coming to London to take up employment. The problem is not confined to Welsh girls, but it extends also to girls coming from the North-Eastern coalfields. It is, however, particularly obvious where Welsh girls are concerned, any visit to Paddington Station when the excursion trains come in will convince any of our readers.

It is difficult to argue that girls should not go out into the world to earn their own living, particularly when family circumstances at home render their means of livelihood precarious in the extreme. But clearly there should be some limit of age, and desirably some limit of occupation. The National Vigilance Association, apart from its station work, which is of greater value from the preventive point of view than is commonly recognized, lays stress on two points. Firstly girls coming to London should assure themselves beforehand that the situation to which they are proceeding is a safe and desirable one; second, since many social workers exist for the purpose of helping these girls, it is desirable that those social workers should do something more than offer through the printed word to assist them. Personal contact should be established by means of friendly visits. We have made enquiries for many years past, and an experiment in the manner of paying visits is now in process, since the names and addresses of a number of such girls are regularly given to the Central Council for the Social Welfare of Girls and Women in London and the *London Welsh Girls Friendly Aid Society*.

(*The Vigilance Record*. January 1930.)

D.6   When I first went there (the tin plate works) I was terrified. It was dirty, noisy. It was hot but you still worked it, because you were born to it — we practically lived next door to the place.

(Oral interview. B.W., Llanelli, 1982.)

D.7   I am the wife of a miner, and many of my people are engaged in the mining industry. I have lived all my life in the mining areas, and as a member of the Women's Co-operative Guild, and of the Labour Party, have had many opportunities of discussing the conditions with other women.

Housing

Women acquiesce in bad housing in Wales because they have no alternative, under the present circumstances due to the extreme shortage of houses, a shortage which was very acute in industrial areas long before the war. The statement made that women acquiesce in bad housing because they like low rent I strongly resent on behalf of the women, as they have had to pay a very big increase in rent this last ten years for the same houses and conditions. I quote Rhondda, for example, being one of the largest mining areas in Wales.

> Population: 165,051 (1918 estimate)
> Number of inhabited houses: 28,384
> Number of miners: 44,460 (estimate)
> The estimated need for houses at present is 1,500 to 2,000.

Houses that have been condemned before the war (not fit for human habitation) are still occupied owing to the shortage, and most of them occupied by large families.

(Evidence of Mrs Elizabeth Andrews. *Report and Minutes of Evidence of the Royal Commission on the Coal Industry.* Cmd.359,360, 1919.)

D.8   Housing accommodation and the rent paid for it are of the utmost importance to working women, and that they have taken a keen interest in these matters has been evidenced by their views expressed at many housing Conferences held in different parts of the country, and by the issue of pamphlets

The Labour Woman

Edited by Dr. Marion Phillips, M.P.

Vol. XVIII. No. 6

June, 1930

PUBLISHED BY THE LABOUR PARTY

WHO RULES THE WORLD ?

A Monthly Journal for Working Women

Paul Nash illustration for a cover of *The Labour Woman.*

setting forth the requirements of a working woman's home. In these homes the children are born, brought up, and are nursed through their illnesses. All the family life is lived within its four walls, and within them the woman does the washing, the cleaning, the cooking, the mending, and the housekeeping, with its bewildering problem of making both ends meet, besides looking after the needs of each member of the family. It is little wonder, therefore, that the Central Committee and the Sectional Councils of the Women's Co-operative Guild, representing 52,000 wives and mothers, have passed a resolution declaring that the housing of the people at rents within their capacity is a matter of vital national concern, and that if any improvement of real worth is to be made, it is absolutely necessary for the Government to tackle the question on a large scale for the whole of the country.

(*The Vote*, 9 February 1923.)

D.9 I think it may be said that the following points embody the demands of women, particularly of working women, for better housing.

1. Houses should not be built in rows, but semi-detached or in blocks of four. Fortunately the former arrangement is now a thing of the past.
2. The typical house should contain a parlour, but in every scheme there should be a small proportion of single, large living-room houses.
3. A bathroom separate from the scullery should be supplied and, in most areas, preferably an upstairs bathroom.
4. The w.c. should be in a separate room from the bathroom.
5. Each house should have an efficient supply of hot water to sink, bath and lavatory basin.
6. The entrance lobby or hall should be large enough to accommodate coats, umbrellas and small type of pram.
7. No living-room should be less in area than 170 sq.ft.,

no parlour less than 120 sq.ft., no scullery less than 80 sq.ft.

8. If the w.c. is downstairs the house should be so planned that the living-room is not a passage-way between the bedrooms and the w.c.

9. The scullery should be planned to provide convenient space for sink, copper, cooker, and a table.

10. In addition, there should be storage space, either off the back lobby or outside the house, for cycles, garden tools, etc., so as to preserve tidiness in the back premises.

11. Three bedrooms should be the minimum, and in every scheme a certain proportion of four-bed-roomed houses should be provided. The floor area of the largest bedroom should not be below 150 sq.ft., nor the smallest below 65 sq.ft.

(*The Welsh Housing Association Year Book*, 1921.)

D.10 245. *Llanberis* — Houses in some instances are so wet that the walls cannot be papered. Sacking has first to be nailed to the walls, and paper is then pasted on to the sacking. In some houses, layer after layer of paper has been pasted on to the sacking, and these conditions harbour germs and dust. One house was so damp that it could not be papered, and instead it was tarred inside. There are houses where sacking is laid under the ceiling so as to catch the dust, and there the dust has collected in such quantity that the sacking sags. In some cases the roof is leaking, and buckets have to be used to catch the water when it rains.

249. *Criccieth* — A house, occupied by a husband and wife, three children over ten and five children under ten. The accommodation is one living room, one sleeping chamber, one attic bedroom or grog-loft, and two shelters in the garden. The attic room or grog-loft, was described to us by the witness as a 'hell-hole'. It was occupied by the children, who were stated to have been lying there all day long up till quarter to half-past five on the day when he visited it. Five of the children are on the

dispensary register as contacts, and one of them has been at a
sanatorium.

(*Report of the Committee of Inquiry into the Anti-Tuberculosis Service
in Wales and Monmouthshire*, 1939.)

D.11   A woman in Caerphilly has five children, the eldest 13. Her
health is good except for teeth. She says she is on her feet for $16\frac{1}{2}$
hours a day, sometimes more, and about leisure she writes —
'After my children go to bed, I gets two hours rest, if call it rest,
I am mending my children's clothes and tidying in those few
hours I get.'

(M. Spring Rice, *Working Class Wives: Health and Conditions*,
1939. Reprinted London, 1981, p.111.)

D.12   The outstanding fact about many of these homes was that the
men in them appeared to have higher standards of personal
cleanliness than those reflected by their living conditions. It
seemed, very largely, their womenfolk who had lost all pride in
personal appearance and the appearance of the home. Men folks
were obliged to go out of doors, even if only to the
Employment Exchange; this was a reason for washing and
dressing up. The women had not this incentive. Their outings
extended little beyond the small shops at the corner of the street,
and to these they could 'slip-down' without washing. To them
there seemed little point in washing the children, as they just got
dirty anyway. All this is highly regrettable and, quite apart from
unemployment and bad housing conditions, many of the
women, even if given the opportunity and money for improved
standards, would find it an exceedingly difficult task to break
away from their acquired habits. But we must face the fact that
to live constantly on a depressed standard of living, where life is
a hand-to-mouth existence, is, except for the bravest souls, to
experience the bitterness of defeat.

(Pilgrim Trust, *Men Without Work*, Cambridge, 1938.)

D.13   As soon as the whistle went they put chairs outside their front
doors and sat there waiting till the men came up the Hill and

149

home. Then as the men came up to their front doors they threw their wages, sovereign by sovereign, into the shining laps, fathers first and sons or lodgers in a line behind.

(Richard Llewellyn, *How Green Was My Valley* (1939), New English Library edition, 1984, p.7.)

D.14   Mrs C. lives in a 'nicely situated villa' in a 'nice quiet spot' in Caerphilly. She has one child and her husband is a collier. Her housekeeping is £2 10s. od. from a full working week but she says her husband is delicate so she sometimes only gets 30/-. She is 29 years old.

Below is her average of living per week, 'when times are good':

	s.	d.
Rent	10	0
Light	2	0
Coal	2	0
Firewood		6
Clothing Club	1	6
Boot Club	1	6
Insurance	1	0
Milk	1	6
Meat	3	6
Groceries (on the average)	18	6
Bread	3	0
Fish	1	6
Vegetables	1	3
Sunday meat (about)	2	6
	£2 10	3

Breakfast: Bread and butter for all, but porridge for change.

Dinner: Fresh Veg. when possible to get with potatoes and little meat, sometimes suet pudding.

Tea: Bread and butter and cake when possible with little jam.

Supper: Very little supper. Very little tinned food
            used.

(M. Spring Rice, *Working Class Wives; Health and Conditions*,
              1939. Reprinted London, 1981, pp.178–9.)

D.15   Mrs L. C. of Cardiff, says she has been ailing since marriage. She
        was a housemaid in private service before and was never ill. She
        is now 39. She has had six children (all still living at home) and
        one miscarriage; she has a fair house but no bathroom or hot
        water, which she misses 'sadly'. She is badly constipated and has
        piles and has had bad backache 'ever since her first confinement
        which was a difficult one'. She now has also palpitation and
        cardiac pains. For none of these has she consulted anyone, but
        she listens to the wireless talks on health. She makes no
        complaints and after her remark about the lack of hot water and
        a bathroom she says hopefully 'things will ease up a bit soon
        when the children grow older'. She is however only 39 and her
        two youngest children are 4 and 3!

(M. Spring Rice, *Working Class Wives: Health and Conditions*,
              1939. Reprinted London, 1981, p.79.)

D.16   Miss Megan Lloyd George well deserved all the congratulations
        she received after she had made her maiden speech last Monday
        on the Government's new Housing Bill. She welcomed that Bill
        as a new crusade against slums because it dealt with the problem
        in rural areas. She thought it was not possible to over-emphasize
        the problem of housing in the towns, but they could and did
        under-emphasize the gravity of the problem in the rural areas;
        and she mentioned the fact that the agricultural worker was still
        the lowest paid worker in any industry. Referring to a report
        made some years ago in her own constituency of Anglesey, she
        said it was shown that the death-rate from *tuberculosis* among
        women was the highest but one on the list for the whole of the
        administrative counties in England and Wales, and yet the
        death-rate of the men came only twenty-second on that very
        black list. There could be only one explanation of that — bad
        housing. The greater risk to health was for the woman who

spent the greater part of her life in those squalid, dark, ill-ventilated cottages, and, of course, what applied to the woman also applied to the young children. She also welcomed the Bill because she felt that it was the largest scheme for unemployment that had yet been put forward.

('Miss Megan Lloyd George's Maiden Speech', reported in *The Vote*, II, April, 1930.)

D.17 We are told that the high maternal mortality in Wales is receiving the special attention of the Department. It should surely receive the special attention of the citizens throughout the Principality. Whereas in other directions mortality rates are decreasing, we are in Wales losing mothers at a preventable rate, and continuing year by year to do so.

The problem cannot be solved through one approach, since the contributing causes are many. The apathy of certain among the public bodies (upon which women are for the most part conspicuous by their absence), the insanitary conditions due to bad housing and to over-crowding, the lack of an adequate supply of trained midwives (especially in scattered rural areas), the lack of the provision of facilities for ante-natal work, the prejudices and ignorances in some cases of the women themselves — all these are contributing factors. There are others which are as yet imperfectly recognized, but whatever the causes scandal of maternal mortality in Wales is a challenge to every thinking woman and should convince public opinion of the urgent need of the greater co-operation of women in public affairs.

(*The Woman's Leader*, 12 December 1924.)

D.18 South Wales, 22 March 1921.

What I would like to know is how I can save having any more children as I think I have done my duty by my country having had 13 children — 9 boys and 4 girls and I have 6 boys alive now and a little girl who will be 3 years old in May. I buried a dear little baby girl three weeks old who died from the strain of whooping cough. I have not had much time for pleasure and it is telling on me now I suffer very bad from varicose veins in my legs and my ankles gives out and I just drops down. I am pleased to tell you that I received one of those willow plates from the News of the World for mothers of ten.

(Letter from Mrs R.G. to Marie Stopes, in R. Hall (ed.), *Dear Dr Stopes: Sex in the 1920s*, 1978, pp.17–18.)

D.19   How often in this tour have elderly women not said, 'You've come too late to help me, Comrade, but give me some papers for my girls. I don't want them to have the life I've had.'

(*The New Generation*, January, 1924.)

D.20   'There can be no question that a large number of married women are anxious to obtain reliable information about methods of preventing conception', stated Dr Ralph M. F. Picken, medical officer, reporting to Cardiff Health Committee to-day.

He anticipated, however, that the establishment of a birth control clinic would alienate 20 per cent of the women and children who were served at the present clinics, and therefore, if the city council decided to establish a birth control clinic, it should be in separate premises.

'Some members may want to consult their constituents and others their consciences', said the chairman, Alderman John Donovan, adjourning the decision till next Monday, in view of the importance of the subject and the feeling which would be roused.

'It has been maintained', said Dr Picken in his report, 'that the use of contraceptives is associated with damage to health.

Advocates of birth control clinics claim that their methods, if the advice is properly given and strictly followed, are not attended by such results.

On the other hand, it must be remembered that an alternative to birth control is being widely practised, namely, self-induced abortion, and leads not infrequently to death, and still more commonly to permanent damage.'

(*Daily Herald*, 21 April 1932.)

D.21   The deputation took place yesterday. The chief constable heard our complaints about the wholesale distribution of and selling of contraceptives in the town (Merthyr) by means of a slot machine and packing of sheaths in packages of cigarettes, sweets, etc.

(Family Planning Association Archive.)

D.22   For over a quarter of a century I have spent the summer in that queen of Welsh watering places, Aberystwyth. Walking along the promenade one day this summer I saw the welcome announcement that the Women's Freedom League had arrived and were going to hold their first meeting that night on the promenade. My thoughts went back to some seven or eight years ago, when Miss Clark and Miss Munro held their first meeting in Aberystwyth educating the public to the just claim of votes for women, and the violent opposition they met with, and how, in spite of the most hostile reception at several meetings, the opposition was eventually broken down and enthusiasm reigned instead.

 For three summers the Women's Freedom League have not held a campaign in Aberystwyth, and I waited with eagerness for their first meeting, punctually at 8 p.m. Miss Clark taking the chair, she spoke of the great strides women had made during the past four years. It was a deplorable fact that it had taken a European war to make the country realize the capacity of the women; it had been there all the time, and only wanted the opportunity. She pointed out that since the last campaign in Aberystwyth several millions of women had been enfranchised, and hoped that the enfranchised women were going to use their vote for their unenfranchised sisters and work for full equality and equal opportunity between men and women.

('An Impression of the Aberystwyth Campaign' by 'A Visitor' in *The Vote*, 26 September 1919.)

D.23   Once I was living in Wales and could see much more clearly the absolutely humiliating and devastating effect of unemployment on people particularly in the valleys, where all hope seemed to be gone. Men were standing on the street corners, pale, in

mufflers and absolutely not knowing what to do with themselves — people really hungry. Well you couldn't not take part
in any activity which would make people themselves feel that at
least they were fighting back and also you felt it was absolutely
essential to get other people to understand the enormity of the
situation.

(Oral interview, 1985, with Dora Cox, participant in the 1934
Tonypandy to London *Hunger March*.)

Debating the Evidence

As Deirdre Beddoe argues, it has long been a justifiable complaint that
the history of women has been shamefully neglected, reflecting the
wider inequalities of a society in which women rulers, women politicians
and women priests, to name just the most obvious of the establishments,
have either been extremely few in number or unthinkable. Fashions in
history have changed considerably over the last decades. There has been
an urgent movement to rescue whole sections of neglected society from
what E. P. Thompson has called 'the enormous condescension of
posterity'. In the case of women's history, that condescension is slowly
giving way to informed judgement.

Source D.1
Why do you think the editorial staff of the *Western Mail* in 1919 were
men?

Source D.2
Having read Document 2 have you in any way revised your thinking in
relation to Document 1?

Source D.3
The author uses this document to support the view that Welsh women
were trained for work outside Wales. However, there is information in
this document which might be used to support another generalization
that Dr Beddoe makes in the same paragraph about the conditions of
women domestic workers. What further information would be required
before this material could be adequately used? If you knew that large

1934, Welsh hunger marchers. (*Source: Dora Cox.*)

numbers of teachers (men and women) educated in Wales in the inter-war years were also forced to find work outside Wales would this influence your assessment of the document and the conclusions drawn from it?

Sources D.4 and D.5
How far are these documents mutually reinforcing?

Sources D.4 and D.6
What information essential to our evaluation of these sources is missing from these documents?

Source D.7
Mrs Andrews is, we are told, a member of the Labour Party — indeed she occupied the position of Women's Organizer for Wales. The *Sankey Commission* was set up to decide on the future control of the coal mining industry after the war. The Labour Party wished the State to take over the coal industry and the private owners, whose control had been wrested away for part of the war, wanted the industry to revert to private hands. In what way might Mrs Andrews's Labour Party affiliation have affected her evidence on housing? What does the document tell us about the Labour Party's attitude to women?

Sources D.7, D.8, D.9, D.10
What similarities and differences are there in the way in which these sources on housing may be used to support the general statements about the state of Welsh housing in the inter-war period?

Sources D.11 and D.12
What possible reasons are there for the apparent incompatibility between these two sources?

Source D.13
This is a short excerpt from one of the most famous novels written about the mining valleys of Wales. How far would this extract be sufficient to convince you of the supreme position of 'mam' in the Welsh household?

Sources D.14 and D.15
From the documents alone, what is it possible to deduce about M. Spring Rice?

Source D.16

The author uses this document to illustrate the prevalence of *tuberculosis* among women in Anglesey. What else does it tell us about women?

Sources D.17 to D.21

How far do these documents complement or contradict each other?

Source D.22

What problems of interpretation does this source present?

Source D.23

What are the major problems for the historian of twentieth-century Welsh history who uses oral evidence of this kind? How far are the same problems evident in using autobiography?

Discussion

The majority of the sources which Dr Beddoe uses are literary and newspaper sources. We should not be surprised. We need statistical information to provide the basic facts — for example, the numbers of women in specific jobs — we are then enabled to say that the largest proportion of Welsh women in employment between the wars were in domestic service, but this is merely the starting point in this essay. The author's main concern, more than is the case with any of the other essays, is with *attitudes* — of the press, of women's organizations, of politicians, of novelists. D.1 immediately points up the problem of interpretation associated with such sources. First, the *Western Mail* demonstrates a significant bias against women, the kind of bias which newspapers have against various groups and classes. But there is more, because the language in which this is expressed is such that the present-day *Western Mail* would never countenance. While it is possible that the *Western Mail* might still argue that a social group was being paid 'artificially inflated high wages' the paper would not dare to say today of women that, 'they have not a sufficient grasp of economic factors to appreciate . . .' Such a document prompts us to an exercise in empathy as well as interpretation. Document D.2 similarly projects us into a world of widespread domestic help foreign to present experience.

Oral evidence (D.4, D.6) is fraught with difficulties of interpretation.

How accurate is the recollection? How selective is the memory of the bad times and the grim experience? Yet, corroborated, it has an impact and an immediacy in depicting the reality of an individual experience which more formal records cannot match. And there *is* some corroboration in Document D.5. In stating that 'girls coming to London should assure themselves beforehand that the situation to which they are proceeding is a desirable one', the implication is that there are jobs which are highly undesirable for whatever reasons. Indeed the unwitting testimony in the very existence of the *Vigilance Record* is that the fate of some girls seeking work in London meant that there was much to be vigilant about. Documents D.7 to D.15 relate to the problem of health and housing in Wales in the Depression. They provide (Document D.10, for example) a salutary reminder that it was not only industrial south Wales which saw extreme poverty. Royal Commission reports indicate, unwittingly, some of the concerns of the government in Wales. The Welsh Housing Association Year Books inform us not only of the general concern of women over housing conditions but the specifications considered desirable in well-planned houses. In this respect D.9 would seem to be at variance with D.12 in that the former stresses, unintentionally, that the concept of improved housing is certainly central to working women's thinking, while D.12 gives the impression of women who have crumbled before the onslaught of deprivation, malnutrition and the type of exhaustion that is detailed in D.11.

The polarities of historical evidence are very well represented in an extract from a novel (D.13) and a household budget (D.14). It is salutary to remember that *How Green Was My Valley* has probably done more for the mythology of the Welsh 'mam' than anything, yet it hardly seems to square with D.12. But there are inadequacies in D.14, too. What can that 'nicely situated villa' be? What was the average wage of a shopkeeper or a bank manager in Caerphilly in 1939? The *relativities* of housing, food and clothing are highly significant to our interpretation, as would be some indication of the kind of diet considered adequate and healthy.

With the documentary material discussed so far it may, perhaps, be legitimate to question whether taking the women's perspective alone distorts our view of, for example, attitudes to housing, or the extent of demoralization, especially when the perspective is that of working-class women alone. Did more affluent women share a sense of exploitation? When we get on to those documents dealing with birth control they again tend to be associated with the women of Wales in the Depression. Whether it was the enormity of the effect of the Depression or the condescension of men to women that gave rise to the information in this range of documents is not answered by the documents themselves. Can it ever finally be answered by the historian?

Wales and Film

PETER STEAD

The public showing of motion-pictures had first become a popular form of urban entertainment in the last years of the nineteenth century and then later, in the period following the First World War, it rapidly developed into the major form of mass entertainment in most of the world's industrial and urban regions. At the turn of the century south Wales had been as dynamic an industrial region as any in the world and so it was hardly surprising that, as far as the commercial exhibition of films was concerned, Cardiff and Swansea were as advanced as any other towns outside the major centres of London, Paris and New York. In fact, so popular were motion pictures in south Wales that one local showman, William Haggar, was inspired into making fictional feature films that were as ambitious and polished as the world's best. After 1918 Wales experienced a period of economic decline and south Wales was no longer a trend-setting urban area but, of course, the inhabitants of Welsh towns retained their urban appetites and expected to be entertained in as varied and sophisticated a way as the rest of the world's population. Above all, they wanted to see the best and most recent films.

The statistics of film-going in the inter-war years are quite massively intimidating: by 1939 some 23 million tickets were being sold every week in British cinemas, already in 1934 there was one cinema seat in south Wales for every ten persons and one for every thirteen in north Wales. The many contemporary surveys indicated that the basis of cinema's popularity was a pattern in which younger people went more often than the middle-aged or elderly and in which workers and their families went more often than middle-class professional groups. From the very earliest days of the century both the showmen-entrepreneurs who ran cinemas and the production companies which provided the films had battled to increase their profits and improve their social prestige by attracting a wider range of social groups, so lessening their dependence on those at the

E.1   bottom of the social scale (E.1). To achieve this end they had constructed increasingly attractive and comfortable cinemas and this was especially the case after the coming of talking pictures at the end of the 1920s. By the 1930s every urban area had a number of cinemas which ranged from the rough 'industrial halls' (as they were called) to the very smart and exotic Odeons, but in any case nearly every cinema, however luxurious, still catered for those who could only afford to sit in

E.3   the front of the stalls (E.3). The statistics suggest that the showmen had won their battle for a mass audience but their victory was never total for whilst most adolescents and courting couples, and many young married couples, became regular film-goers the cinema had never fully convinced either educated people or religious groups that it deserved to be regarded as a serious or respectable activity. By the late 1930s most politicians and social leaders had come to see that the cinema probably provided harmless entertainment for workers, adolescents and the unemployed but there was always a general wish that those classes would engage in more worthwhile and demanding activities. Religious leaders, having seen the cinema replace the chapel in the lives of most young people, concentrated their efforts on ensuring that at least there would be no performances

E.2   on Sundays (E.2).

As soon as the popularity of films had become evident, politicians and reformers had taken steps to ensure that this new form of entertainment would not corrupt. From the earliest days British and American film companies had been told that their films could not be sexually explicit or politically contro-versial. Producers were always far too well aware that the authorities were eager to pounce and, in any case, respectable films were precisely what they themselves needed in their campaign to bring in a better class of audience. In America, there were always enormous pressures on film-makers whilst in

Britain the industry had, in 1912, set up its own Board of Film Censors which ensured, in a quite informal and unofficial way from that time on, that there would be nothing offensive or controversial in films that went on general release. The film companies and the authorities conspired, then, to ensure that entertainment would be the main aim of the cinema in the English-speaking world and that seemed to be a formula that met with the approval of the great mass of film-goers. Reformers and radicals were always pressing for films that would instruct, improve or challenge but showmen, politicians and the regular audience seemed satisfied with sheer entertainment. All the evidence suggests that what people wanted to see when they went to the cinema were well-made fictional films with a strong narrative line, an emphasis on adventure, romance or humour, and a cast of attractive stars. For economic reasons the production of this kind of feature film had become concentrated in Hollywood, California and, throughout the inter-war years, the massive film audience in Britain associated the best in film entertainment with the five or six major Hollywood studios. For the most part, British films were thought of as supporting films or fill-in items, so most British film-goers would never have expected to see films set in their own communities or dealing realistically with the social and political problems of their everyday lives. Obviously, to be successful, feature films had to measure up to certain standards and had to deal with characters, emotions and incidents that were rooted in real life, but there is no evidence that the mass audience expected or desired a realistic depiction of their own social experiences.

Of course, British film audiences were not subjected to an unrelieved diet of feature films and, by the 1930s, most cinemas would have been showing the regular newsreel bulletins produced by the various newsreel companies in London. The newsreels made much of their depiction of actuality and competed with each other to be as up-to-date as possible: signature tunes, background music, very official-sounding commentators and bold captions were all used to heighten the tension and to create a sense of journalistic urgency and yet, in reality, they hardly dealt with contemporary issues at all. No

A poignant image from the 1930s — empty coal trucks from Ralph Bond's 1937 film *Today We Live*.

other form of film was so highly censored and the efforts made
by the government to prevent the filming of the *Hunger Marches*
serves as a reminder that the newsreels had been instructed to
exclude any depiction of controversial political and industrial
materials (E.4). Politically, the newsreel companies contented

E.4

themselves with support for the king and his government and
with general remarks about the British genius for avoiding
confrontation. In any case the newsreels were always meant to
be entertaining and they always ensured that political headlines
were accompanied by human-interest stories. Their approach
was essentially tabloid, as the example of their treatment of

E.5

Wales so clearly illustrates (E.5). Perhaps because of the rather
unusual nature of the protest, the newsreel companies gave a
full and sympathetic coverage to the stay-down strikes by Welsh
miners in 1935, but otherwise cinema-goers would only have
seen the depressed valleys on the occasion of visits by the Prince
of Wales and by far the most frequently filmed event in Wales
was Cardiff's annual Corpus Christi procession. The generally
bland nature of British newsreels was underlined by the great
critical acclaim given to the American newsreel series, *The
March of Time*, and one 1937 issue of this newsreel dealt in some
detail with the Welsh coal trade, actually depicting *Arthur
Horner* and other miners' leaders. Of course these imported
newsreels would only have been seen in a few selected cinemas
but, even then, they would have been seen by more people than
the various independent newsreels made by the Communist
Party and other groups on the left.

Such was the dominance of Hollywood and of the feature
film in the 1930s that a group of British film-makers, inspired in
particular by the Scottish political scientist John Grierson, set
out to create a new kind of non-fictional film in which there
would be a creative or artistic treatment of actuality. For this
new genre, Grierson derived the term 'documentary' and
throughout the 1930s British documentary film-makers proceeded to make short films about everyday aspects of life in
Britain. Some of the most important and critically acclaimed of
these films were to deal either wholly or in part with the coal-
mining valleys of south Wales. Film directors went to south
Wales at first because they wanted dramatic shots of working

miners, but later they went to make films about the relief agencies working amongst the unemployed. Whatever the initial consideration however, the films made about south Wales reflected more than anything else the way in which unemployment amongst miners had become a political and cultural reference point for so many intellectuals. South Wales had become a national 'problematic' and film-makers soon saw the possibility of using the visual drama of both unemployment and the scenery in south Wales as the basis of powerful cinematic images. Shots of the unemployed searching for coal on the tips of south Wales were destined to become the most dramatic image of the Depression in the United Kingdom, but again the irony is that films like *Today We Live* and *Eastern Valley* were seen more frequently in London's art cinemas than they were in south Wales itself, and the same was generally true

E.16   of several other forms of independently-made films (E.16).

The vast majority of British cinemas were owned either by major companies or by independent entrepreneurs and in both cases the film programme would have been largely determined by national distributors who would have been linked in turn with the production companies. In general, the proprietors and managers of individual cinemas had little say in what films they exhibited, although they lost little opportunity in making known what they took to be their patrons' preference for well-made American films and their accompanying dislike for documentaries. In south Wales there was one interesting variation on this pattern, for the thirty or so Welfare and Workmen's Halls that were fully equipped as cinemas afforded local committees some say in the selection of films. Evidence suggests that at least some of the committees did attempt to introduce more serious films into their programme but the very fact that the halls were equipped to show 35mm films meant that, for the most part, they had to rely on precisely the same films that were distributed to the commercial cinemas. These were subject to all the normal constraints of censorship. The irony was that most independent and propaganda film was available only on 16mm film: these films were much less heavily censored but organizations wishing to show them had to rely on using halls that were not regular cinemas and even then there

An audience in a cinema in the 1930s. (*Source: BBC Hulton Picture Library.*)

E.7   were often problems with the authorities (E.7). These irregular film showings were always expensive and difficult to organize and they were never popular with a public who had been spoilt by the comfort and excellent projection facilities of proper

E.6   cinemas (E.6).

Until the mid-1930s very few people in Britain or America had taken film seriously either in terms of artistic content or social comment. As the decade proceeded so critics began to detect that American films had improved and began to appreciate in particular the ways in which many of these American films fed off energies in contemporary American society. There was, as always, an admiration for the polish and style of the American product but now in addition there was an appreciation of new elements of realism. What had been vital was the coming of sound which had led to a more realistic style of acting and then had encouraged writers and actors to rely increasingly on other idioms of contemporary American urban life. The other great influences were the phenomenon of mass unemployment and then of President Roosevelt's New Deal, both of which encouraged some producers to set their stories against a background of social tension and dislocation. As always with Hollywood, the emphasis was still on narrative, on personal redemption and on melodrama, but in a significant number of films these traditional features were now linked up to contemporary social issues. This was particularly true of a small number of what were called 'social problem' films which used their stories to condemn evils such as the prison chain-gangs and mob violence or which relied on the setting of a strike or a protest. These films were in fact a good deal more conventional than they seemed but, viewed alongside the larger number of crime and urban problem films and in particular the social comedies of Frank Capra, they confirmed that Hollywood was capable of fairly intelligent social comment and also underlined precisely what was wrong with British films. By 1938 most of the leading British critics were crying out for some measure of

E.8   social significance in British films (E.8).

It was against this background that Wales really made its debut in the movies. *The Citadel*, which was made in 1938, was not only the first important feature film to deal with contemporary Welsh society but it was also widely regarded as one of the best British films ever made. It tells the story of a doctor who struggles to find his true values after having had his initial idealism dented by the stupidity and prejudices he encounters during his first job in the south Wales valleys. The film was acclaimed by the critics because, quite unusually for a British film, it had a serious message (it was making a plea for a national system of public medicine), but even more because that message was carried along by a good strong story and set first in a very recognizable south Wales and then in an equally recognizable London. *The Citadel* is a good film and it is important to understand those factors which suddenly allowed such an effective social drama to be made in 1938. In part the answer lies in the growing influence of Hollywood within the British film industry as such and indeed it can be argued that *The Citadel* was really an American social problem film made in Britain: it was produced by an American company (MGM) and directed by *King Vidor* who had already made some of Hollywood's most famous social problem films.

American companies were making films in London so as to get around quota restrictions and the great benefit of their films was the enormous emphasis they could place on the quality of their productions: everything about *The Citadel* suggested a new emphasis on quality. The other reason why *The Citadel* was made was because as war became an increasing certainty there was undoubtedly a slight relaxation in censorship and *Vidor*'s film was one of a number made at that time which took up relatively radical positions on certain issues. Not that censorship had been entirely relaxed, for MGM and *Vidor* were still careful to ensure that the radical critique of private medicine came as part of the hero's redemption rather than from any political organization. In fact, *Vidor* was very much an American rural Progressive and as such had little sympathy with labour unions and in *The Citadel*, in order to emphasize the initial idealism of his hero, he is quite prepared to suggest that the miners' own organization was reactionary and corrupt and a real obstacle to medical progress. In other words, *Vidor* was only interested in a south Wales setting in order to facilitate his narrative and he was quite prepared to distort and ignore the

(*Source: Weintraub Entertainment (Administration) Limited.*)

real nature of voluntary medical schemes and of trade unionism. His film was based on an autobiographical novel by the radical Scottish doctor, A. J. Cronin, but of course MGM were less interested in the precise details of the novel than they were in enjoying the publicity and prestige of having made a film of such a well-known and admired book. This was another well-known Hollywood technique guaranteed to bring in those too respectable and serious to go the cinema regularly.

As *The Citadel* was completed, a British company was already filming *The Stars Look Down*, a novel in which Cronin had made a case for the nationalization of the mines. The story was set in the Durham coalfield, but American reviewers always referred to the film's Welsh setting and certainly the presence of *Emlyn Williams*, together with the general subject matter, gave the film

E.9 a very Welsh atmosphere (E.9). In subsequent interviews, the director, Carol Reed, always stressed that he was not interested in any political message but nevertheless the case for national-ization is very effectively made in a number of scenes. What is certainly true is that the emphasis is on melodrama, and once again the union is depicted as a stupid and reactionary organization; quite incredibly there is no suggestion that the miners' union had long been pressing for nationalization. Every important idea has to emanate from the hero in true Hollywood

E.10 style (E.10).

Just as the war began, Ealing Studios completed a film called *The Proud Valley* which told of a fight to save a Welsh pit from closure. In the original script it was intended that the miners would occupy the pit and then run it themselves but in the final film it was the onset of war which gained a reprieve for the workforce. The most remarkable feature of the film was the way in which a black sailor, played by Paul Robeson, comes to the Valley and fits into the community both as a miner and as a

E.11 soloist with the local choir (E.11). Throughout the film the singing creates a marvellously warm sense of communal, racial and class solidarity, but remarkably there is no hint of trade union organization and all initiatives have to come from individual miners. *The Proud Valley* was directed by the young Englishman, Pen Tennyson, and, whilst it has considerable charm, it was less well written and acted than the two Cronin films and much of the dialogue and characterization are hopelessly stylized and provide an early example of the caricatured way Welshness was to be depicted in British films E.12 for the next twenty years (E.12). This flurry of social-problem films reached its apogee in 1941 with John Baxter's film of Walter Greenwood's novel *Love on the Dole*. Throughout the 1930s the censors had not allowed a film to be made of this story of the unemployed in the North of England and even now Baxter's film was to have few sequels: from 1941 the emphasis was on the production of films about the people of Britain winning the war and, in fact, it was to be another twenty years before the film companies returned to look closely at industrial communities in Britain.

In America too the sense that war was imminent encouraged Hollywood to extol the virtues of the common man and films were made of John Steinbeck's novel *The Grapes of Wrath* and Richard Llewellyn's *How Green Was My Valley*. Twentieth Century Fox's film of Llewellyn's novel is probably the most famous and popular film ever made about Wales. It was shot in Hollywood on a ludicrously artificial set and it dealt in all the sentimental clichés that so many critics thought of as the hallmarks of American cinema. Yet the director, John Ford, remembering the Ireland of his ancestors, was able to convey such a powerful sense of family and community that many film-goers around the world were overwhelmed and thereafter could E.13 only think of Wales in these terms (E.13, E.14, E.15).
E.14
E.15

Sources

This press report from the early days of cinema illustrates the fears that some people had about the social impact of films: even in the 1930s many respectable people were prejudiced against the cinema in this way:

E.1   At Swansea Quarter Sessions on Friday last 'penny horribles' and bioscope pictures of burglaries were said to have influenced two youths in committing a number of burglaries and stealing jewellery. Their names were Pendarvis Tagholm and David John Harris and they at once pleaded guilty. For the Prosecution it was stated that the prisoners appeared to have entered on a career of crime after reading sensational fiction, their favourite work being *The Life of Charles Peace*. Detective Sergeant Howard said that the boys had seen bioscope pictures of a burglary and they stole a revolver and dagger to arm themselves like the hero of the pictures. The Recorder in binding the prisoners over under the Probationers Act said that if they went into a music-hall or any place of that kind or entered a public-house within the next two years they would be brought up and sentenced.

(*The Bioscope*, 9 October 1908.)

In the 1930s politicians and social reformers expended a great deal of energy worrying about whether the unemployed were spending their time doing useful things. In this extract we see that cinema-going was still not really thought of as a worthwhile activity:

E.2   It is certainly no new contribution to state that young people like to go to the Cinema. Where there is a choice of visiting several cinemas, frequent visits, as long as finances allow, are customary. About 22 per cent of the sample were in the habit of visiting a cinema at least twice a week.

In what lies the special appeal of the cinema? The views expressed by these young people can be summarized as follows:

a) The cinema is a form of escape — 'something to get your mind off things'.

b) It portrays a romantic 'wish-fulfilment world'.

c) The modern cinema is a comfortable building. Many of these young people confessed to receiving a 'thrill' from the carpets and comfortable seats.

d) Because of the darkness, it is possible to go to the cinema after 'slipping on your coat'.

e) Cinema topics are news. It appears just as necessary for these young people to be able to discuss the latest film as it is for others to be able to talk about the best-seller in literature.

Haggar's Cinema, Aberdare. (*Source: Aberdare Central Library.*)

Many of the cinema attenders revealed a technique of criticism of the films which they saw. Too many, however, went to the cinema even when they confessed they knew that no good film was showing. If the cinema invariably showed films of a high standard, the regular attendance of these young people could be understood and appreciated. It is to be regretted, however, that their participation even in this form of leisure activity has become 'routine' and not actuated by intelligent interest.

(A.J. Lush, *The Young Adult in South Wales*; Being A Report Prepared in Co-operation with Young Men in Cardiff, Newport and Pontypridd. Under the Auspices of The Carnegie United Kingdom Trust, 1941.)

To bring in a better class of customer the showmen built grander and grander cinemas and as they were opened to the public had to be assured that they were being offered only the very best:

E.3   In the construction of this beautiful theatre every care has been taken to erect it on the most modern lines. 'Safety' combined with beauty has been the ideal, and this has been achieved in every detail in the Building. Nothing has been left to chance in order to make the edifice a safe and comfortable one for Patrons. It has seating capacity for 3,000 people and the two Cafes will accommodate 300.

No efforts will be spared in providing the best Talking and Silent Films and the Grand Organ Music will be a feature that will certainly appeal to Swansea and West Wales Patrons who are renowned for their love of good Music . . . Indeed it can confidently be said that it is one of the finest Cinemas in the Provinces, both from the point of view of elevation and internal arrangements.

The Woodwork is carried out in Teak with Burr Walnut panels and Cellulose treated. The Facade and Interior Decorations have been treated in the Renaissance style with Celtic motifs introduced into the fibrous work. A panel in Bas-relief depicting the Gorsedd Ceremony of the Welsh Druids has been introduced over the Proscenium Arch with the organ grilles suitably disguised on either side. Two additional panels with subjects of local interest form part of the design of the Boxes, one on each side of the Proscenium. Electric Light Fountains form a pleasing feature of those Boxes.

(*The Plaza Cinema, Swansea*, Souvenir Brochure, Inaugural Ceremony, 14 February 1931.)

The Newsreel companies appreciated that they should not film controversial social and political stories but in the 1930s the *Hunger Marches* of the unemployed seemed too good a story to miss. The final rallies of the Marchers in Hyde Park always occasioned the sharpest tension between the film world and the authorities:

E.4 An example of the kind of thing that may happen unless we have some hold occurred in 1932 in conjunction with the demonstrations by the so-called '*Hunger Marchers*'.

Some very unfortunate films were taken and exhibited which, by isolating small incidents, gave an entirely exaggerated impression of what was going on and made it look as if the Police were being unnecessarily violent and brutal. The Companies then operating were therefore asked to abstain from taking any pictures of the demonstrations and they all willingly agreed except one — the Paramount Company — who took films and sent them to America where they were widely exhibited.

An opportunity of 'retaliating' upon the Paramount Company occurred almost at once when they asked for some special facilities to photograph the Lord Mayor's Show.

These facilities were refused and the Company were told in effect when they protested that if they would not put themselves out a little to help us, we should not be inclined to afford them any special assistance.

(Home Office Minute, (H.O.45), signed by Sir Philip Game, Commissioner of Police of the Metropolis, 28 October 1938.)

E.5 Not the slightest mention on any of the film news reels of the *Hunger Marchers* or of the tremendous London demonstrations. I have been looking out for them in the London cinemas but cannot find a trace: and I suppose the same is true of all the provincial cinemas . . .

So the distortion and suppression on the news reels goes on . . . In this way the film magnates suppress vital news and so hope to mould opinion along lines favourable to capitalism and capitalist repression of all forms of working-class action. It would be interesting to discover whether this suppression of a vitally important newsreel item was due to the action of the film companies themselves, or to intervention by the Censor or a direct approach by the Government.

At any rate — however it was contrived — the *Hunger Marchers* and the demonstrations and the baton charges are not news; but the visit of Princess Ingrid and her relationship to the Duke of Connaught and Queen Victoria is very important news, as also is the visit of the Arsenal Football team to France, and a woman swinging by her teeth over New York . . . and so on through the whole gamut of piffle and snobbery.

(*Daily Worker*, 7 November 1932; Home Office Files (H.O.45).)

A number of organizations and especially the Communist Party arranged screenings for 16mm versions of Russian and German films that had not been granted a certificate by the censors in their 35mm form or had not been taken up by commercial cinemas. Independent newsreels would also be shown. Even then the authorities could make difficulties as the Peace Pledge Union found in 1939:

E.6   '*Potemkin*', '*Free Thaelmann*' and '*Rhondda*' will be on tour in South Wales during February with full amplified musical accompaniment. Low inclusive charge for all organizations, miners' lodges, etc. Reserve your show now.

(Advert for Kino Films, *Daily Worker*, 17 January 1936.)

E.7   P.P.U. local organization in Cardiff wished to hold a film show on December 16th. The films in question were *Kamaradschaft* and three P.P.U. shorts of appeals by Dick Sheppard, Lansbury and Stuart Morris. All on 16mm non-flam. stock.

. . . at the film show two cops and one fireman were present. The fireman insisted that the operator make a roped-off enclosure around the projector, and that he should have a sand bucket and a fire extinguisher somewhere handy. The operator complied with these requirements to save a row and the risk of having the show stopped. The fireman also asked a lot of questions about fuses, double pole switches, etc. in the projector circuit. The operator was able to make sufficiently satisfactory answers to these questions.

The point is that this visit by the police and the fireman is *ultra vires*. The police appear to have been acting under Part Two of the Cinematograph Regulations 1923 . . . pursuance of the Act of 1909. The Act of 1909 relates solely to *inflammable films* . . . The action of the police and fire authorities in attempting to enforce flam. film regulations on a non-flam. show, is therefore *ultra vires* and illegal. What about a protest to the Chief Constable and letters to the Cardiff papers?

(Memo to National Council of Civil Liberties Central Committee, 3 January 1939. NCCL Files, Hull University Library. The full letter is published in Don MacPherson (editor), *Traditions of Independence*, British Film Institute, 1980.)

E.8   The chief reason, apart from occasional examples of sheer technical inability, for the conspicuous lack of success which attend most British films lies in their remoteness from the lives of the people . . . This is not the case with American films. They are not afraid to pillory any aspect of American life that suggests itself. Crime, graft, poverty, slums — all have been exposed to the world via Hollywood. In this country we are more genteel . . . It might be said that the road to the cemetery of British films is littered with the half-chewed bones of history . . . It surprises me that no producer has thought of making a film around a coal mine. The stories of Rhys Davies could be adapted. Producers need to emerge from their stupid little world of make-believe and start catering for the people who do most to keep them going.

(David Thomas. Letter to *Daily Worker*, 9 May 1938.)

E.9   This smashing filming on Cronin's five year-old novel of the Welsh coal-fields [*sic*] could never have happened in Hollywood. It is grim, ruthless, relentless, full of the dark stenches of slimy mines . . . It takes a savage crack at selfish capital . . . M.G.M. acquired it, then hesitated to release it. Its sneers at capital left the movie moguls worried. But here it is two years later. It never will be box-office, but it is an outstanding film achievement for the discerning.

(Review of *The Stars Look Down* in *Liberty Magazine*, 16 August 1941.)

E.10   This is what is most likely to happen to the work of any Socialist novelist when translated into capitalist film. His ideas with all the Socialism subtracted can so easily be made fascist. This after all is what capitalists today would like . . . that the State should seem to have the responsibility for the welfare of industry and that they would still enjoy their profits.

(Elizabeth Young, *Tribune*, 26 January 1940. Review of *The Stars Look Down*.)

E.11   'If it had been a film about any other subject I would not have come — not if you were to pay me thousands for it. But (he told Balcon) because you've got the courage to make a film about a piece of the country that's neglected and forgotten until another explosion or disaster awakens public interest for a day or two then I'll stay and work with you . . . As a child I've covered dead men's faces down the mines. I've been sent to tell the women about the death of their men in the pit. I've been storing all these experiences up . . . Now it's as if the sluice gates were opened.'

(The writer Jack Jones, referring to *The Proud Valley*, on his involvement with Ealing Studios, *Western Daily Mail*, 10 June 1939.)

E.12   It is unfortunate for everybody concerned in *The Proud Valley* that *The Stars Look Down* preceded it: if that fine film had not set a standard this picture of a Welsh mining village would have seemed a worthy, if rather dim, little picture: one might have been tempted to overpraise it for the sake of a few authentic scenes with a G.P.O. touch — the meeting, for example, of the miners' choir to prepare for the Eisteddfod. No picture of a mining district ever seems to be complete without a disaster (we have two in this picture): the warning siren is becoming as familiar as the pithead gear shot against the sky — and that has joined the Eiffel Tower and the Houses of Parliament among the great platitudes of the screen; and yet a far worse tragedy in a district like this must be just inaction. This, perhaps, is the theme of the picture — women pretending sickness when the rate-collector calls, credit petering out at the general store, but too many red-herrings scent the storyline beside the disasters: colour prejudice is dragged in for the sake of Mr Paul Robeson who plays the part of a big black Pollyanna, keeping everybody cheerful and dying nobly at the end (Mr Robeson's fat sentimental optimism seemed to me a little revolting); and the theme dies out altogether at the close with patriotic speeches and crisis posters and miners dying for England!

(Graham Greene, *The Spectator*, 15 March 1940.)

E.13 'I am disappointed in the script, mainly because it has turned into a labor story about real living people. I think we should take a revolutionary viewpoint of the screenplay of this story and we should tell it as the book does — through the eyes of Huw, the little boy . . . If we use this technique we can capture much of the wonderful descriptive dialogue of the book, particularly when the boy talks about the valley and about his father and mother . . . I get the impression that we are trying to do an English *Grapes of Wrath* and prove that the mineowners were very mean and that the labourers finally won out over them. All this might be fine if it were happening today, like *Grapes of Wrath*, but this is years ago and who gives a damn? The smart thing to do is try to keep all the rest in the background and focus mainly on the human story as seen through Huw's eyes.'

(Producer Daryl F. Zanuck's reaction to Ernest Pascal's initial script of *How Green Was My Valley*: Mel Gussow, *Don't Say Yes Until I Finish Talking. A Biography of Daryl F. Zanuck*, 1971.)

E.14 *How Green Was My Valley* is technically one of the finest flowerings of the sound motion picture. In the rather rambling memories of a man recalling his boyhood in a little Welsh mining town, memories as unplotted as might emerge in anyone's fond recollection, John Ford has found something to put his best craftsmanship and feeling into, and no one has better craftsmanship in movies, nor sounder and tenderer feeling, than John Ford at his best.

There is inescapably, a unifying mood, lyric and nostalgic, and the final, vivid memory of the picture is of a family which the pressure of change and changing ways broke up and scattered. The music does as much as anything to create and sustain this mood, along with the device of using the voice of Huw grown up, to keep in our mind what we see is what he most poignantly remembers of his boyhood. The Welsh singers are always in the background for atmosphere, and the emotional lift, sad or gay, that such singing gives to the screen's action.

(James S. Hamilton in the American *National Board of Review Magazine*, Vol.XVI, No.8, 1941. The film was 'Rated Exceptional'.)

E.15   An awkward film to review. Most of the film is so good that it is difficult to understand why the rest should be so bad. I should think it is the first real film about ordinary people that has come from Hollywood. That is, a film of ordinary people living their ordinary lives. There is no epic trek across a continent, no battle against Fascist cops as in *The Grapes of Wrath*, no romantic boozing in the tropics, no fights over luscious dames or against bombers — Nothing that happens is out of the ordinary.

There is a lot of rough stuff in the film. The long shots of the much publicized mining-village set are atrocious. The mining cottage interiors are about the size of a football pitch. A lot of the acting is not of the best, but it always seems to be difficult for actors to play ordinary people, and there are always the two fake slopes in the background. But the good stuff bears down all the faults and you remember with a great deal of pleasure *How Green Was My Valley* as a rich and human film of ordinary people.

(*Documentary News Letter*, Vol.3, No.2, February 1942.)

E.16   *Eastern Valley* has been made by the Strand Film Company to describe the activity of a society called the 'order of friends' in a distressed Welsh area. The older men have been given the chance to work on the land without losing their unemployment pay. The object is a psychological one — they receive no pay: but the whole community of unemployed families benefit by cheaper goods. The film has been directed by a newcomer, Donald Alexander. He has learnt from Anstey the value of direct reporting; the appalling cottages held up by struts from falling, dwarfed by the slagheaps; the trout stream turned into a drain, one empty fag packet floating down between the old tins; the direct interview with the wife of an unemployed man; but he has learnt too from Basil Wright how to express poetically a moral judgement. Life as it once was before industry scarred and mutilated the valley; life as it is, life as it should be.

(Graham Greene, *Night and Day*, 16 December 1937.)

Debating the Evidence

There have always been pictorial sources from which the social historian has been able to gain invaluable insights. Indeed with such sources we revert to pre-history because the cave paintings of Lascaux or Altamira long pre-date any written record. Yet, despite paintings and woodcuts and lithographs, the invention of still photography and film photography constitutes something of a quantum leap in historical source material. The movies changed lifestyles and historians' interpretations of lifestyles.

Source E.1
Why might you be prepared to attach particular weight to the information conveyed in this document?

Source E.2
In what ways may this document be giving us much significant information about south Wales in the Depression?

Source E.3
What does this document, ostensibly limited in information to describing the Plaza Cinema, Swansea, tell us about Welshness and contemporary conceptions of Welshness?

Sources E.4 and E.5
Home Office records, like those of all government departments, are
closed to the public (including professional historians) for at least thirty
years from the time they came into existence. How does this knowledge
affect our assessment of these documents? What is the significance of
Document E.5, a newspaper, being found among Home Office papers?

Sources E.6 and E.7
What information is needed about the *Daily Worker* and the Council for
Civil Liberties before the historian can derive full benefit from the
information contained here?

Sources E.8 and E.9
In view of the information available in earlier documents, particularly
E.2, how far do you accept the view expressed by David Thomas in this
letter (E.8)? How far are your views modified by E.9?

Sources E.10, E.11, E.12
What are the strengths and weaknesses of these sources as historical
evidence for the historian of film of Wales in the 1930s?

Source E.13
Daryl F. Zanuck was a Hollywood film producer, here talking about a
script of a novel about the south Wales valleys. The distorting prisms
through which views of south Wales might pass are made obvious here.
How valuable are the facts here — and our knowledge of the
distortions?

Sources E.14, E.15, E.16
Life as it once was before industry scarred and mutilated the valley: life
as it is, life as it should be (E.16). Which of these three do we learn most
about?

Discussion

There is a fundamental incongruity about this material which is not the
case elsewhere in this book. A historian discussing film, without his
readers having seen the movies he is discussing, is perhaps at as much of

a disadvantage as the music historian whose readers have not heard a note of the composers' work. Many will have seen those three seminal films, *The Stars Look Down*, *Proud Valley* and *How Green Was My Valley*. The advice to those who have not is that Peter Stead's essay and his documents make them required viewing. Of course, many of the documents presented here have an impact as historical evidence in their own right. The prejudices of early twentieth-century society — epitomized in its law-enforcers — are all the more forceful in that they are recorded in a publication (E.1) which publicized the development of bioscope pictures. The document provides an incidental if salutary reminder that public opinion on this matter seems to rest on similarly unproven assertion nowadays.

There is a moral stance in other documents, very significantly in a document of record (E.2). The core of the document is the views of young people frequenting cinemas. There is no reason to doubt that these opinions were accurately summarized and recorded by A. J. Lush, whose socialist sympathies provide further authentication in that he would have wanted more elevated reasons from them. Indeed this is reinforced by Lush's highly subjective comment: 'it is to be regretted that their participation even in this form of leisure activity has become "routine" and not actuated by intelligent interest.' It is fascinating to compare this high-mindedness with that expressed in E.8. The perception of this correspondent to the communist *Daily Worker* is that films should be socially critical — a view wholly consistent with the attitude of the *Daily Worker* which was that the 'crime, graft, poverty and slums' of 1930s' Britain should be constantly highlighted. However, the caution which the historian needs to exercise is amply demonstrated in that the seeming logic of the sentiment that 'producers need to emerge from the stupid little world of make-believe and start catering for the people who do most to keep them going' (E.8) is contradicted by E.2's record of what cinema-goers in the south Wales of the Depression actually said they wanted from the cinema — escapism, warmth, comfort, darkness. The way in which the *Daily Worker* could so easily be right and wrong in the space of a paragraph is graphically illustrated in E.4 and E.5. News was suppressed — but the real villain as far as Paramount was concerned was the British government, governing in this instance by blackmail. Indeed the ironies inherent in these documents are enhanced in E.3. Here, in 1931 at the height of the Depression is the opening of a plush, luxurious, no-expense-spared cinema. True, Swansea and the anthracite end of the coalfield were far less badly hit than the eastern valleys of Wales, but this kind of self-advertisement must have jarred with the unemployed. The concessions to Welshness are equally fascinating — epitomizing escapism once again in a world of Celts and bards. Still, this in itself is indicative that some Welsh sentiment was felt appropriate in the predominantly American world of Swansea cinema.

The views of Wales have been filtered through a complex variety of media down the centuries. None has been as powerful as the moving picture. It may be that more people in America and Britain have been conditioned in their vision of Wales by *The Proud Valley* and *How Green Was My Valley* than by any other medium of information. Ultimately, sources E.8 to E.16 leave us with a fascinating paradox. The artistic imagination can be harnessed to a depiction of reality of experience which is dramatically effective (E.9). *Proud Valley* produces now a minor schizophrenia in Welsh people. They still share, at least in communal memory, Jack Jones's experience. Yet we cannot ignore the analysis of as talented an artist as Graham Greene, a perspective made all the more pointed by the realization of how far film material has been filtered by the time novelist, script writer and eventually director have got their hands on it (E.13). Film — newsreel, documentary or feature — enhances graphically our perception of how the reality of the past so tantalizingly eludes our grasp, whatever the richness of the source material.

Writing Wales

DAVID SMITH

The most famous writer to emerge in Wales between the two world wars was Dylan Thomas (1914–53), whose *18 Poems* (1934) immediately proclaimed his precocious, bubbling-over talent to the world. Yet, at first sight, Dylan Thomas, *the* Welsh poet as the world came to decide, is not representative of his people or their country. He was neither Welsh-speaking nor nationalistic — 'Land of my fathers, and my fathers can keep it' — left Wales and formal education as soon as he indecently could and only returned for comfort, nostalgia and fantasy. He knew next to nothing of the racking social and economic dislocation affecting industrial Wales to the east and north of Swansea and even less of its politics of protest and rebellion or accommodation and despair. In a radio broadcast of 1946 he recalled the poetry of social protest that had already been marked out as typical of the 'Angry Thirties' and paraphrased the themes he found in the work of his Welsh contemporaries — though it was really Alun Lewis (1915–44) of whom *he* spoke:

> They spoke, in ragged and angry rhythms, of the Wales they knew: the dole queues, the stubborn bankrupt villages, the children, scrutting for coal on the slag heaps, the colliers' shabby allotments, the cheap-jack cinema, the whippet races, the disused quarries, the still pit wheels, the gaunt tin-roofed chapels . . . the hewers squatting in the cut . . . the scummed river.

None of this imagery figures in his own work. He openly

acknowledged it as alien to him. However, in that same radio
F.14   talk (F.14) he lingered over the details of his own, local Wales
and 'the fine, live people' who were, for him 'the spirit of Wales
itself'. We can see now that Thomas's suburban Wales in which
private, familial satellites circle, without touching, the larger,
public society is more central to the twentieth century Welsh
experience than once seemed possible. It is the world of slate
quarries, of collieries, tin plate mills and terraced streets that
seems like History, not the world of semi-detached and private
dreams and shrinking communities. We may not always
recognize a public Wales in Dylan Thomas but we can surely
detect in his shadow-play the Wales that lurked outside the
door. Writers do not document reality, they interpret it. If they
are good enough they manage to explain it: through unexpected
connections, unbidden thoughts, unwanted juxtapositions of
ideas, images, people and events. They would be only newspapers if they pretended that a collection of random facts
reflects reality. Instead they strive to refract actuality until it
takes on a meaningful shape in the mind. They seek the form
that will suggest the significance of the experience. And since
the inter-war years were so adept at creating their own
mythology of words and pictures, later writers often needed to
peel away the layers to remind us that life was unclear, petty,
funny, confusing and overwhelming, not fixed and certain. Like
Dylan Thomas they emphasize the vision of the child to make
the public domain freshly available. Dannie Abse (b.1923) and
Alun Richards (b.1929) were, like Thomas and Alun Lewis,
relatively affluent in a grotesquely deprived society but in
F.15   Abse's autobiographical novel (F.15) and Richards's story of a
F.16   life (F.16) the towns and children of Cardiff and Pontypridd
witness, from their vantage points of their satellites, the world
they were in but not of.

The post-war world was present in parts of Wales just as it
was, in a higher scale, on the 'arterial roads', housing estates and
light industry factories of the Midlands and the south-east of
England. Our post-war writers, though, have often seemed
obsessed with the culture and society Wales has left behind. It is
a commonplace that many 'contemporary' novels really concern
themselves with a previous generation. Certainly Welsh writers

between the wars were preoccupied with explaining the dramatic shifts of fortune which had occurred in Wales from the late nineteenth century onwards. Towards the end of the period a number of novelists wrote books which we can now acknowledge as fables about a Fall from Grace (Richard Llewellyn's 1939 elegy *How Green Was My Valley*) or on the theme of Knowledge is Power (Gwyn Thomas's 1949 historical fiction on the proletarianization of the Welsh, *All Things Betray Thee*), all of which strove to give some meaning to the disturbing chaos of Welsh life. The roots of the disaster (material and spiritual) were located outside the period in which they had become apparent. *Kate Roberts* (1891–1985) published *Traed Mewn Cyffion* in 1935 but the novel deals with the unremitting hardship of life in the quarry villages of north Wales before the First World War. Her first readers would have been aware of the collapse of that slate economy and the distinctive communities they had once sustained, of the responses of some, such as one son, William, who argues for socialism and eventually migrates to the coalfield, and of others, the schoolteacher son, Owen, who contemplates the death of his other brother, Twm (T.G.), and considers a future of struggle (F.1). *Kate Roberts* herself had been actively involved in Welsh Nationalist politics from the early days of *Plaid Cymru* and her novel, with its past echoes, had in 1936, the year *Saunders Lewis* and his two companions committed a symbolic act of arson against the bombing school put in the Llŷn peninsula, a future resonance. For many Welsh-language writers at this time it was only the past that could be summoned up to expose what they saw as the rootless misery of a present existence that threatened the very identity of Wales as they defined it.

F.1

This dilemma was posed in another way by Geraint Goodwin (1903–41) in the novel he published in 1936, *The Heyday in the Blood*, where the contemporary bustle of modern life mocks the optimistic, progressive outlook of the pre-1914 Welsh who tried 'to lead' Wales and defeats the sons of the fathers until they begin to look, unabashed, in the mirror (F.2). Goodwin is especially interesting because of the skill with which he depicts the collision, in confined space, of two eras, two tongues, two cultures and two nations. He transposes this into the divisions

F.2

that Llew discovers in himself. There is, here, neither the absolute dismissal of a Dylan Thomas nor the absolute loss stated by a *Kate Roberts*. In the quest for re-definition of identity it may be that Goodwin and the Newtown in Powys he depicts, balances in more than a geographical sense between 'Wales' and 'England'.

The exchange of Time and Space by physical uprooting, by occupational shift, by experience of war and struggle, or by educational and professional mobility, has been a process with which the modern Welsh have been very familiar. There have been moments, though, when the pattern of change, rooted in traditions and radiating outwards at the same time, seemed both normal and acceptable. Raymond Williams (b.1921) is another Welsh writer whose perspective from the frontiers of Wales (near Abergavenny in his case) has been sharpened by its focus on the interaction of past and future in the present lives of his characters in the novel *Border Country* (1960) in which an academic interested in population movement into industrial Wales in the last century comes, slowly, to terms with the relationship of his own life and work to that of his railwayman father, Harry, who is an industrial worker in a rural society after the First World War (F.3).

F.3

Border Country is a fine example of an extraordinarily sophisticated depiction of the parallel lines along which private lives and public events can run. Its central drama, nonetheless, is the *General Strike* of 1926 whose infinite possibilities for effecting revolutionary change are brought to a finite point of action before the lines run on again. Williams is concerned to show us, in 1960, the manner in which the very marginality of the railwaymen's actions in 1926 (only in support of the miners) is expressive of a working-class solidarity that goes beyond economic gain or the cohesion of any located industrial mass. The real defeat of the strike in 1926 is not denied but nor is its indication of already achieved communities and for the potential identity of individuals *within* communities. Looking back, Williams underlines the running history of 1926 by making its significance neither dependent on geographical centrality nor chronological immediacy (F.4). Even so, the *General Strike* did occupy directly the minds of contemporaries who realized what

F.4

Lewis Jones (centre) greets Arthur Griffiths on his release from prison in 1936. (*Source: South Wales Miners' Library.*)

a turning point it was in the confident militancy of the British working class.

Naturally, this proved to be a central concern of the writers who addressed themselves to the lives and hopes of the bulk of the Welsh population in the coalfields of south Wales. They became known as the first generation of 'Anglo-Welsh' writers because they wrote in English about a largely English-speaking people who thought themselves to be Welsh in the same manner as did their authors. By the end of the 1930s little magazines such as Keidrych Rhys's *Wales* (founded 1937) and Gwyn Jones's *The Welsh Review* (founded 1939) were proclaiming this flood of work inside and beyond Wales. Much of it reflected prevailing tastes for epic romance, social naturalism and documentary realism and was, too hastily, dismissed later as merely clumsy in its attempt to give literary representation to its content of strikes and social struggles. The full scale of the achievement of such 'raw' writers as Jack Jones (1884–1970) and Lewis Jones (1897–1939) has only been properly assessed when the task they set themselves, of writing panoramic social history as novels, has been put back into the context of their own infant literary traditions and the complex history they chose to unravel. What was already starkly obvious in the 1930s was that these writers, too, had lost worlds to look back upon. The loss was recent. The implications staggering.

Times Like These (1936), Gwyn Jones's period novel of 1926 tells of the ordinariness of life in Jenkinstown but it also highlights the burning, angry determination of those who thought, momentarily, that natural justice and the power of F.5 unity were on their side (F.5). The same kind of testimony could be revealed by extracts from Jack Jones's *Black Parade* (1935) or Lewis Jones's *Cwmardy* (1937) where documentary reportage of action and rhetoric are similar despite different political lessons being drawn. Undoubtedly, though, the most subtle and enduring work to take the *General Strike* as its subject is the magnificently varied verse-drama *The Angry Summer* (1943) which many critics now recognize as Idris Davies's (1905–53) F.6 masterpiece (F.6).

The *General Strike* and *miners' lock-out* brought the post-war militancy of south Wales to an abrupt close. This, in turn, seemed to usher in the dog-days of industrial decline. Now, not even the vaunted prosperity of the coalfield was there to be measured against any alleged loss of standards, culture or language. The febrile politicization of south Wales was seen as the other side of this false coinage and anglicization, proletarianization and industrialization indicted as the trinity of a false God. The stated policy of *Plaid Cymru* was to de-industrialize the south, diminish the existence of the 'rootless' proletariat by returning workers to the land and of course restore the culture that was only possible through the possession of the Welsh language. This combination of politics and morality offered an organic vision to replace the mechanistic nightmare that it saw in the Welsh present. The vision and the nightmare were both apocalyptic in the verse of the nationalist writers *Saunders Lewis* (1893–1985) and J. Kitchener Davies (1902–52) (F.7, F.8).

F.7
F.8   Other Welsh-language writers, whilst sharing the sense of lost opportunities, were less dismissive of the worth of all those ordinary, wasted lives. Again, from the vantage point of post-war writers, like the popular novelist T. Rowland Hughes, it was the vanishing of both material and spiritual wealth in the eldorado of the south that was astonishing to his quarryman hero, William Jones. On the other hand, William Jones's stay in the home of his brother-in-law, Crad, and sister Mary in Bryn Glo gives him a sympathetic outlook on the '*Shonis*' of the

F.9   deracinated south (F.9). The humanistic acceptance and the bleak dismissal of this strange cosmopolitan race with Welsh roots is, perhaps, best seen as a conflict between older and newer forms of nationalist writing about Wales. It is not the close detail that is as important as the gloss put on an accumulation of all such details.

Two poets who considered the Depression years as an effect on their own valleys were Alun Lewis and *Gwenallt* (1899–1968). The latter, a conscientious objector in the First World War, grew up Welsh-speaking in the industrialized Swansea Valley where he embraced a fundamental *Marxist* creed. Gradually he reunited this with, and then replaced it by, Christian faith and planted the latter in his memory of, and hopes for, neighbourhood and family. The poem, 'The Dead',

F.10   (F.10) dates from his 1951 volume *Eples* (Leaven). Alun

F.11 Lewis's much more anthropological poem 'The Mountain Over Aberdare' (F.11) dates from the late 1930s but is, again, a war poem in the sense that it summed up attitudes that prevailed about the hopelessness and passive suffering of the unemployed. Charity alone seems able to dispel the Lost Age.

After the Second World War the inter-war period in Wales was, too quickly and glibly, reduced to an anteroom in which the denizens of that Lost Age waited for the coming of social welfarism and state interventionism. As a result a great deal of the tonality of the period was lost. The generalizing poets — concentrating in elegy or epic on the clinching image — were taken as suppliers of detail as well as form. To this extent it was only when historians began to construct a new historiography of these years in Wales that a fuller picture became more clear. It is within that context — and asking of novelists and poets: Who is writing? when? with what motives? and under what difficulties of genre, tradition and language? — that literature in and about the inter-war period must now be judged. It is also, in part, an explanation for the re-discovery of the novels of Lewis Jones and the resurrection of the critical reputation of Gwyn Thomas (1913–81).

Jones, in *Cwmardy* (1937) and *We Live*, wrote, in the snatches of time he found between being a leader of *hunger marches* and acting as a Communist County Councillor in Glamorgan, novels that tried to show the people of the Rhondda overcoming de-humanization by poverty and defeat through their revolt. He took, in *We Live*, the huge marches against the 1935 *Unemployment Assistance Bill* as his theme in a crucial chapter. Len, his collier-hero who will die fighting in the *Spanish Civil War*, and his radicalized wife, Mary, who will take over Len's political role, are not content to wait and moon in a Lost Age

F.12 (F.12). Gwyn Thomas, who participated in these marches on his return from Oxford University, did not publish anything until 1946. Then came a flood of short stories, novellas and novels that commented on the history of the modern Welsh by using the device of a black comic satire. Before he discovered this style, fuelled by a 'sidling, malicious obliquity', he wrote a quasi-naturalistic novel about the 1930s in south Wales. It centred on three brothers — Alf, an unemployed collier;

Hugh, a student and Herbert, a small grocer — and their views on the abyss into which the industrial valleys had fallen. *Sorrow For Thy Sons* was written in 1937 and first published in 1986. The novel's climax, though reached by a slightly different route from that of Lewis Jones, is the *1935 demonstrations* (F.13).

That novel is of vital interest not only for its contemporary witness and outrage but also because it foretold the way in which Welsh writers would seek to come to terms with the meaning of such a dramatic era in Welsh history. Gwyn Thomas, like his contemporary Dylan Thomas, went on to build a distancing surrealism that acted to inform through caricature. It was contemporary immediacy that acted on him until he transformed it into a style that was a surrogate for the actual; in the 1980s our writers, intent on explaining us by our origins, remain obsessed with the inter-war years as the revealed history of the period acts on us in its demand for re-assessment.

Emyr Humphreys (b.1919) writes in English from that tradition of Welsh-language concern which must explicate the industrial-urban life of the Welsh in order to take a particular kind of Welsh identity forward. *The Best of Friends* (1978) is in an on-going sequence of novels that are an examination of the lineaments of Wales this century. The Welsh Nationalist, Val Gwyn, and the Communist, Pen Lewis, argue out the issues of the 1930s as seen forty years on as they seek to prevent a bailiff removing furniture for debt from the home of Dick Jenkins of F.17 Cwm Du (F.17). The incident is real: based on the action taken by *Arthur Horner* (Communist President of the *South Wales Miners' Federation* from 1936) in Maerdy, Rhondda, in the early 1930s. The debate is Emyr Humphreys's projection of the event. This is a methodology, fraught with tension, that the fiction writer uses again and again: it is a dive into historical actuality to re-shape it that Raymond Williams lays bare in his 1986 novel *Loyalties*, a work that spans 1936 to 1984, and takes in the politics of those who tried to control or order what others experienced but could not always articulate. Bert, who fought in Spain and in Normandy, lies dying, after a lifetime of work underground, in Dan-y-Capel in 1968. He sits up in bed to give F.18 his son, Gwyn, a pair of binoculars (F.18). The objects are freighted with a History that historians cannot reach. Perhaps only in the reaches of the literary imagination can lives be made whole again. Certainly historians need to read and interpret the texts that seek to imagine realities that otherwise lie in pieces like torn, discarded newspapers.

Sources

F.1 Dechreuwyd Ysgol Nos yn yr ardal, a dysgid Saesneg a rhifyddiaeth ynddi. Yr oedd Saesneg yn help i chwi fynd trwy'r byd, ac yr oedd rhifyddiaeth yn beth reit handi. Yr oedd eisiau codi'r gweithiwr o'i safle bresennol. Yr oedd eisiau rhoi cyflog byw iddo. Wedi dysgu ychydig mwy o Saesneg nag a ddysgwyd iddynt yn yr Ysgol Elfennol, daeth y bobl ieuainc i ddechrau darllen am syniadau newydd a enillai dir yn Lloegr a De Cymru. Lle y buasai eu tadau (y rhai mwyaf byw ohonynt) yn dysgu syniadau Thomas Gee ac S.R., daeth y plant (y rhai mwyaf byw ohonynt hwythau) i ddysgu syniadau Robert Blatchford a Keir Hardie.

Dechreuodd rhai o'r bobl ifanc gyfarfod yn y cwt torri barf, ac aed ati i ffurfio Cangen o'r Blaid Lafur Annibynnol. Wiliam oedd prif yrrwr y symudiad. Eu prif waith oedd ceisio darbwyllo eu cyd-chwarelwyr i ddyfod i berthyn i Undeb y Chwarelwyr. Ni cheid safon cyflog heb hynny. Ym mrwdfrydedd cyfiawnder yr hyn y safent trosto, teimlent y byddai pob chwarelwr yn rhedeg i dalu. Yna ni byddai anhawster o gwbl mewn sefyll yn erbyn gostwng cyflog. Eu siom gyntaf oedd gweld diffyg sêl eu cyd-weithwyr; rhai'n anfodlon rhag tynnu gwg y meistri, eraill yn methu gweld pa ddaioni a ddeuai ohono, y lleill yn ddifater. Ychydig a gafwyd yn selog. Talai rhai, megis Ifan Gruffydd, o ddyletswydd. Teimlent y gallai fod yn beth da yn y pen draw, yn amser rhywun arall efallai, ond nid yn eu hamser hwy.

Felly, daeth y to yma yn yr ardal i gymryd diddordeb yn y Gweithiwr. Caent eu syniadau o lyfrau Saesneg ac o bapurau Cymraeg oedd yn adlais o'r papurau Saesneg. Daeth y Gweithiwr yng Nghymru i'w ystyried ar yr un tir â'r gweithiwr yn Lloegr. Iddynt hwy yr un oedd ei broblem ym mhob gwlad, a'r un oedd ei elyn — sef cyfalafiaeth. Darllenai Wiliam bopeth y

Kate Roberts. (*Source: Welsh Arts Council.*)

câi afael arno ar y pwnc o un safbwynt. A phan ymgodymai ef â'r problemau hyn ni ddywedodd neb wrtho i'r feri chwarel y gweithiai ynddi gael ei gweithio ar y cychwyn gan y chwarelwyr eu hunain, a rhannu'r elw rhyngddynt.

A daeth newid ar eu crefydd. Astudiodd eu teidiau a'u neiniau, a ddechreuodd yr achosion Anghydffurfiol ar hyd ochrau'r bryniau, eu diwinyddiaeth yn ddwfn. Yr oedd defosiwn ac aberth yn eu crefydd. Yr oedd eu hwyrion yn amddifad o'r defosiwn, ac nid oedd cymaint o alw am aberth. Dalient i astudio diwinyddiaeth, ond megis peth oer ar wahân iddynt hwy. Ymddiddorent mewn pynciau fel Person Crist, Yr Ymgnawdoliad, Rhagluniaeth, Yr Iawn, fel pynciau a roddai gyfle i'w deall, ac nid fel pynciau oedd a wnelont â'u bywyd hwy, ac yn yr ystyr yma yr oedd gan y pynciau afael yn yr ifanc fel yn yr hen a'r canol oed. Fel y newidiai cyflyrau eu bywyd bob dydd, fel yr âi'r byd yn wannach, daeth newid hefyd yn eu hagwedd at bynciau crefydd. Yn yr ifanc y daeth y newid hwn. I rai oedd â'u bryd ar godi'r gweithiwr, dyletswydd dyn at ei gyd-ddyn oedd yn bwysig bellach, a daeth y Bregeth ar y Mynydd yn bwysicach nag Epistolau Paul. Newidiodd eu hagwedd at bregethwyr. Y pregethwyr gorau'n awr oedd y rhai a bregethai am onestrwydd cymdeithasol a dyletswydd dynion at ei gilydd. Fe foddheid yr ieuanc trwy alw Crist yn Sosialydd. Ond mater o ddiddordeb i'r deall oedd hyn eto, ac nid mater o gredo. Symudasid eu diddordeb o Grist y Gwaredwr i Grist yr Esiampl. Nid effeithiai hynny ar eu bywyd. Mwynhaent bregeth dda o'r pulpud, a dadl dda yn yr Ysgol Sul. Nid oedd ganddynt weinidog i gydweld nac i anghydweld ag ef.

Yr oedd eu diddordeb mewn gwleidyddiaeth yn un ochrog. Yr oedd yr hen a'r canol oed yn Radicaliaid, am y credent mai dyna oedd orau i'r gweithiwr. Plaid y 'bobl fawr' oedd y Blaid Doriaidd, a holl amcan y bobl fawr oedd cadw'r gweithiwr i lawr. Yr oedd Rhyddfrydiaeth wedi ennill tir byth er 1868, a daliai'r chwarelwyr i sôn am ryddid y gweithiwr a safon byw. Yn awr dyma do o bobl ifanc yn dysgu darllen Saesneg ac yn darllen am bobl oedd yn dechrau blino ar Ryddfrydiaeth ac yn dweud mai rhwng Cyfalaf â Llafur y byddai brwydr fawr y dyfodol, ac nad oedd Rhyddfrydiaeth yn ddim ond enw arall ar gyfalafiaeth. Yr oedd yr hen dipyn yn ddrwgdybus ohonynt, a chilwgai blaenoriaid a phobl flaenllaw'r capel yn agored oherwydd cysylltid enw'r blaid newydd hon ag anffyddiaeth. Ni ddaeth hyn ag anghydwelediad teuluol i'r Ffridd Felen, oherwydd nid oedd yno argyhoeddiadau crefyddol na gwleid-yddol dwfn.

Ni thyfodd Cangen Moel Arian o'r Blaid Lafur Annibynnol yn fawr o ran rhif, ac araf oedd cynnydd eu dylanwad. Ond yr oedd yr ychydig a berthynai iddi yn selog. Ceisient gael aelodau newydd, a cheisient gael y chwarelwyr yn Undebwyr. Bu nifer o fân streiciau yn yr ardaloedd yn ystod y blynyddoedd hyn, ond nid o dan nawdd Undeb y Chwarelwyr y deuai'r dynion allan, ond ohonynt eu hunain, ac ychydig iawn a gâi fudd Undeb. Ai telerau cyflog yn waeth o hyd, ac ni wellhai pethau ar ôl streic. Ofer oedd darbwyllo'r dynion na cheid isrif cyflog heb Undeb. Un o'r rhai mwyaf siomedig oedd Wiliam y Ffridd Felen. Siaradai a dadleuai ar bob cyfle dros y blaid newydd. Câi bobl i gydweld ag ef, ond nid i gyd-weithio.

. . . .

Yr un noson eisteddai Owen yn y gegin ar ôl i'w dad a'i fam fyned i'w gwelyau. Ni fedrai feddwl am gysgu oherwydd y cynnwrf yn ei feddwl. Yr oedd bron fel y diwrnod y daeth y newydd am ladd Twm. Gadawodd ef a'i fam i'w teimladau lifo trosodd. Er hynny, ni theimlai ef yn well. Eithr yn lle bod ei feddwl ar ei frawd yn unig, rhedai i bob cyfeiriad yn awr. Yr oedd y swyddog pensiynau wedi taflu carreg i ganol llyn, ac ni fedrai Owen ddweud yn lle y gorffenai'r cynnwrf. O'r blaen llanwai colli ei frawd holl gylch ei feddwl a'i deimlad. Yr oedd fel petai'r Rhyfel wedi bod yn gwylied eu teulu hwy a tharo Twm er mwyn dial arnynt.

O hyn ymlaen fe fyddai marw ei frawd yn beth caled, oer ar ei galon, ond fe fyddai ei feddwl yn gweithio i gyfeiriadau eraill. Cyn hyn, nid effeithiodd y Rhyfel arno ond yn oddefol. Dioddefai ef fel rhyw dynged anosgoadwy a ddaeth ar y byd, gan ofni a gobeithio; ofni y deuai ar warthaf eu teulu hwy, a gobeithio na ddeuai. Yng nghanol hyn i gyd, gwelsai lawer o garedigrwydd yn gymysg â siarad gwirion, dwl. Clywsai am ddynion yn ymgyfoethogi ar y Rhyfel; fe'u gwelsai o bell. Ond heddiw fe ddaeth i ymyl gweithred greulon gan un o'u pobl hwy eu hunain, megis. Yn rhyfedd iawn, nid ofn i'w fam ddyfod o flaen ei gwell am hitio'r dyn oedd arno, ac ni phoenai ychwaith pe na chawsai ei fam ddim dimai o bensiwn, ond yr oedd creulondeb y peth ei hun yn boen arno. Dyna fel yr oedd rhyfel; nid y lladd a'r dioddef oedd yn greulon yn unig, eithr pethau achlysurol fel hyn. A dyna ei fam yn gorfod cael un i gyfieithu'r newydd am ladd ei fab.

Chwysodd wrth feddwl am y peth, ac aeth y gegin yn annioddefol. Rhoes fflam bach ar y lamp, aeth allan a throi i gyfeiriad y mynydd. Yr oedd yn noson olau leuad, ac yr oedd y ffordd yn llwydwen o dan ei draed. Codai dafad yn awr ac yn y man yn ddistaw o'i gorweddle wrth glywed sŵn ei droed, a rhedai i rywle arall. Yr oedd sŵn y ffrydiau mor dawel nes gwneud iddo feddwl mai troi yn eu hunfan yr oeddynt ac nid llifo. Eisteddodd ar garreg fawr. Gorweddai'r pentref odano fel gwlad y Tylwyth Teg dan hud y lleuad. Yma ac acw fel smotiau duon yr oedd tai'r ffermydd bychain, a chlwstwr o goed o'u cwmpas yn cysgodi'r gadlesi a'r tai. Ar y tai eraill disgleiriai'r lleuad, a rhedai ei goleuni'n rhimyn ar hyd llechi'r to. Yr oedd cysgodion y tai yn hir o'u blaen, ac edrychai'r caeau'n felyn yn y goleuni. Yn y gwaelod isaf yr oedd cae ŷd yn ei styciau. Yr oedd y tir o gwmpas lle'r eisteddai ef yn gochddu, a gwyddai Owen fod yr holl dir, cyn belled ag y gwelai ei lygaid, felly i gyd — tua chan mlynedd cyn hynny. Yr oedd y bobl a oedd yn gyfrifol am droi lliw'r tir yn wyrdd yn gorwedd erbyn hyn ym mynwent y plwy, yn naear frasach y gwastadedd a orweddai rhyngddo â'r môr. Daethai rhai ohonynt o waelod y plwy i drin tir y mynydd ac i fyw arno, ac aethant i'w cynefin i dreulio'u 'hun hir'.

Ac nid o flaen ei lygaid yr oedd gwaith y dwylo caled hynny. Gallai ddychmygu am wledydd lawer ar hyd y byd, trefi mawrion a rhesi dirifedi o dai a llechi Moel Arian ar eu to, a'r un lleuad ag a ddisgleiriai ar dai Moel Arian heno yn taflu ei phelydrau i lithro hyd do'r tai hynny, yng ngwledydd byd.

Troes ei olygon at domen y chwarel. Heno nid oedd ond clwt du ar ochr y mynydd. Yr un bobl a oedd yn gyfrifol am godi tyddynnod ar fawndir oedd yn gyfrifol am domen y chwarel hefyd. Rhwng y ddau yma y bu'r pentrefwyr am gan mlynedd yn gweithio'n hwyr ac yn fore, nes mynd â'u pennau at lawr cyn bod yn bobl ganol oed. Tybiasai rhai ohonynt yr osgoent hyn i'w plant drwy eu hanfon i ysgolion a swyddfeydd a siopau.

Daeth ei feddyliau'n ôl at ei deulu ei hun. Yr oeddynt hwy yn enghraifft gyffredin o deuluoedd yr ardal, pobl wedi gweithio'n galed, wedi cael eu rhan o helbulon, wedi ceisio talu eu ffordd, wedi methu'n aml, a phan oedd gorffen hynny mewn golwg, a gobaith i'w rieni gael tipyn o hawddfyd, dyma gnoc hollol annisgwyl.

Cofiai glywed Ann Ifans yn dweud rywdro, dillad mor grand oedd gan ei fam pan ddaeth i'r ardal gyntaf. Ni châi ddillad newydd byth yn awr. Fe gafodd rai ar ôl marw Twm, ond ni wisgasai mohonynt byth oddi ar hynny. Cofiai mor dda yr edrychai y diwrnod gwobrwyo hwnnw yn yr Ysgol Sir. Ef yn unig o'r teulu a geisiodd wneud rhywbeth i roddi hwb ymlaen iddynt, er nad efe oedd yr unig un a allai wneud. Ni chyfrifai hynny'n rhinwedd. Meddalwch ydoedd, a dim arall. Ni allai beidio. Ffurf ar ei hunanoldeb ydoedd. Tynnai rhywbeth ef at ei fam er pan oedd yn blentyn. Yr oedd arno eisiau ei chariad yn gyfangwbl, ond nis câi byth. Câi ei charedigrwydd a'i gofal, ond nid ei chariad. Tybed a deimlai'r plant eraill yr un fath? Ag eithrio Elin, nid oedd cartref yn ddim i'r plant eraill. Meddyliai Owen weithiau fod Twm yn nes at galon ei fam na'r un arall o'r plant, ond nid oedd ganddo braw o gwbl o hyn. Mae'n debyg mai'r un fath y teimlasai hi pe collasid ef — Owen — yn y Rhyfel.

Yr oedd ei rieni'n dawedog ynghylch eu teimladau bob amser, ac anodd oedd gwybod beth a rôi bleser iddynt. Mwynhaent lawer o bethau, ond gwyddai i sicrwydd mai edrych ymlaen yr oedd y ddau at y dydd pan fyddent yn glir â'r byd a chael mwynhau seibiant diwedd oes yn ddi-boen. Yn hyn o beth nid oeddynt lawer gwahanol i weddill y ddynoliaeth. Dyna a wnâi eu profedigaeth yn ddwbl galed ym meddwl Owen. Pan oedd bod yn glir â'r byd yn y golwg, dyma ergyd hollol annisgwyl.

. . . .

Ac fe agorwyd ei lygaid i bosibilrwydd *gwneud* rhywbeth, yn lle dioddef fel mudion. Yr oedd yn hen bryd i rywun wrth-wynebu'r holl anghyfiawnder hwn. Gwneud rhywbeth. Erbyn meddwl, dyna fai ei bobl ef. Gwrol yn eu gallu i ddioddef oeddynt, ac nid yn eu gallu i wneud dim yn erbyn achos eu dioddef. Wiliam oedd yr unig un o'i deulu ef a ddangosodd wrthwynebiad i bethau fel yr oeddynt, oni wnaethai Sioned. Efallai mai dangos ei gwrthwynebiad i fywyd ei theulu yr oedd hi, drwy fyw yn ôl safonau moesol hollol wahanol. Troesai Twm ei gefn ar gartref a dangos y medrai ei adael, beth bynnag. Yr oedd ef, Owen, yn llwfr, dyna'r gwir. Fe adawodd i'w fam hitio'r dyn pensiwn heddiw, yn lle ei hitio ei hun. Nid aeth erioed i ffwrdd o'i gartref, i nac ysgol na choleg, heb i'w hiraeth wneud iddo daflu i fyny.

Edrychodd ar y wlad. Ar wahân i oleuadau gwan y dref, ni allasai neb ddweud bod rhyfel yn unman. Yr oedd yn syndod meddwl bod gan ryw gongl fechan ddiarffordd fel hyn o Gymru ran yn y Rhyfel o gwbl. Ac eto, cyrhaeddai crafangau'r anghenfil hwnnw i gilfachau eithaf y mynyddoedd. Ychydig wythnosau'n ôl diangasai bachgen o'r ardal o'r fyddin, a llochesodd am wythnos yn nhyllau'r creigiau, gan fyned adref at ei fam i swper bob nos. Ond daeth gwaedgwn y fyddin o hyd iddo, a gwelwyd ef yn myned i'r stesion rhwng dau filwr a golwg y gorchfygedig arno. Ymhen tridiau daeth gair i ddweud ei fod wedi ei ladd yn Ffrainc, ac yr oedd ei deulu a'r rhan fwyaf o'r ardal yn ddigon diniwed i gredu hynny. Paham na chodai'r ardal yn erbyn peth fel hyn? Ond i beth y siaradai? Un ohonynt oedd yntau. Credai weithiau y buasai'n well pe cadwasai eu hynafiaid yr ochr arall i'r Eifl yn Llŷn a thrin y tir yn unig.

Ond efallai ei fod, wedi'r cyfan, yn disgwyl bywyd rhy grwn, rhy orffenedig, ac yn rhoi gormod o goel ar y gredo y deuai pethau'n iawn ond iddo wneud ei ddyletswydd. Yr oedd llinynnau bywyd rhai pobl ar hyd ac ar led ym mhob man, a dim gobaith dyfod â hwy at ei gilydd.

Cododd oddi ar y garreg, a gwelodd fod rhywbeth yn gynefin iddo ynddi. Craffodd, a gwelodd fod enwau llawer o blant yr ardal wedi eu torri arni, a'i enw yntau yn eu plith. Yr oedd pedwar ohonynt wedi eu lladd yn y Rhyfel. Yr oedd T.G. yno'n eglur, ac yn perthyn i gyfnod diweddarach na chyfnod O.G. Cofiodd mai dyma'r garreg y rhoddent eu beichiau grug arni pan aent i dynnu grug at ddechrau tân, cyn rhoddi'r hwb terfynol iddynt ar eu cefnau cyn cychwyn i lawr ffordd y mynydd. Wrth gerdded i lawr yr un ffordd yn awr, cofiai am

aroglau'r grug ac aroglau mawn — y grug yn crafu ei wddf a'r
pridd yn mynd i lawr rhwng ei grys â'i groen, a'i ddychymyg
yntau'n creu miloedd o forgrug gydag ef.

Pan gyrhaeddodd y tŷ, yr oedd y gath yn eistedd ar garreg y
drws. Rhwbiodd yn anwesol yn ei goesau, a dilynodd ef i'r tŷ a'i
chynffon i fyny. Troes yntau'r fflam i fyny, a rhoi pwniad i'r tân.
Daliai'r gath i hel yn ei goesau a chanu'r grwndi. Eisteddodd
yntau yn y gadair freichiau, ac estyn ei bibell i gymryd smôc, y
gyntaf y diwrnod hwnnw.

(Kate Roberts, *Traed Mewn Cyffion*, Abertawe, 1936, tt.91–4 a
188–93.)

(A night school was started in the district at which English and
Arithmetic were taught. A knowledge of Arithmetic was useful,
and English allowed you to make your way in the world. It was
necessary to raise the worker from his present position. He
should have a living wage. After learning a little more English
than they learned in the Elementary School, the young people
began to read about new ideas that were gaining ground in
England and South Wales. Where their fathers (the more
interested ones) had absorbed the ideas of Thomas Gee and
S.R., their children grasped the ideas of Robert Blatchford and
Keir Hardie.

Some of the young men began to meet in the barber's hut and
they set about forming a branch of the *Independent Labour Party*.
Wiliam was the moving spirit behind it all. Their chief task was
to persuade their fellow-workers to join the Quarrymen's
Union. They would not have a standard wage without that. Full
of enthusiasm for the justice of their cause, they felt that every
quarryman would rush to join, and then there would be no
difficulty in resisting any attempt to lower their wages. Their
first disappointment was seeing the lack of zeal of their fellow-
workers. Some were afraid of attracting the owners' animosity;
others questioned what possible good could come of it; others
were just not interested. Only a few were keen. Some, like Ifan
Gruffydd, paid up out of a sense of loyalty. they felt that it might
prove to be a good thing in the long run, in the distant future,
but not in their own lifetime.

Thus it was that the present generation came to take an

interest in the plight of the worker. They gathered their ideas from English books, or from the Welsh papers that echoed the English ones. The worker in Wales came to be recognised along with his counterpart in England. It was the same problem in every country, with the same enemy — Capitalism. Wiliam read everything about the matter that he could lay his hands on. And while he was wrestling with these problems nobody bothered to tell him that the very quarry in which he was working had, in the beginning, been worked by the quarrymen themselves, sharing the profits.

Their religious outlook also changed. Their grandfathers and grandmothers — the pioneers of the Nonconformist causes scattered on the hillsides — had a profound knowledge of theology. There was devotion and self-sacrifice in their religion. But the grandchildren had lost the spirit of devotion and there was little call for sacrifice. They continued to study theology, but only coldly, as something remote from their lives. They too were interested in such topics as the person of Christ, the Incarnation, Predestination and the Atonement, but only on an intellectual level rather than as concepts having a real bearing on their lives. As the conditions of their everyday lives changed, as their world seemed to be collapsing, so their attitudes towards religion changed. The change was most evident in the young. To those intent on improving the condition of the workers, a man's duty to his fellow-men was the important thing, and the Sermon on the Mount became far more important than Paul's Epistles. Their attitude towards preachers changed. The best preachers were those who preached about social justice and man's duty towards his fellow-men. The young were placated by calling Christ a Socialist. Yet this too was a matter for the intellect, not one of belief. Their interest moved from Christ the Redeemer to Christ the Example. This did not impinge upon their lives. They enjoyed a good sermon from the pulpit and a good debate in the Sunday School. But they did not have a minister with whom to agree or disagree.

Their interest in politics was partisan. The old and the middle-aged were Radicals because they believed that was best for the workers. They regarded the Tory party as the party of the Ruling Class whose sole object was to keep the worker down. Liberalism had gained ground steadily since 1868 and the quarrymen still talked about workers' freedom and his living standards. Now here was a generation of young people learning to read English and getting to know about people who were beginning to tire of Liberalism, maintaining that the great battle of the future would be between Capitalism and Labour, and that Liberalism was only another name for Capitalism. The older people were a bit suspicious of them, and the deacons and more prominent members of the chapel openly showed their disapproval because they linked the new politics with atheism. This, however, did not bring dissension into the Ffridd Felen family for they did not have deep religious or political views.

The Moel Arian branch of the *Independent Labour Party* did not attract a large membership, and the growth of influence was very slow. But the few who belonged to it were very zealous. They constantly sought new members and encouraged the quarrymen to join the Union. During these years there were frequent minor strikes in the district, but these were not organised by the Union of Quarrymen. The men came out on their own initiative, very few of them receiving financial help from the Union. The men's wages continued to fall and things did not improve after a strike. It was useless trying to convince the workers that they would never be able to negotiate a minimum wage agreement without a strong Union. One of the most disappointed was Wiliam. Whenever he had the opportunity he spoke and argued on behalf of the new party. Usually he managed to get people to agree with him, but they still refused to become active members.

. . . .

That same night, Owen was sitting in the kitchen after his mother and father had gone to bed. He could not think of sleep because of the deep disturbance in his mind. It was almost like the day when the news came that Twm had been killed. He and his mother had allowed their feelings to flood over them. And yet he did not feel better for it. Instead of being concentrated on his brother, his thoughts now ran in all directions. The pensions officer had thrown a stone into the middle of a pond and Owen could not tell where the commotion would end. Before this, his brother's death had filled the compass of his thoughts and feelings. It was as if the War had singled out their family and struck down Twm in revenge on them all.

From now on his brother's death would lie hard and cold on his heart, but his mind would work in other directions. Until now the war had affected him only passively. He had endured it with fear and hope as some inevitable fate that had fallen on the world, fearing that the worst would happen to his family and desperately hoping that it would not. In the midst of it all he had seen a lot of kindness mixed up with foolish, silly talk. He had heard of War profiteers; he had even seen them from a distance. But today he had come face-to-face with a cruel action performed by one of his own people, as it were. Strangely enough, it was not that he was afraid of his mother being taken to court for hitting the man, neither was he worried lest she not receive the pension, but it was the cruelty of the whole thing that hurt him deeply. That was how it was in war; it was not only the killing and the suffering that was cruel, but also incidents like this. And there was his mother having to have somebody translate into Welsh the news that her son had been killed!

The thought of it made him sweat, and the kitchen became insufferable. He turned down the lamp and went out in the direction of the mountain. It was a clear moonlit night and the path was a greyish white underfoot. Now and again a sheep rose from its resting place, disturbed by the sound of his tread, and ran somewhere else. The streams flowed so quietly; it was as if they were just swirling around and not scudding along. He sat down on a big stone. The village lay beneath him like a fairyland under the spell of the moon. Here and there, like dark smudges, were the little farmhouses and their yards, sheltered by their clumps of trees. The moon shone on the houses, the light reflected from their slate roofs. The houses cast long shadows before them, and the fields looked strangely yellow in that light. In the bottom field of all the corn stood in stooks. Around him, where he sat, the land was reddish black and Owen knew that all land, as far as the eye could see, had been like that once — about a hundred years before. Those who had toiled to turn that barren land into green pastures were by now lying in the parish cemetery in that more fertile soil that lay between him and the sea. Some of them had come from the bottom of the valley to cultivate the high mountain land and to rear their families, and then returned to their original environment for their 'long sleep'.

And yet the real handiwork of those toil-worn hands was not visible to him. In his mind's eye, he could visualise many countries all over the world, where there were great cities with countless streets, and they had Moel Arian slates on their roofs. And the same moon which shone on the houses in Moel Arian tonight would be casting its beams to slide over the roofs of those houses in distant lands.

He turned his eyes towards the quarry tip. Tonight it was but a black patch on the mountainside. Those same people who had wrested the small farms from the mountain peat-lands had been responsible for the quarry tip too. Between these two, for a hundred years, the villagers had worked from dawn to dusk making their backs bend before they reached middle-age. Some of them had hoped that, by sending their children to schools, to offices, shops, they would escape from it all.

His thoughts came back to his own family. They were typical of the families of the district, a hard-working people who'd had their share of trouble, trying to pay their way and frequently failing, and then when there was an end to debt in sight and the prospect of an easier life for his parents, here was a cruel unexpected blow.

He remembered Ann Ifans once saying what grand clothes his mother had when she first came to the district. She never had new clothes now. She had some after Twm's death but had never worn them again. He remembered how well she looked on that prize-giving day at the County School. He was the only one who had tried to make things easier for his parents, although he was not the only one capable of doing so. He did not consider that a virtue — he was soft, that was all. He could not help it. In a way, it was his selfishness. He had felt strongly attracted to his mother since he was small; he wanted all her love for himself, but he never got it. He had her generosity and her care, but not her love. He wondered if the other children had felt the same. Apart from Elin, home was nothing to the others.

Sometimes Owen suspected that Twm had been nearer to his mother's heart than all the other children, but he had no proof of that. Probably she would have felt the same if she had lost him — Owen — in the war.

His parents had never been ones to show their emotions, and it was difficult to know what really gave them pleasure. They enjoyed many things, but he knew for certain that what they looked forward to most of all was to be free from debt and to enjoy a retirement without worry at the end of their lives. In this way they were not very different from the rest of mankind. That was why Owen thought this calamity was such a grievous one for them. When freedom from debt was in sight, they were struck down by this unexpected blow . . .

. . . .

And his eyes were opened to the possibility of doing something instead of simply enduring like a dumb animal. It was about time that somebody challenged this injustice and did something about it. Come to think of it, that was what was wrong with his people. They were courageous in their capacity to endure pain, but would do nothing to get rid of what caused that pain. Wiliam was the only member of the family who had stood out against things as they were, unless you could say that Sioned had done so. Perhaps she was showing her antipathy towards the way his family lived, by living her own life according to completely different standards. Twm had turned his back on the home and had shown that he was capable of leaving it. He, Owen, was a coward, that was the truth of it. He had let his mother hit that pensions officer this morning, instead of hitting him himself. He had never left home, to go to school or college, without feeling homesick to the point of vomiting.

He looked around him at the countryside. Were it not for the dimmed lights of the town, nobody could say there was a war on. It was difficult to believe that a little out-of-the-way corner of Wales had a part to play in the War. And yet the vile tentacles of that monster reached into the deepest recesses of the mountains. A few weeks ago, a local boy had deserted from the army and had hidden for a week in a cave, going home to have supper with his mother every night. But the army bloodhounds had discovered him, and he was seen being led to the railway station looking like one defeated. Within three days news came that he had been killed in France, and his family and most of the people in the locality were innocent enough to believe it. Why did they not rise up against such things? But what was he saying? He, himself, was one of them. Sometimes he thought it would have been better if his ancestors had stayed on the other side of the Eifl mountains in Lleyn and just tilled the soil.

But perhaps, after all, he expected too rounded and complete a pattern of life, taking it for granted that things would turn out all right if only he did his duty. But there was no hope of knitting-up the ravelled threads of people's lives.

He got up from the stone and saw that there was something familiar about it. Examining it closely, he saw that a number of names had been scratched upon it, his own amongst them. Four of them had been killed in the War. T.G. was there, clearly to be seen, but more recently than O.G. He remembered that when they used to fetch heather to light the fire in the morning this was the stone on which they had rested their loads before humping them higher on their backs and setting off on the track down the mountain. Walking down the same way now, the smell of heather and peat came to him again — the heather scratching his neck and the peat trickling down between his shirt and skin so that it seemed to him like thousands of ants.

When he arrived home, the cat was sitting on the door-step. It rubbed itself fondly against his legs and followed him into the house with its tail high in the air. He turned up the flame in the lamp and gave the fire a poke. The cat continued to press itself against his legs, purring contentedly. He sat down in the armchair and reached for his pipe to have a smoke, the first that day.)

(Kate Roberts, *Feet in Chains*, (Trans. Idwal Walters and John Idris Jones), Cardiff, 1977, pp.64–6 and 130–3.)

F.2   He had made up his mind that he would not go to the Red Lion again — at least, not for a long time. It was a gesture on his part that he found very hard to keep up. The Red Lion had been a second home to him as long as he remembered. Not until now did he realize quite how much it meant. That was why he had gone back into himself — why he began to think about life.

He had left the 'intermediate' six months before, having failed the London Matric. three times, and the headmaster having held out little hope of him ever getting it. He had not even a Welsh matric. The way to Aberystwyth College was thus closed, and with it the jobs a Welsh degree carried — the teaching and the preaching, for neither of which he had any special desire. And unlike the lads who left the elementary school, he could not now be apprenticed to a trade. He was halfway up a ladder, and there he had to stay.

His father had been one of the Young Men of Wales. In his dark, bitter, fuming eyes, his long narrow face, his lean spindle body, one glimpsed the passion that was to devour him. He came at a time when the country was turning anxiously, as though in sleep. The young man, his soul aflame, had proclaimed the new birth. And as the pulpit went hand in hand with politics, he forgot the wedded bride for this new mistress, more provocative, more tantalizing and with the infinite promise of greater reward. He neglected his God, but he served his country, and his pastorate in this little town had been the penalty of that neglect.

It was there that he met his wife — Twmi's sister — a farmer's daughter, with the soft, easy paganism of the earth, red and glowing as a sunset in her ripening beauty. The easy, placid sensuality of her overwhelmed him as a flood; he yielded himself up in the naked frenzy of his spirit — this other world, infinitely dark and menacing, that he was to know. They had never met — they were as two people shouting at one another across an abyss.

He died of what, in rural Wales, they called galloping consumption when Llew was a year old. The mother brought up the boy. She never married again, though she could easily have done so, and with the family money left her and the small pension from the Church Benevolent Fund, she was just able to manage. But now that Llew had left school and was of an age to work, this grant had been stopped, and this was a growing source of reproach to the lad.

This, and the breach with Beti, made him think about life —

his life — for the first time. There were only two paths open to him, as he saw it — the army, or the City Police Force in a place like Birmingham or Manchester where there was a prospect of promotion. He set his face against both.

And yet he would have done anything to get away. He did not belong. That was why he was always heading for the Red Lion, which was Wales proper — an instinct as sure, as unanswerable, as makes the duckling in a brood head for water.

The little town stood there under its cloud of smoke which lifted and blew towards the mountains, towards the coloured valley, like a signpost between two worlds. It belonged to neither. In the respite it had, it grew of itself, grew as a fungus grows, quick in its humidity. Industry had come there, the wheels had turned, the people had gone into the mills, had left the mills, when they fell derelict.

In its heyday, it had within itself aspired to greatness. The mills were throbbing, the new Severn fresh from the mountain uplands, and before it was to expend its strength in the low-lying valleys, had been barricaded with weirs. Money flowed. On market-days, the butter women lined the kerb; all the week money and drink flowed in the ale- houses — there were scores, small and petulant like blisters in the streets.

Then the prosperity had suddenly gone, receded as a tide recedes, leaving this little town between two worlds neither land nor water, like a piece of flotsam, on the drying beach. It had gone back into itself, its people were 'townies'. They never belonged — belonged to anything but themselves.

On fair days and at the auctions, the people beyond them mingled — mingled, but never met; the hill farmer driving in his flock of Welsh mountain sheep, the mountain ponies, wild and unbroken, from the hard springing sour green pastures of the uplands; the Border farmer with his sleek, sweat-dropping Herefords, his Kerry-hills. They elbowed one another in the Smithfield, they were prey for the same dealers, but they were as remote, as unbridgeable in their distance, as the two poles.

That was the land the lad had grown in — Powys, once one of the three proud territorial divisions of the Cymru, named by them the *Powys, Paradwys Cymru* — 'Powys, the Paradise of Wales' — now frayed and broken in the east where the invader had come up the low-lying fertile valleys, come in possession, but not conquest.

Life — a portentous thought, and one that annoyed Llew! Far more important was to get away. And next in importance was to have some money by him. The sixpences and shillings his mother doled out to him were not enough even for his present requirements. A seat in the pictures among the 'class' — the small tradespeople who were the 'class' — was one and threepence: the rest, the rag-tag and bobtail, were herded in a pen to shout and whistle and stamp their feet at sixpence a head. He had no views as between the one and the other — they were all the same to him — but he had decided views on the difference between a one-and-threepenny seat and a sixpenny one.

And so 'life' now loomed up very ominously. He took stock of himself and knew that he could do nothing. But he was not in the least dismayed, for at the same time he was equally sure that he could do everything.

One of his best friends was secretary of the provincial eisteddfod. They would walk up and down the High Street discussing things, the fantastic world the County Library had opened up for them both — Anatole France and Tchekov, and the great god Tolstoi before whom they were both constrainedly silent, while boys ran backwards and forwards with penny slips shouting: 'Footba' results — footba' results'.

Llew would break off and listen. Even the unemployed went on a gala day to see Wolverhampton Wanderers. The world of fact was very different from this world of fiction. He had gone beyond them — these people who were neither Welsh nor English — but they had gone beyond him. He had never been to the Shrewsbury Flower Show.

His friend kept on talking, but he was not listening. He leaned his arms on the stone bridge. Even the Severn got away — Shrewsbury — Hereford — wherever it was.

'Well, have a shot, Llew', he was saying, 'nothing to beat'.

Llew looked at him absently.

'And its three quid. Three quids iss three quids.'

They were both Welshmen; they formed a colony on their own in this little town. At mention of three quids Llew came back to earth. He reached for the official programme his friend carried.

'How much time?' he asked.

'A week.'

'They are getting frisky,' he said. 'Short story! They'll be having a play next.'

'Pooh,' said the other man, 'move with the times. They are having Ibsen's *Pretenders* for the National.'

'No joke?' asked Llew anxiously. 'You mean I got nothing to beat?'

'You try,' answered his friend with a wink. Then he added: 'Three quids iss three quids. There's no joke *there*.'

He took the programme. If it had been upholstery or metal work it would have been all the same to him, except that he could do neither. But then he had never written a story in his life. He had always been top in English, but being top in English was not writing a story that would win three pounds at an eisteddfod.

Writing had seemed so remote, so foolish a thing that it had never once entered his head, how ever many the schemes he had drawn up for his betterment. There were the local reporters who sat at a green baize table under a platform, with pencils sharpened at each end, people who caused a certain awe, it was true, but people whom he had never once considered joining. Nor did he now.

Below them was the fair ground, wet and desolate, a reach of clinkers on the river bank, with black puddles here and there where the rain had sluiced. It was an empty place now. Beyond the weir was the gas-works, fuming on the river bank, and beyond that again a skin yard.

'I'll try,' he said.

He had been afraid of making a fool of himself, that was all. It seemed a bit soft and sloppy.

'The Chair's a cert,' said his friend.

Llew was not listening. He had not even a remote interest in poetry.

'Yes?' he said, for something to say.

'There's a poet for you, man,' replied his companion warmly.

Llew looked at him in question.

'Evan Edwards — that keeps the mill at your uncle's,' he explained. 'Hope of Wales, that man iss.'

'Yes?' said Llew, his eyes narrowing. There was that baleful light in them that people did not like.

'Know him?' said the other man.

'Yes and no,' answered Llew casually. 'I see him about.'

They dropped the subject and walked slowly back through the town.

The excitement worked in Llew. It was a new toy to him — a fresh release for his energies. Whether it was the three pounds or the thought of beating other people at their own game, he did not know, but the project, which he had nearly turned down with contempt, had now taken firm hold. He was like that in all things — there were no half-measures for him.

But it was not so easy to get started. That quick, instinctive self — the unanswerable self in him — had no place now. It was one thing to be oneself, but it was another thing to transfer oneself onto paper. The process choked him — the whole thing was unreal and foolish, he tried to tell himself, hurling the twentieth bit of paper across the room. He had always suspected as much, and now he knew it.

He worked in his father's study — 'Dad's room' — unaltered, unchanged, through the lad's life. The dark oak secretaire was still locked; within, all the rhetoric, the passion, the zeal of that young life, now mute and tongueless; a few scraps of paper scribbled over, underlined, margined in red — little drawings of men streaming along the edges, when he had paused for the new thought, the burning phrase, which, caught and circumscribed, flew over the paper in a scrawl, as though impatient of the ink.

All done now; nothing that interested Llew, nothing that interested his mother, but for some strange streak of sentiment, reverence, perhaps, for his memory, had been kept.

Around about were all his books. Theological commentaries jostled one another along the shelves, political tracts, modern-day heresies. There was Locke and Spinoza, Hazlitt and William James, Cromwell's letters and speeches, a whole shelf of Carlyle. There were Welsh books, Dafydd ab Gwilym and Goronwy Owen, breasting the poets; many books on the old sources of

Celtic literature, then so painstakingly unearthed: Renan's *Poetry of the Celtic Races,* and much else. It was as though the ghost of the mind, of the spirit, of the man who once inhabited the room, were walking within its walls.

Above the mantlepiece was a college photograph in a green frame, yellow moulded around the edges; a group of young men, posed and ponderous, in the quadrangle. One or two of them had become famous; the rest were forgotten. And there was his father, with that straight, staring look, as though looking beyond the camera, into truth itself. There were the hard-lined, searching eyes of genius.

Llew got up and looked straight at his father. Before, he had been a word, a memory, a legend. Now he saw him face to face. And he felt ashamed. Something in his father's straight staring gaze, looking out at him from that old, mouldering print, moved him in a way that nothing else could have done.

He began again. He threw the half-finished story away in disgust — the voluptuous woman who moved from Paris to Monte Carlo and back to Paris like a shuttle-cock, who sat sunning herself under palm trees and in orange groves, who sipped absinthe and whose collection of lovers, for ever being added to, caused even Llew to raise his eyebrows in wonder.

He had never thought of writing about Wales. It was like looking at one's own face. But he knew nothing else, and what he *knew* was at least real to him. He thought of a true story, and every detail came out clear, everything fell into place.

(Geraint Goodwin, *The Heyday in the Blood*, 1970, pp.134–42.)

F.3   Once they were up on the road, Harry and Ellen could look out over the valley and the village in which they had come to live. To the east stood the Holy Mountain, the blue peak with the sudden rockfall on its western scarp. From the mountain to the north ran a ridge of high ground, and along it the grey Marcher castles. To the west, enclosing the valley, ran the Black Mountains: mile after mile of bracken and whin and heather, of black marsh and green springy turf, of rowan and stunted thorn and myrtle and bog-cotton, roamed by the mountain sheep and the wild ponies. Between the black ridges of Darren and

Brynllwyd cut the narrow valley of Trawsfynydd, where the ruined abbey lay below the outcrop of rock marked by the great isolated boulder of the Kestrel. Fields climbed unevenly into the mountains, and far up on the black ridges stood isolated white farmhouses and grey barns.

Within its sheltering mountains, the Glynmawr valley lay broad and green. To a stranger Glynmawr would seem not a village, but just thinly populated farming country. Along the road where Harry and Ellen walked there were no lines of houses, no sudden centres of life. There were a few isolated houses by the roadside, and occasionally, under trees, a group or patch of five or six. Then lanes opened from the road, to east and west, making their way to other small groups, at varying distances. To the east, under the wooded ridge, lay Cefn, Penydre, Trefedw, Campstone. To the west, under the wall of the mountains, stood Glynant, Cwmhonddu, The Pandy, The Bridge, Panteg. The village was the valley, the whole valley, these scattered groups brought together in a name.

To Harry and Ellen, this was not strange country. Harry had been born in Llangattock, only seven miles north-west, and Ellen in Peterstone, three miles farther north. A river runs between Llangattock and Peterstone, and that is the border with England. Across the river, in Peterstone, the folk speak with the slow, rich, Herefordshire tongue, that could still be heard in Ellen. On this side of the river is the quick Welsh accent, less sharp, less edged, than in the mining valleys which lie beyond the Black Mountains, to the south and west, but clear and distinct — a frontier crossed in the breath. In 1919, a year before coming to Glynmawr, Harry and Ellen had been married in Peterstone church. They had known each other as children, and were engaged when Harry came home from France with a bullet through his wrist. He had gone back, been gassed, so that one lung was permanently damaged and he could not smoke. After the wedding he had gone back to the railway, where before the war he had been a boy porter. He had become a porter-signalman and been moved from station to station in the mining valleys, Ellen moving with him in lodgings. Now, with the signalman's job in Glynmawr, there was a chance to settle, to move nearer home. As they walked, carrying their things, they were facing the northern ridge beyond which their own villages lay.

The narrow road wound through the valley. The railway, leaving the cutting at the station, ran out north on an embankment, roughly parallel with the road but a quarter of a mile distant. Between road and railway, in its curving course, ran the Honddu, the black water. On the east of the road ran the grassed embankment of the old tram-road, with a few overgrown stone quarries near its line. The directions coincided, and Harry, as he walked, seemed to relax and settle. Walking the road in the October evening, they felt on their faces their own country: the huddled farmhouses, with their dirty yards; the dogs under the weed-growing walls; the cattle-marked crossing from the sloping field under the orchard; the long fields, in the line of the valley, where the cattle pastured; the turned red earth of the small, thickly-hedged ploughland; the brooks, alder-lined, curving and meeting; the bracken-heaped tussocky fields up the mountain, where the sheep were scattered under the wood-shaded barns; the occasional white wall, direct towards the sun, standing out where its windows caught the light across the valley; the high black line of the mountains, and the ring of the sheep-wall.

At the end, past the grey school and the master's cottage, they could hear the river as it came towards the road, and soon they could see it, fast-flowing and stonestrewn below them, and there ahead was the first chapel, alder-shaded, and beyond it the other chapel, larger and better-built, its graveyard tidier. The lane ran up steeply from the road, and from its high banks the trees arched over. They turned up the lane and climbed steadily. Then round a long curve the pitch eased away, and the tree-line opened. The patch of eight houses lay ahead: set so that looking to the north and west the spurs of the mountains lay open in the distance. Harry stopped, put down the leather box, and looked round. 'All right, last bit,' he said after resting, and they walked on to the houses.

(Raymond Williams, *Border Country*, London, 1964, pp.30–3.)

F.4 In the spring of 1926, in Glynmawr, the green of the meadows was fresh and cool, and the blossom was white in the orchards, and on the thorns and crabs in the hedges. Along the banks of the roads the violets were hidden in overgrowing leaves, but the primroses were out, though not so thickly as on the banks of the railway, where they flowered most richly, as if the cuttings and embankments had been made for them. All over the valley, and far up on the mountains, innumerable birds sang and flew. The Honddu was high, as it had been since midwinter. The low-lying cottages near the river had already been flooded.

Here was the ordinary history of the valley, sheltered and almost isolated under its dark mountains. But now, with this May Day, a different history exerted its pressures, and reached, with the railway line, even this far. The troubled years of strike and lock-out, which had affected the village only slightly, moved now to their crisis, and touched this valley under its lonely mountains. As April ended, the Government's subsidy to the coal industry ended with it. The miners refused the owners' new terms, and lock-out notices were already posted at the pits. Up beyond the mountains, little more than ten miles from this farming valley, lay the different valleys, where the pits and the colliers' houses were crowded. At dusk, above Darren, the glow of the steel furnace spread up each evening into the sky, and many turned now to watch it more seriously, and to think of the black valleys that lay hidden beyond. There was the trouble, that the eye could almost see, and in the papers the trouble was recorded, to be read in the sun of mid-morning among flowers and blossoming trees.

The coal negotiations in London had broken down. That afternoon, at two o'clock, the executives of all unions affiliated to the Trades Union Congress were meeting again in the Memorial Hall. That night, when Harry went to work, two telegrams had reached the Glynmawr branch of the National Union of Railwaymen, and had been pinned up on the noticeboard in the box. Morgan showed them to Harry, who went across and read them.

> *Negotiations with Government on miners' dispute having broken down, Executive Committee now considering our attitude along with other unions. Circular letter in post outlining position, meantime our members must continue their ordinary work.*

> *Spasmodic action can only defeat our object. Prepare your members
> for action, but only on instructions from this office.*

The second, and later, telegram read:

> *Executive instructs all our members not to take duty after
> Monday next. Arrangements to be made locally so that all men
> will finish their turn of duty at their home station on Tuesday
> morning. Circular in post.*

Harry stood re-reading the telegrams, above the low fire.

'*General Strike* then, is it?'

'Aye,' Morgan said. 'And about time.'

Harry turned and took off his coat. 'All right,' he said. 'It's
straightforward enough for us.'

'So long as we know what we're doing,' Morgan said,
coming nearer. 'Only I tell you Harry, this is no ordinary bit of a
strike. This is us against the Government, no penny-an-hour
job.'

Harry rubbed his hand over his face, 'We're with the miners,
isn't it?'

'Aye, but with them why? Because we're the working class,
Harry, united for common action. The miners are fighting their
own battle against their employers. We're not, mind. We're not
fighting the companies, we're fighting the Government.'

'The country they said,' Harry answered, half to himself. He
wanted, in one way, to hear Morgan talk, yet the real argument
was in his own mind, and in different terms.

'The country, Harry! We're the country. And mind you, if we
come out, let's realize it's that we're saying. We're saying that
we're the country, we're the power, we the working class are
defying the bosses' government, going on to build our own
social system.'

'I don't know about that,' Harry said.

'How many know it, I wonder? Do the union leaders know
it? Have they got the courage? We're not miners see, Harry. We
got no right to strike, only for the working class.'

'I'll stand by the miners, if it comes to it.'

Morgan looked at him, doubtfully, and then threw up his
hands.

'If that's all it is, mun, we shall lose. We're out for the power, the power in our own hands.'

(Raymond Williams, *Border Country*, London, 1964, pp.81-2.)

F.5   The afternoon's gathering was an unparalleled one, dwarfing even the celebrated meeting on Red Sunday. The amphitheatre spilled over with men, some of whom had pressed behind the same hand card of Lewis the Boots on which the speakers stood. Others lined the low bluff behind, and to these the orators occasionally turned with an embracing gesture, to pull them into the body of the meeting. No one there but felt it a momentous occasion.

Edgar's speech was again the event of the day. 'Men,' he began as before, 'Fellow-workers — you are here to-day in such numbers because you realise that you are facing a crisis in trade union history. Last July we met here in a meeting, great but not as great as this, because our livelihoods were at stake. Men — I tell you that the situation that we thought grave then, we should think a trifle to-day. We stood then, confident of a quick victory, with every union man in the country standing behind us. To-day we stand with the capitalist class confident of a quick victory, and not a single comrade of the unions with us in the struggle. We working men have seen a great vision; we saw it become real; and we saw it smashed to smithereens. That vision was the *General Strike* — Labour Militant. Men — you and me, we are left alone to-day to fight our own battle. Only the miners are militant, but they — thank God! — are solid and strong. We have seen this last fortnight that when all the forces of the owners are supported by a repressive Government, when Labour has no chance to put its case to the country by wireless or newspaper, Labour must be defeated.' He raised his hand. 'For why? Because the unions were not staunch? No. Because the railwaymen and the dockers and the tinplaters and the transport men wouldn't stick it out? No. But because every man, woman, and child in this country who was not for the miners was against us. In the past the country has been more or less passive. It was the Government and hunger broke us in 'Twenty-One. But this time you have seen the rank and file of

Gwyn Jones. (*Source: Welsh Arts Council.*)

the middle class and all its hangers-on up against the rank and file of the workers, because in Great Britain to-day the nation is willing to see the miner a serf and his family paupers. Every night of the strike you heard with me on the wireless how your hopes were being ruined, not by the owners, but by clurks with motor cars, boys and girls from the Colleges who have never done a day's work in their lives, and by the bright young things, as they call theirselves, who found the *General Strike*, when you and me had staked all we got in the world, just a big joke. Joke!' He laughed his harsh laugh. 'I can think of other jokes! The owners we have always known against us. If they can kick us in the face, they will; and we expect them to. And we know that here in South Wales we got the most inhuman lot of brutes for owners that this country has seen since the passing of the Factory Acts. Even their fellow-owners are ashamed of um! The Government we have known against us. We know that more than ever since we know the preparations made for this strike. There was never any hope from them, never any hope of a fair deal, and perhaps now, when too late we are looking back, we can see that a lightning strike would have been our best weapon.'

There was a muttering of hear-hears.

'But that's over and done with. What we got to grasp now is that we are alone, and the country thinks us beaten. I don't blame the other unions — though I do feel somehow that if the miners had been backing the others, we wouldn't have gone back in a hurry. You got to remember how many have lost their jobs because they came out with us. I'll have something to say about that later. But at the moment, there it is, men — the miners stand alone, and the country thinks you are licked, and that like the N.U.R. you'll go back on your bended knees, hat in hand, and ask their mighty reverences the owners if they'll please let you go down the pits and cut um coal for what they please to offer. That's the situation. You know what they offer — an hour on the day, and much more than a penny off the pay. Your earning power will be cut in proportion to your labour by almost one-quarter, for you lose almost two-and-ninepence in the pound, and work one-seventh as long again to get that seventeen-and-thruppence. Eight hours, they do argue — and let me tell you that that Eight Hours' Bill is on the way. That's your impartial Government for you — going ahead with an industrial bill to lengthen hours during the strike! They think we're licked, you see. They think we'll take it lying down. It's only the miners — we've smashed the rest, and now we'll smash them. We'll show these trade unions what we think of them!' He paused. 'That's the situation. Now, what are we to do?'

'Stay out!' shouted voices from all over the meeting place.

'See um all in 'ell!'

'Chuck our tools into the river and see the pits to the devil!'

All these shouts were from the younger men. Miners like Oliver, equally or more determined, had nothing to say. Edgar raised his hand for silence.

'There's one trade union unbroken in Great Britain — the home of trade unionism. The eyes of the workers all over the world have been on us — are on us. They are wondering what will happen here. Will the miners, who have always been the first attacked, surrender? Will they humbly beg pardon for what they have done? They were holding big dances in the West End on the night of the twelfth because all save the miners were beat — are they going to hold more dances any night now and knock back the wine because the miners too are on their knees? It is for you to decide. Don't let's be afraid to face facts. They're not very nice, I can promise you. On the one hand is hardship and privation, every man's hand against you, a struggle dragging out to I don't know where. There's no strike pay in the Federation's funds. Nineteen twenty-one cost seven million pounds to the unions, and we've never picked up since then. You'll have to tighten your belts and suffer in silence. Your wives and kids can go on the parish — you can't. Those with savings will spend them. You'll have all this, and at last you will win your fight. On the other hand — '

'Why all this talk?' shouted Ike Jones, on his feet. 'Why gas, gas, gas? Put it to the meeting — back to work or stay out! We don't want all this talk!'

Edgar tried to speak again, but failed. For a minute or two there was a general uproar, with fierce arguments everywhere. Then, when this settled down somewhat, Josh Green shouted:

'So you'll stand by the Federation?'
   'Ay, we will! Ay-Ay-Ay!'

(Gwyn Jones, *Times Like These*, London, 1979, pp.172–5.)

F.6   5

What will you do with your shovel, Dai,
And your pick and your sledge and your spike,
And what will you do with your leisure, man,
Now that you're out on strike?

What will you do for your butter, Dai,
And your bread and your cheese and your fags,
And how will you pay for a dress for the wife,
And shall your children go in rags?

You have been, in your time, a hero, Dai,
And they wrote of your pluck in the press,
And now you have fallen on evil day,
And who will be there to bless?

And how will you stand with your honesty, Dai,
When the land is full of lies,
And how will you curb your anger, man,
When your natural patience dies?

O what will you dream on the mountains, Dai,
When you walk in the summer day,
And gaze on the derelict valleys below,
And the mountains farther away?

And how will the heart within you, Dai,
Respond to the distant sea,
And the dream that is born in the blaze of the sun,
And the vision of victory?

7
Mrs Evans fach, you want butter again.
How will you pay for it now, little woman

Idris Davies.

With your husband out on strike, and full
Of the fiery language? Ay, I know him,
His head is full of fire and brimstone
And a lot of palaver about communism,
And me, little Dan the Grocer
Depending so much on private enterprise.

What, depending on the miners and their
Money too? O yes, in a way, Mrs Evans,
Yes, in a way I do, mind you.
Come tomorrow, little woman, and I'll tell you then
What I have decided overnight.
Go home now and tell that rash red husband of yours
That your grocer cannot afford to go on strike
Or what would happen to the butter from Carmarthen?
Good day for now, Mrs Evans fach.

31
Let's go to Barry Island, Maggie fach,
And give all the kids one day by the sea,
And sherbet and buns and paper hats,
And a rattling ride on the Figure Eight;
We'll have tea on the sands, and rides on the donkeys,
And sit in the evening with the folk of Cwm Rhondda,
Singing the sweet old hymns of Pantycelyn
When the sun goes down beyond the rocky islands.
Come on, Maggie fach, or the train will be gone
Then the kids will be howling at home all day,
Sticky with dirt and gooseberry jam.
Leave the washing alone for today, Maggie fach,
And put on your best and come out to the sun
And down to the holiday sea.
We'll carry the sandwiches in a big brown bag
And leave our troubles behind for a day

With the chickens and the big black tips
And the rival soup-kitchens, quarrelling like hell.
Come, Maggie fach, with a rose on your breast
And an old Welsh tune on your little red lips,

And we'll all sing together in the Cardiff train
Down to the holiday sea.

41
Here is Arthur J. Cook, a red rose in his lapel,
Astride on a wall, arousing his people,
Now with fist in the air, now a slap to the knee,
Almost burning his way to victory!

And tomorrow in all the hostile papers
There will be sneers at Cook and all his capers,
And cowardly scribblers will be busy tonight
Besmirching a warrior with the mud of their spite.

(Idris Davies, 'The Angry Summer', in *Collected Poems*, ed.
Islwyn Jenkins. Llandysul, 1972, pp.86-7, 88, 103, 110.)

F.7   Mae'r tramwe'n dringo o Ferthyr i Ddowlais,
Llysnafedd malwoden ar domen slag;
Yma bu unwaith Gymru, ac yn awr
Adfeilion sinemâu a glaw ar dipiau di-dwf;
Caeodd y ponwyr eu drysau; clercod y pegio
Yw pendefigion y paith;
Llygrodd pob cnawd ei ffordd ar wyneb daear.

Unwedd fy mywyd innau, eilydd y penderfyniadau
Sy'n symud o bwyllgor i bwyllgor i godi'r hen wlad yn ei hôl;
Pa'nd gwell fai sefyll ar y gongl yn Nhonypandy
Ac edrych i fyny'r cwm ac i lawr y cwm
Ar froc llongddrylliad dynion ar laid anobaith,
Dynion a thipiau'n sefyll, tomen un-diben â dyn.

Lle y bu llygaid mae llwch ac ni wyddom ein marw,
Claddodd ein mamau nyni'n ddifeddwl wrth roi inni laeth o
    Lethe,

Ni allwn waedu megis y gwŷr a fu gynt,
A'n dwylo, byddent debyg i law petai arnynt fawd;
Dryllier ein traed gan godwm, ni wnawn ond ymgreinio i
    glinig,

A chodi cap i goes bren a'r siwrans a phensiwn y Mond;
Iaith na thafodiaith ni fedrwn, na gwybod sarhad,
A'r campwaith a roisom i hanes yw seneddwyr ein gwlad.

II
Cododd y carthion o'r dociau gweigion
Dros y rhaffau sychion a rhwd y craeniau,
Cripiodd eu dylif proletaraidd
Yn seimllyd waraidd i'r tefyrn tatws,
Llusgodd yn waed o gylch traed y plismyn
A lledu'n llyn o boer siliconaidd
Drwy gymoedd diwyneb diwydiant y dôl.

(Saunders Lewis, 'Y Dilyw 1939', *Byd a Betws*, 1941.)

(From Merthyr to Dowlais the tramway climbs,
A slug's slime-trail over the slag heaps.
What's nowadays a desert of cinemas,
Rain over disused tips, this once was Wales.
Pawnshops have closed their doors. Clerks
Of the labour exchange are the chiefs of this prairie.
All flesh has tainted its way on the face of the earth.

The same taint's in me, as I second proposals
In committee after committee, to bring the old land to life.
I'd maybe be better employed on a Tonypandy corner
And my eyes meditating up the valley and down
On the human wreckage adrift in the mire of despond,
One function common to man and the standing slag.

Eyes have been changed to dust, we know not our death,
Were buried by our mothers, had Lethe milk to drink.
We cannot bleed, no, not as former men bled,
Our hands would resemble a hand, if they'd thumbs to go on
    them.
If a fall shatters our feet, all we do is grovel to a clinic,
Touch our caps to a wooden leg, Mond pension and insurance:
Knowing neither language nor dialect, feeling no insult,
We gave our masterpiece to history in our country's M.P.s.

From empty docks the scouring rose
Over dry ropes and the rusted cranes.
Greasily civilised was the flood
Of the proletariat creeping to chipshops.
It crept like blood round policemen's feet.
The spittle of its silicosis spread like a lake
Through faceless valleys of the industry of the dole.)

(Saunders Lewis, 'The Deluge 1939', in *The Penguin Book of Welsh Verse* (trans. Anthony Conran), 1967, pp.246–7.)

F.8   Mi est ti i lawr i Donypandy i'r Streic a'r Streic Fawr,
i'r carnifal jazz, a 'football' y streicwyr a'r plismyn,
at y ceginau cawl a'r coblera,
y ffeiriau sborion i Lazarus gornwydlyd,
gan helpu i ysgubo'r briwsion sbâr o'r bordydd i'r cŵn tan y
    byrddau,
gan arllwys cardodau fel rwbel ar y tipiau
neu hau basic-slag ar erddi 'allotment' o ludw
i dwyllo'r pridd hesb i ffrwythlonder sunthetig.
Yno 'roedd y perthi wedi syrthio a'r bylchau yn gegrwth
a'r strydoedd culion fel twndis i arllwys
y corwynt, yn chwythwm ar chwythwm,
i chwipio'r corneli a chodi pennau'r tai
a chwyrlio dynionach fel bagiau 'chips' gweigion
o bared i bost, o gwter i gwter;
y glaw-tyrfau a'r cenllysg yn tagu pob gratin
gan rwygo'r palmentydd a llifo drwy'r tai,
a lloncian fel rhoch angau'n y seleri diffenest;
a newyn fel brws-câns yn ysgubo trwy'r aelwydydd
o'r ffrynt i'r bac a thros risiau'r ardd serth,
i lawr i'r lôn-gefn at lifogydd yr afon, —
y broc ar y dŵr du sy'n arllwys o'r cwm,
i'w gleisio a'i chwydu ar geulannau'r gwastadedd
yn sbwriel ar ddifancoll i bydru.
A dyna lle'r oeddit ti fel Caniwt ar y traeth,
neu fel Atlas mewn pwll glo
â'th ysgwydd tan y creigiau'n gwrthsefyll cwymp,
neu â'th freichiau ar led rhwng y dibyn a'r môr

yn gweiddi 'Hai! Hai!'
ar lwybr moch lloerig Gadara.

. . .

Cofia di,
'doedd dim raid iti, mwy na'r rhelyw o'th gymheiriaid,
ysgrechain dy berfedd i maes ar focs sebon
ar gorneli'r strydoedd a sgwarau'r dre:

. . .

'Doedd dim taro arnat ti orymdeithio yn rhengoedd y di-waith,
dy ddraig-rampant yn hobnobio â'r morthwyl a'r cryman,

. . .

'doedd dim raid iti
fentro'r *Empire* a'r *Hippodrom* tan eu sang ar nos Sul,
— di geiliog bach dandi ar domen ceilogod ysbardunog
y Ffederasiwn a'r *Exchange* —
ond mi fentraist,
a mentro ar lecsiynau i'r Cyngor tref a'r Sir
a'r Senedd maes-o-law
yn erbyn Goliath ar ddydd na ŵyr wyrth, —

. . .

Do, 'r wy'n adde imi dreio fy mwrw fy hun
i ddannedd y corwynt i'm codi ar ei adenydd
a'm chwythu gyda'i hergwd lle mynnai
yn arwr i achub fy ngwlad.
Cans nid chwythu lle y mynno yn unig y mae'r dymestl,
ond chwythu a fynno o'i blaen lle y mynno;
'Pwy ar ei thymp ŵyr ei thw,' meddwn innau.

. . .

O cae di dy geg â'th hunan-dosturi celwyddog
a'th hunan-fost seimllyd o ffals.
'Rwyt ti'n gwybod mai chwarae pen-ysgafn â gwiwerod
oedd llithro o golfen i golfen;
ac mai chwarae mwy rhyfygus oedd hofran yn y gwynt
fel barcut papur, a bod llinyn yn dy gydio di'n ddiogel wrth y
     llawr,
lle'r oedd torf yn crynhoi i ryfeddu at dy gampau
ar *drapeze* y panto a'th glownio'n y syrcas.
Nid marchogaeth y corwynt, ond hongian wrth fwng
un o geffylau bach y 'roundabout' oedd dy wrhydri,

ceffyl-pren plentyn mewn meithrinfa,
a sŵn y gwynt i ti'n ddim ond clindarddach miwsig recordiau
    periant sgrechlyd y ffair wagedd.

(From J. Kitchener Davies, 'Sŵn y Gwynt sy'n Chwythu', in
Mair Davies, *Gwaith James Kitchener Davies*, Llandysul, 1980,
                                                          tt. 19–20.)

(You went down to Tonypandy for the Strike, and the General
    Strike,
for the jazz carnival, and the football of strikers and police,
to the soup-kitchens and the cobbling,
the jumble-sales for sore-ridden Lazarus,
helping to sweep the spare crumbs from the boards for the dogs
    under the tables,
pouring alms like rubble on the tips
or sowing basic slag on allotment gardens of ashes
to cheat the arid earth into synthetic fertility.

Then the hedges had fallen and the gaps were gaping
and the narrow streets were like funnels for the whirlwind's
    pouring, blast upon blast,
to whip the corners and raise the house-tops,
whirling wretches like empty chip-bags
from wall to post, from gutter to gutter;
the cloudbursts and the hailstones choking every grating
splitting the pavements and flooding through the houses,
and clanging like a death-rattle in the windowless cellars;
and famine like a stiff brush sweeping through the homes
from front to back and over the steep garden-steps,
down the back-lane to the river's floods,—
the wrack and black water pouring from the cwm,
to be battered and spewed to the level land's hollow banks,
rubbish abandoned to rot.

And there you were like Canute on the shore,
or like Atlas in a coal pit
with your shoulder under the rocks holding back a fall,
or with your arms outstretched between the crag and the sea
shouting Hey! Hey!
in the path of the lunatic Gadarene swine.

Remember,
there was no need for you, more than the rest of your fellows,
to scream your guts out on a soap-box
on the street-corners and the town squares;
no call for you to march in the ranks of the jobless,
your dragon-rampant hobnobbing with the hammer-and sickle;
there was no need for you
to dare the packed Empire and the Hippodrome on Sunday
    evening,
— you a dandy bantam on the dung-heap of the spurred cocks
of the Federation and the Exchange —
but you ventured,
and ventured in elections for the town Council and the County
    and Parliament all in good time
against Goliath in a day that knows no miracle.

Yes, I confess that I tried to hurl myself
into the whirlwind's teeth to be raised on its wings
and be blown by its thrust where it willed
as a hero to save my land.
Since it not only blows where it will, the tempest,
but blows what it will before it where it will;
'Who at its birth knows its growth,' I said.

O shut your mouth with your lying self-pity
and your false unctuous boasting.
You know it was a giddy game with squirrels
to slip from bough to bough;
and a more reckless game to hover in the wind
like a paper kite, a string tying you safe to the ground,
where the crowd gathered to marvel at your feats
on the pantomime trapeze and your clowning in the circus.
Not riding the whirlwind, but hanging to the mane
of a little roundabout horse, that was your valour,
a child's wooden-horse in a nursery,
and the sound of the wind no more to you than the crackle of
recorded music from vanity fair's screeching machine.)

(From J. Kitchener Davies, 'The Sound of the Wind that is

Blowing', (trans. Joseph P. Clancy), in *The Valleys*, John Davies and Mike Jenkins (eds.), Bridgend, 1984, pp.35–6.)

F.9   Ar ôl brecwast aeth William Jones allan am dro, gan fwriadu dringo'r llwybr i'r mynydd. Ond wedi iddo gyrraedd pen yr ystryd, troes i'r chwith ac i lawr i'r pentref i gael golwg mwy hamddenol ar y lle. Chwaraeai twr o blant ym mhob heol, ac yn eu plith yr oedd cŵn y greadigaeth. Ysgydwodd William Jones ei ben yn drist: beth a ddywedai Mr Lloyd? Pan gyrhaeddodd y brif heol, gwelodd ddwy siop wrth ochrau'i gilydd â'r ddau air TO LET yn fawr ar eu ffenestri, ac yr oedd un arall, siop esgidiau, yn wag tros y fforddd iddynt. Pur dlawd yr ymddangosai eraill, a hysbysai amryw eu telerau arbennig — hyn-a-hyn ar law a hyn-a-hyn yr wythnos: gallech brynu rhywbeth, o fwced i biano, felly. Nodiodd William Jones ar ŵr bach cyflym a godai ei ben, yn wên i gyd, o'r papur Sul yr oedd newydd ei brynu. 'Bora bach ffein?' meddai yntau, gan ateb ei gwestiwn ei hun ag 'Odi, wir, w!' a gwên arall ar gynnwys y papur. Newyddion da o lawenydd mawr am *Golden Streak*, efallai. Pam na roesai'r dyn goler a thei am ei wddf? Yn enwedig ar fore Sul fel hyn.

   Wrth ddynesu at y *Workmen's Hall*, syllodd William Jones yn ddig ar y dwsin o lanciau a merched ifainc a cyfarfuasai yno i gychwyn ar eu beiciau i lan y môr neu rywle. Ni hoffai eu coesau noethion na'u gyddfau isel na'u sŵn gorlawen. Yna oedodd ennyd ar y bont i wylio lliwiau'r olew a nofiai ar dywyllwch araf yr afon islaw. Yr oedd siop yr Eidalwr gerllaw ar agor, a chlywai chwerthin a chlebran uchel ynddi. Oni wyddai'r taclau ei bod hi'n ddydd Sul? Troes William Jones yn ei ôl yn bur anhapus ei feddwl.

   Cafodd y teulu wrth eu brecwast o weddill y *sausage* a ddygasai Wili John o siop y cigydd. Yr oedd dagrau ar ruddiau Eleri.

'Hylo, be' sy?' gofynnodd ei hewythr.

'O, meiledi yn daer am gael gadal yr ysgol,' meddai ei mam, 'Mae hi'n bedair ar ddeg ac yn sâl isio mynd i weithio. I b'le, dyn a ŵyr.'

'I Lunden, fel Rachel.'

'Hogan tros y ffordd sy wedi mynd i weini at ryw Iddewon yn

Llundain,' eglurodd Meri. 'Ac mae hi bron â thorri'i chalon
yno, yn ôl 'i mam.'
' 'Dyw hi ddim,' meddai Eleri'n ystyfnig.
'Be' wyddost ti? Dos di ymlaen hefo dy frecwast a phaid â bod
yn fabi 'rŵan.'
'Dere di 'nawr 'rwan,' meddai ei thad mewn cymysgedd rhyfedd
o'r ddwy dafodiaith.
'Mae'n ddigon inni weld Arfon a Wili John wedi gadal yr
ysgol,' chwanegodd ei mam wrth Eleri, 'heb orfod gwrando
arnat ti'n swnian. Dy le di ydi gwneud dy ora' yno, gan dy fod
ti'n cael cyfla i fynd yn dy flaen. Yntê, Wncwl William?'
'Ia . . . Ia, wir,' meddai William Jones yn ddwys.
    Rhyw sylwadau o eiddo Arfon am dyrfaoedd a phrysurdeb
Llundain oedd achos yr helynt. A dwyawr ganddo i aros am ei
drên ar ei ffordd adref, aethai am dro i ganol y ddinas, gan
ryfeddu at y goleuadau amryliw a droai nos yn ddydd, at y
lluoedd o bobl ym mhobman, at y ceir yn gwibio yma a thraw.
Troes i mewn i dŷ-bwyta anferth am gwpanaid o goffi, ac yno yr
oedd darluniau a goleuadau cywrain ar y muriau, cannoedd o
bobl wrth y byrddau, ac, mewn ffrydlif o olau a newidiai ei liw
bob ennyd, fand o wŷr yn chwarae a chanu, pob un ohonynt yn
gwisgo crys o sidan melyn. Teimlai Arfon yn euog wrth ofyn
am ddim ond cwpanaid o goffi yn y fath blas o le, yn arbennig a'r
dyn a weinyddai arno'n gwisgo ffrynt wen galed a bwa du.
Cafodd fwy na gwerth ei dair ceiniog yn gwylio'r bobl o'i
amgylch, y gymysgfa ryfeddaf a welsai neb erioed. Bwytâi un
gŵr swper anferth gan ddal i ysmygu ei sigâr yr un pryd rhwng
pob cegaid o fwyd; gwelai un arall gerllaw iddo, dyn â barf laes,
aflêr, yn darllen yn uchel o lyfr o'i flaen ac yna'n annerch y byd
yn gyffredinol, gan grychu a dadgrychu ei drwyn yn ffyrnig.
    Cuddiodd William Jones y wên a ddeuai i'w wyneb wrth iddo
ddilyn Crad a'r plant tua'r capel, ddeng munud yn rhy gynnar.
Yr oedd cerdded Crad yn wahanol i'r hyn ydoedd y noson gynt,
yn fwy defosiynol, yn drymach, yn arafach, a lled-ddisgwyliai
i'w frawd yng nghfraith agor ei lyfr emynau a ledio emyn yng
nghanol yr ystryd. Hwy oedd yr unig rai yn y capel am rai
munudau, ond dechreuodd y gynulleidfa fechan ymgasglu cyn
hir. Gwyliodd William Jones hwy'n mynd i'w seddau — pobl
ganol oed neu rai hyn bron i gyd, a daeth cwestiwn yr hen

Ddafydd Morus yn ol i'w feddwl. Beth a ddeuai o'r capeli ymhen ugain mlynedd, tybed? Clywsai lawer o sôn am gynulleidfaoedd mawrion y Sowth, am bregethwyr yn ysgwyd tyrfaoedd, am ganu a ymchwyddai'n donnau ysblennydd. Ond yma, ym Mryn Glo, gwelsai mai'r papur Sul a beicio i lan y môr a siop yr Eidalwr a ddenai'r ieuainc — yn y bore, beth bynnag: ond efallai y byddai pethau'n o wahanol erbyn y nos.

. . . .

Treuliasai'r chwarelwr dros flwyddyn ym Mryn Glo, a dysgasai lawer am fywyd y cwm a fu unwaith mor brysur a llon. Diar, mor ddifeddwl oedd ef yn Llan-y-graig wrth ddarllen ambell lythyr oddi wrth Meri. Soniai hi fod Nymbar Wan wedi cau a'r pentref bron i gyd yn ddi-waith, ond ni sylweddolodd ef lawn ystyr y newydd. 'O, maen' nhw'n cael y *dole*,' meddai Bob Gruffydd, ac aent wedyn i son am y plyg a dorrent neu am y das wair a aethai ar dan yn yr Hendre. A phan glywsai fod Arfon yn Slough a Wili John yn negesydd i gigydd Bryn Glo — wel, gellid cydymdeimlo â bechgyn â rhyw ysfa am adael yr ysgol ynddynt: felly'n hollol y teimlai William Jones yn Standard V. Codasai Mr Lloyd yn y capel un nos Sul i ddarllen rhyw gylchlythyr yn gofyn am gynhorthwy i Gymoedd y Dirwasgiad, a darllenodd ei lais cwynfanllyd ef yn hollol fel petai'n apêl oddi wrth bwyllgor y teparti. Tair ceiniog a roes William Jones yn y casgliad hwnnw, gan deimlo bod pobol bowld y Sowth 'na wedi clochdar digon yn y tywydd teg a 'rŵan, pan oedd tipyn o gwmwl . . . Clywsai rywun yn y caban-bwyta'n dweud bod miloedd ohonynt yn llifo i Gaerdydd a hyd yn oed i Dwickenham i weld Cymru'n chwarae Rygbi. Os oedd ganddyn' nhw arian i betha' felly . . . Ni wyddai William Jones fod belt y Shoni a grochlefai ar y cae Rygbi yn un go dynn amdano, a bod mwy o londer yn ei lais nag o obaith yn ei galon. Ni wyddai chwaith fod rhai ohonynt yn cerdded bob cam i Dwickenham, siwrnai o ddau can milltir. Yn awr, wedi rhyw bymtheng mis ymhlith y segurwyr anorfod, rhyfeddai fod eu hysgwyddau mor ysgwar a'u cyfarchiad mor llawen. Tynnai William Jones ei gap — ei fowler, yn hytrach — i Shoni.

Ac i Feri'n fwy na neb. A'i phlant yn ennill rhyw gymaint, a'i brawd yn cyfrannu'n weddol hael at dreuliau'r tŷ, nid oedd hi'n gorfod cynilo a chynllunio fel y gwnâi cannoedd o wragedd o'i chwmpas, ond casglai ei brawd i fywyd fod yn fain iawn ar y teulu am gyfnod hir. Rhyw dri neu bedwar diwrnod yr wythnos a weithiai Crad am ddwy flynedd cyn i Nymbar Wan gau, a cherddai'n ffyddiog i'r pwll lawer bore i ddim ond i weld y lampman yn ysgwyd ei ben. 'Dim gwaith 'eddi' — ac i ffwrdd ag ef adref yn araf a phrudd, ond cyn gynted ag y deuai i Nelson Street, plastrai wên ar ei wyneb a cheisiai feddwl am bethau digrif i'w dweud wrth Feri a'r plant. Yn arbennig wrth Arfon, y bachgen â'r llygaid treiddgar, dwys, a gariai ei lyfrau i'r Ysgol Ganolraddol yn bur ddiysbryd weithiau. Ac â rhyw ddoethineb tawel yn ei gwedd, daliodd Meri, fel miloedd o wragedd eraill drwy'r cwm, i lanhau ei thŷ a dyfeisio prydau bwyd maethlon ond rhad a thrwsio neu ail-wneud llawer dilledyn. Galwai Shinc yn aml ar y dechrau i ddadlau tros wrthryfel, a neidiai ei eiriau fel gwreichion oddi ar eingion: âi Meri ymlaen â'i gwaith. Weithiau, wrth gwrs, troai dewrder Crad yn surni a'r gŵr di-hîd yn fingam, a dychrynai hi ar adegau felly. 'Dyn a â allan i'w waith ac i'w orchwyl hyd yr hwyr,' meddai rhwng ei ddannedd un bore wrth gychwyn allan i wario awr yn Neuadd y Gweithwyr. Yr oedd rhyw olau dieithr yn ei lygaid ac ynni chwyrn yn ei gam, a dilynodd Meri ef o hirbell rhag ofn y bwriadai gyflawni rhyw drosedd ffôl. Ymlaen ag ef drwy'r pentref a heibio i'r orsaf ac ar hyd y ffordd tuag Ynys-y-gog, gan gerdded yn gyflym a phenderfynol. I b'le yr âi? Gwelodd ei gamau'n arafu cyn hir, ac yna safodd i bwyso'n erbyn y clawdd ac i syllu'n hir i lawr i'r afon oddi tano. Brysiodd hi tuag ato, ac edrychodd yntau'n euog arni.

'I b'le 'rwyt ti'n mynd, Crad bach?' gofynnodd.

'I ddeud y gwir, 'wn i ddim ar y ddaear, dim on bod yn rhaid imi fynd i rwla.'

'Ond i b'le?'

'Wn i ddim ar y ddaear, hogan, ond pan es i o'r tŷ, yr oeddwn i am gerddad a cherddad a cherddad. 'Doedd o ddim coblyn o ods i b'le. Ond ydw' i'n un gwirion, 'r hen gariad!' A dug y pwl o chwerthin y Crad a adwaenai yn ol iddi.

(T. Rowland Hughes, *William Jones*, Liverpool, 1944, tt.88–90 a 242–4.)

(Breakfast over, William Jones went out for a stroll, meaning to go up the path leading to the mountain. But on reaching the top of the street he turned left and went down into the village, in order to study it more at his leisure. Swarms of children, accompanied by all the dogs in Creation, were playing in the streets, and William Jones shook his head sadly: what would Mr Lloyd say? When he came to the main street he saw two shops side by side, with the words TO LET in large lettering across their windows, and another — a boot and shoe store — standing empty across the road. Other shops looked wretchedly shabby and several bore announcements of their conditions of sale — so much down and weekly instalments of so much — one could buy anything, from a bucket to a piano, in this way. William Jones nodded to a brisk little man who looked up, all smiles, from the Sunday paper he had just bought. Nice fine mornin'?' said the latter, answering himself with a Yes, indeed, mun!' and another smile at what he read in the paper. Glad tidings of great joy about Golden Streak, perhaps. Why wasn't the man wearing a collar and tie? Especially on Sunday morning like this.

As he approached the Workmen's Hall William Jones glared indignantly at a party of youths and young girls who had gathered there before going off on their bicycles down to the sea. He didn't like their bare legs, their low-necks and their riotous merriment. He lingered on the bridge, watching the coloured patches of oil floating on the dark surface of the sluggish river beneath. Bracchi's shop, close by, was open, and he could hear the sound of laughter and loud voices inside. Didn't the creatures know it was Sunday? William Jones retraced his steps, feeling very unhappy in mind.

He found the family breakfasting off what was left of the sausages brought by Willie John the day before. There were tears on Eleri's cheeks.

'Hullo, what's the matter?' her uncle asked.

'Oh, milady is very anxious to be allowed to leave school,' her mother replied. 'She is sixteen, and ill for wanting to go to work. To where, goodness knows.'

'To London, like Rachel.'

'A girl over the way who has gone into service at some Jew's house in London,' Mary explained. 'And she is nearly breaking her heart there, according to her mother.'

'She isn't,' said Eleri obstinately.

'What do *you* know? Go you on with your breakfast and don't be a baby, now.'

'Come on, now; now then,' put in her father, in an astonishing mixture of the Northern and Southern dialects.

'It's enough for us to see Arfon and Willie John left school,' her mother added to Eleri, 'without having to listen to your whining. *Your* place is to do your best there, since you have got a chance to get on. Isn't it, Uncle William?'

'Aye . . . aye, indeed,' said William Jones gravely.

A chance remark by Arfon about the crowds and bustle of London had been the cause of the trouble. Having two hours to wait for his train he had gone for a walk into the heart of London, marvelling at the multi-coloured lights that turned night into day, at the dense crowds of people everywhere and the traffic speeding by in every direction. He had gone into a huge restaurant for a cup of coffee, where there were pictures and curious-looking lights on the walls. The tables were packed with people and, in ever-changing floodlighting, an orchestra, every member of which was wearing a yellow silk shirt, was playing and singing. Arfon had felt very guilty when he asked for nothing but a cup of coffee in such a palace, the more so because the man who brought it was wearing a dress shirt and black bow-tie. He got more than full value for his threepence by watching the people around him, the strangest mixture one ever saw. One man was eating a huge supper and puffing at a cigar between each mouthful; while another, with a long, untidy beard, who was sitting nearby, was reading aloud from a book propped up in front of him and then addressing the world in general, while furiously wrinkling and unwrinkling his nose.

William Jones hid a smile as he accompanied Crad and the children to chapel, ten minutes too early. Crad's gait was very different from what it had been the night before; it was more solemn, more measured, slower; and his brother-in-law half expected him to open his hymnbook and lead a hymn in the middle of the street. They had the chapel to themselves for a few minutes, but it was not long before the rest of the congregation

— few in number — trooped in. William Jones watched them as they went to their seats — nearly all of them of middle-age or elderly, and the question put by old Dafydd Morris recurred to his mind. What would become of the chapels in twenty years time? he wondered. He had heard much talk about the large congregations in South Wales, preachers swaying huge crowds, magnificent singing that rose and swelled in mighty waves. But here, in Bryn Glo, he had seen that it was the Sunday newspaper, the bicycle ride down to the seaside and the shop kept by an Italian that drew the young folks — in the morning, at any rate: perhaps though, it would be different at night.

. . . .

The quarrymen had now been more than a year in Bryn Glo, and had learnt much about the life of the valley once so happy and full of activity. *Diar*, how unmindful he was in Llan-y-graig as he read an occasional letter from Mary. She would mention that Number One colliery was closed and nearly the whole village out of work, but the full meaning of her news was lost upon him. 'Oh, they are getting the dole,' Bob Griffiths would remark and then they would proceed to talk about the block of slate they were breaking up, or the haystack in Yr Hendre that had caught fire. And when he had heard that Arfon was in Slough and Willie John errand-boy to a Bryn Glo butcher — well, one could sympathise with boys itching to leave school: William Jones had felt exactly the same when he was in Standard V. Mr Lloyd had stood up in chapel one Sunday night to read out a circular letter appealing for help for the Depressed Area valleys, and his querulous voice sounded exactly as though he was reading out an appeal from the tea-party committee. William Jones had contributed threepence to that collection, feeling that those bold people in the South had cackled quite enough in the fine weather, and now, when it was a bit cloudy . . . he had heard someone in the mess-hut say that thousands of them were streaming down to Cardiff and even to Twickenham to see the Welsh team play rugby. If they had the money for things like that . . . William Jones didn't know that the '*Shoni*' who shouted himself hoarse at the Rugby International had tightened his belt several holes, and that there was more merriment in his voice than hope in his heart. Nor did he know that some of them had footed it the whole two hundred miles to Twickenham. Now, after some fifteen months among these men, idlers by force of circumstance, he was lost in wonder at their defiant squareness of shoulder, their cheery hail of greeting. William Jones took off his cap — or rather his bowler — to *Shoni.*

And even more so to Mary. Now that her children were earning a trifle, and her brother bearing a very fair share of the household expenses, she was no longer compelled to skimp and plan to the same extent as so many housewives around her, but her brother gathered that the family were for a long time in very straitened circumstances. Three or four days a week had been the extent of Crad's employment before Number One shut down and on many a morning he had trudged hopefully to the pithead only to see the lampman shake his head and to hear 'No work today'. Slowly and sadly he would go back home, but as soon as he reached Nelson Street he would clamp a broad grin on his face and cast about for something to say that would amuse Mary and the children. In particular to Arfon, the boy with the grave, penetrating look, who took himself off with his books to the Intermediate School in utter dejection at times. And Mary, quietly discerning like countless other women throughout the valley, diligently applied herself to keeping the house clean, thinking out cheap but nourishing meals and mending or re-making sundry garments. Jenk, when the slump began, would often look in and urge revolt, his words leaping forth like sparks from an anvil: Mary just carried on with her work. There were times, of course, when Crad's courage turned to bitterness, his care-free smile to a wry grimace, times when Mary was thoroughly alarmed. 'Man goeth forth unto his work and to his labour until the evening,' he muttered through his teeth one morning as he went off to while away an hour in the Workmen's Hall. There was a strange, wild light in his eyes, a compelling urge in his step, and Mary followed him at a distance, fearing that he contemplated doing something foolish. On he went through the village, past the station and along the road to Ynys-y-gog, walking fast and resolutely. Where could he be going? She saw him slacken speed; then he stopped, leaned against the wall and gazed for long down into the river below. She hurried up to him and he looked at her guiltily.

'To where are you going, Crad bach?' she asked him.

'To tell the truth, I don't know at all, only that I must go *somewhere*.'

'But to where?'

'I've no idea, girl, but when I went from the house I wanted to walk and walk and walk. It didn't matter a bit to where. Aren't I a stupid one, old sweetheart?' And a gale of hearty laughter brought back to her the Crad she knew.)

(T. Rowland Hughes, *William Jones*, (trans. Richard Ruck), Llandysul, 1953, pp.99–101 and 267–9.)

F.10   Bydd dyn wedi troi'r hanner-cant yn gweld yn lled glir
Y bobl a'r cynefin a foldiodd ei fywyd e',
A'r rhaffau dur a'm deil dynnaf wrthynt hwy
Yw'r beddau mewn dwy fynwent yn un o bentrefi'r De.

Wrth yrru ar feisiglau wedi eu lladrata o'r sgrap
A chwarae Rygbi dros Gymru â phledrenni moch,
Ni freuddwydiais y cawn glywed am ddau o'r cyfoedion hyn
Yn chwydu eu hysgyfaint i fwced yn fudr goch.

Ein cymdogion, teulu o Ferthyr Tydfil oeddent hwy,
'Y Merthyron' oedd yr enw arnynt gennym ni,
Saethai peswch pump ohonynt, yn eu tro, dros berth yr ardd
I dorri ar ein hysgwrs ac i dywyllu ein sbri.

Sleifiem i'r parlyrau Beiblaidd i sbio yn syn
Ar olosg o gnawd yn yr arch, ac ar ludw o lais;
Yno y dysgasom uwch cloriau wedi eu sgriwio cyn eu pryd
Golectau gwrthryfel coch a litaniau trais.

Nid yr angau a gerdd yn naturiol fel ceidwad cell
A rhybudd yn sŵn cloncian ei allweddi llaith,
Ond y llewpart diwydiannol a naid yn sydyn slei,
O ganol dŵr a thân, ar wŷr wrth eu gwaith.

Yr angau hwteraidd: yr angau llychlyd, myglyd, meddw,
Yr angau a chanddo arswyd tynghedfen las;
Troi tanchwa a llif-pwll ni yn anwariaid, dro,
Yn ymladd a phwerau catastroffig, cyntefig, cas.

Gwragedd dewrfud â llond dwrn o arian y gwaed,
A bwcedaid o angau yn atgo tan ddiwedd oes,
Yn cario glo, torri coed-tan a dodi'r ardd
Ac yn darllen yn amlach hanes dioddefaint Y Groes.

Gosodwn Ddydd Sul y Blodau ar eu beddau bwys
O rosynnau silicotig a lili mor welw â'r nwy,
A chasglu rhwng y cerrig annhymig a rhwng yr anaeddfed gwrb
Yr hen regfeydd a'r cableddau yn eu hangladdau hwy.

Diflannodd yr Wtopia oddi ar gopa Gellionnen,
Y ddynoliaeth haniaethol, y byd diddosbarth a diffin;
Ac nid oes a erys heddiw ar waelod y cof
Ond teulu a chymdogaeth, aberth a dioddefaint dyn.

(D. Gwenallt Jones, 'Y Meirwon', *Eples*, Llandysul, 1951,
tt.9–10.)

(With his fiftieth birthday behind him, a man sees with fair
    clarity
The people and surroundings that made him what he is,
And the steel ropes that tether me strongest to these things
In a village of the South, are the graves in two cemeteries.

I'd ride a bike pilfered from scrap, or with a pig's bladder
Play rugby for Wales; and all that while,
Little thought I'd hear how two of my contemporaries
Would spew into a bucket their lungs red and vile.

Our neighbours they were, a family from Merthyr Tydfil,
The 'martyrs' we called them, by way of a pun,
And five of them by turns had a cough that crossed the fences
To break up our chatter and darken all our fun.

D. Gwenallt Jones (Gwenallt). (*Source: Welsh Arts Council.*)

We crept in the Bibled parlours, and peeped with awe
At cinders of flesh in the coffin, and ashes of song,
And there we learnt, over lids screwed down before their time,
Collects of red revolt and litanies of wrong.

Not the death that goes his natural rounds, like a gaol warder,
Giving notice in the clink of his damp keys,
But the leopard of industry leaping sudden and sly
That strikes from fire and water men to their knees.

The hootering death: the dusty, smokeful, drunken death,
Death whose dreadful grey destiny was ours;
Explosion and flood changed us often into savages
Fighting catastrophic and devilish powers.

Mute and brave women with a fistful of bloodmoney,
With a bucketful of death, forever the rankling of loss,
Carrying coal, chopping wood for a fire, or setting the garden,
And more and more reading the Passion of the Cross.

This Sunday of Flowers, as we place on their graves a bunch
Of silicotic roses and lilies pale as gas,
Between the premature stones and the curb yet unripened,
We gather the old blasphemings, curses of funerals past.

Our Utopia vanished from the top of Gellionnen,
Our abstract humanity's classless, defrontiered reign,
And today nothing is left at the deep root of the mind
Save family and neighbourhood, man's sacrifice and pain.)

(David Gwenallt Jones, 'The Dead', (trans. Anthony Conran),
in *The Penguin Book of Welsh Verse*, 1967, pp.251–2.)

F.11   From this high quarried ledge I see
The place for which the Quakers once
Collected clothes, my father's home,
Our stubborn bankrupt village sprawled
In jaded dusk beneath its nameless hills;
The drab street strung across the cwm,
Derelict workings, tips of slag

The gospellers and gamblers use
And children scrutting for the coal
That winter dole cannot purvey;
Allotments where the collier digs
While engines hack the coal within his brain;
Grey Hebron in a rigid cramp,
White cheap-jack cinema, the church
Stretched like a sow beside the stream;
And mourners in their Sunday best
Holding a tiny funeral, singing hymns
That drift insidious as the rain
Which rises from the steaming fields
And swathes about the skyline crags
Till all the upland gorse is drenched
And all the creaking mountain gates
Drip brittle tears of crystal peace;
And in a curtained parlour women hug
Huge grief, and anger against God.

But now the dusk, more charitable than the Quakers,
Veils the cracked cottages with drifting may
And rubs the hard day off the slate.
The colliers squatting on the ashtip
Listen to one who holds them still with tales,
While that white frock that floats down the dark alley
Looks just like Christ; and in the lane
The clink of coins among the gamblers
Suggests the thirty pieces of silver.
I watch the clouded years
Rune the rough foreheads of these moody hills,
This wet evening, in a lost age.

(Alun Lewis, 'The Mountain over Aberdare', in *Raider's Dawn*,
London, 1942, pp.62–3.)

F.12   During the week Mary had been busy among the women in the
street, all of whom had pledged themselves to come to the
demonstration. She had been particularly anxious about this, as
she believed that each street should come into a demonstration

as a contingent with its own banner, and not in the usual straggling individual manner. So, immediately after dinner, when Len had gone down to fetch his father and mother, who were to start from the same street as themselves, she went from house to house getting the women ready. In every home she was welcomed either with a smile or a joking remark, the little children, many of them with bare backsides, running to the door to greet her.

Half an hour before the demonstration was timed to start the women and children and the unemployed men in the street were lined up with a red banner at their head with:

'Sunny Bank Women want Bread not Batons'

sewn in white tape. Mary forgot her chest and the conversation with Len on the previous night as she looked behind her at the ranks of men and women who were ready to march. Each pair of eyes gleamed as brightly as her own and every mouth wore a smile, even the little babies', clutched tightly to their mothers' bodies in heavy woollen shawls. One of the Party members from the next street came up with a clarionette and two kettle-drums. The ex-servicemen present soon selected two drum-mers, and in a very short time the air was ringing with the strains of popular songs. The sharp notes of the clarionette kept everyone in tune and the tremor of the drums made feet itch to get into stride. Occasionally the clarionette gave a shrill scream as though its innards were twisted, but no one took any notice of this and kept on singing with unflinching gusto.

At last the music was interrupted by a cheer as Len and his parents came round the corner of the street. Big Jim, failing to walk erect, pretended he was doing so by stretching his head unnaturally far back and twirling his moustache arrogantly. But, not noticing where he was going, he stumbled against a stone in the roadway and would have fallen had not Shân gripped him tightly.

'Holy hell!' he growled under his breath, while at the same time trying to regain his dignified posture. 'These bloody roads are not fit for a dog to walk on, muniferni. It is time that the council do something about it.'

No one heard his words in the excited clamour as the people

prepared for the march off. Jim and Shân were given the place of honour in the front rank because they were amongst the oldest inhabitants of Cwmardy. Len and Mary stood either side of the procession to marshal it. The men with the clarionette and drums waited for the signal, every one held their breath for a moment, then three rolls on the drums, the clarionette blared into action, and the people began their march to the main demonstration. At each street-corner numbers of people saw friends already in the ranks and tried to break in to join them, only to be firmly told that they must go behind as the ranks were not to be broken. Whenever anyone was persistent, the women became vociferous and let the delinquent know, if he was not prepared to go to the rear of his own volition, he would be placed there. Shân and Big Jim, right at the head of the demonstration, with the blood-red banner streaming directly behind them, walked silent and erect, like soldiers, Jim jealously watching every stride she made to make sure she was in step. She stumbled once and, not knowing how, was unable to change her step to answer the music before Jim saw her.

'Change,' he hissed, without turning his head. 'Change, venw, for God's sake. You are a disgrace to the regiment, mun.'

Shân felt deeply the indignity of her position. 'I can't, James bach, I don't know how,' she moaned quietly so that no one but he could hear.

'Iff arn daen, do scotch with both feet at once,' he instructed. She misunderstood him and gave a little hop which only took her slightly in front without bringing her into step. Jim's eyes went blood-shot as he glared at her.

'Fall out,' he ordered. 'Fall out quick to the rear before anybody know you are with me.'

Shân squared her drooping shoulders and planted her feet more firmly into the earth with each stride.

'Never,' she declared emphatically, not caring now who heard her. 'No, not for all the sodgers or sailors in the King's or anybody else's army will Shân fall out. Huh!'

Len happened to come to the front of the procession at this moment and one glance at his parents told him what was brewing. He blew a whistle sharply, the impromptu band stopped playing and the people came to a halt.

'Just a whiff for the stragglers to draw up, so that we can march into the square in order,' Len shouted, at the same time trying to convey with a glance a message to Mary on the other side. She unostentatiously made her way to him and he whispered in her ear. When the signal was given for the restart, Mary was marching between the old couple.

Sunny Bank contingent was the first at the starting point on the square on top of the hill near the pits, but in a very short time hundreds more had gathered and before the pit-hooter blaringly announced that the men were about to come up, the square was packed with men and women. Red banners and streamers speckled the air as the mournful strains of the drum and fife band floated up the hill. Miners in their working clothes and with coal-soiled faces joined the unemployed people, for the march round the valley.

The air was blasted by a roar like thunder when the gallant little group of bandsmen, puffing and blowing, staggered over the crest of the hill and came into sight. Their thirst was quickly quenched by the women, who ran into nearby houses and fetched out jugs of tea, water, and small beer, or whatever other liquid they could get. The lodge officials, some in working kit, now formed up in front with Len and Mary. Jim and Shân fell in the rank immediately behind, their temporary difference forgotten. The people of Sunny Bank made sure their banner was next to the one belonging to the combine committee, this being the only one to which they would grant precedence.

The signal was now given to the band leader, the drums rolled, the fifes began to wail, and the long demonstration against the cuts inflicted on the unemployed began its march around the valley.

At the bottom of the hill, before turning into the square which led to the rubbish dump where the other pit contingents of the combine were waiting, Len looked back. His eyes glowed with what he saw. The street behind him looked like a flowing river of human beings, on which floated innumerable scarlet banners and flags. He looked far into the ascending distance, but failed to see any end. His eyes began to water with the strain and he allowed his ears to continue where the former had failed. Although directly in front of the band, he heard running beneath its trumming wails the deep monotone of countless boots tramping rhythmically on the hard road. The potential power in the sound tickled his throat, sending saliva into his mouth. He had to gulp before he could say in an excited whisper to Mary:

'It's the greatest thing that's ever been. Everybody is on the march. Everybody.' His emotion became too deep to allow for more.

Mary, pride in her every gesture, murmured: 'This is the cure, Len, for me and the people. Unity. Unity in action.' Her voice rose into a shout on this last phrase, and in a moment it was taken up by some young people until it spread all through the ranks like thunder.

'Unity. Unity in action.' The sound of the marching feet was drowned in its tremor.

Mary turned to look at Shân and Jim. The old couple were tight-lipped and silent, but they beamed with happiness, although in Jim's eyes there was also a look of dignity and discomfiture, as though his pride was beating back something he badly wanted to do.

Mary sensed the situation and whispered to Len, who immediately stepped back to his father's side and said: 'There's a urinal lower down, dad. You had better drop out by there and join us on the field.'

Jim kept his eyes fixed on the man in front of him and screwed his mouth up to say: 'What in hell think you I am, Len? Do you think I can't carry three pints without falling out? Huh! I have drunked twenty-three before now and marched eighteen miles afterwards without ever thinking of losing a drop, muniferni.'

Len felt abashed at this retort, particularly when he glimpsed the proud smile of his mother's grim face, and he hastily stepped forward to his own place, where Mary glanced at him enquiringly. He shook his head as an answer to this unspoken query.

By this time the head of the demonstration had reached the square, which was dense with people cordoned off to make way for the demonstration to pass through to the assembling field. Uniformed ambulance men, lining each side of the street, took their places alongside the marching men and women, and in this manner for over half an hour the people of Cwmardy poured through the square which was their ancient battle-ground, into the field where most of their vital decisions had been taken.

A short rest was taken there, while the various bands competed for the loudest playing. The valiant little fife band was lost in the din of different marches blared with brassy resonance into the air, which shook in the martial strains. The various committees now took charge of their own contingents and began marshalling them up, after Mary had had a conversation with the leaders, who agreed that the women should head the march from the field. There was some initial confusion while the people were being sorted out, some women preferring to march with their menfolk, but eventually everything, as far as possible, was in order and ready for the next stage. The bands, each with its own vivid and distinctive uniform, were scattered at regular intervals through the length of the demonstration, adding to its vivacity and colour. A bugle sounded, drums rolled once more, the bands took up the refrain, and the procession began to unwind itself from the field.

The leaders of the combine committee marched in front of the leading band, which was followed by the women, but Shân and Big Jim still remained in the second rank, having with adamant curtness refused to be parted or shifted. The procession marched twelve abreast through the main street, most of whose shop windows still wore shutters as mementos of past battles.

When the front of the demonstration was two miles advanced, and on the summit of the hill to the east of Cwmardy, people were still pouring from the assembling field. Len lifted his head sharply into the air when he fancied he heard the distant strains of music in the direction left of the demonstration. He turned to Mary and the workman next to her.

'Can you hear anything?' he asked.

They both looked simultaneously past Len, and he, seeing their amazement, turned his head to look in the same direction. He drew his breath sharply and his perspiring face went a shade whiter. The mountain which separated Cwmardy from the other valleys looked like a gigantic ant-hill, covered with a mass of black, waving bodies.

'Good God,' the man next to Mary whispered 'the whole world is on the move.'

Mary did not reply for some time, unable to take her eyes from the scene, although her feet kept automatically moving her forward in time with the band. Then she murmured, No, not yet. But the people are beginning to move it now. She said no more, and even the bands were quiet. The people seemed overwhelmed with the mighty demonstration of their own power, which they could now see so clearly. Their voices suddenly became puny, and articulation was left to their feet, which rattled and sang on the roadways with music more devastating in its strength than all the bands in the world.

Len momentarily felt himself like a weak straw drifting in and out with the surge of bodies. Then something powerful swept through his being as the mass soaked its strength into him, and he realised that the strength of them all was the measure of his own, that his existence and power as an individual was buried in that of the mass now pregnant with motion behind him. The momentous thought made him inhale deeply and his chest expanded, throwing his head erect and his shoulders square to the breeze that blew the banners into red rippling slogans of defiance and action. Time and distance were obliterated by the cavalcade of people, whose feet made the roads invisible.

(Lewis Jones, *We Live*, London, 1978, pp.238–43.)

F.13   On their way down the hill the two brothers said very little. Alf dragged at a cigarette that had broken in his pocket. He held his fingers tightly over a puncture in the paper. Hugh had his hands stuck into his overcoat pockets.

'Impossible!' he said.

'What is?'

'Sixty or seventy thousand people on the streets on Sunday. Stupid optimism.'

'The streets are pretty long. There might be room for a couple of thousand more.'

'You've got too much faith in the valley dwellers.'

'It's you've lost touch. You don't know them like you used to.'

'They are not the same as they used to be. I remember a fire in their eyes, strong enough to drive the rainstorms from the pavement. Where is it gone? I see their bodies and their eyes looking as musty and as empty as rooms left idle for thirty or forty years. Poverty has killed them, but they are still standing. They still talk, move and make love the best they can. But the old militancy is dead. The brains of men and women don't produce militancy. It's the speed at which life is lived does that. When the coalowners made a riot out of profit-making, the workers lived in a riot of dissipation or revolt. When the oppressors slackened their tempo, so did the workers.'

'The oppression remains unchanged. It never slackens.'

'Changed in quality then. For so many people unemployment is the end of the world. Why should they struggle to change a world they think is going to end? It's a slow, grinding agony, Alf. First it drives you to thoughts of terrorism. But the oppression of the Labour Exchanges is so subtle, so persuasive, and man's got such an urge to be as the cattle are, that thought soon gives way to a quiet, starving surprised sort of tolerance, an existence that has no interest, no value, no responsibilities.

'When a coal boss closes a pit and tells his workers that they'll have to live on a lower level what he's telling them is that there's no level too low for them to live in. The very first moment a man became unemployed as a result of this God infernally crazy system, every Liberal lover of freedom and progress should have gone and made things easier for the Tories and hung himself on the nearest willow.

'For even ten men to be unemployed is a betrayal by those who order society of everything that humanity is supposed to stand for. We drink in the notion that humanity is supposed to stand for something at our mothers' breasts. But maybe our mothers' breasts are wrong, and humanity stands for nothing more than an incorporation into one iron ball of all these injustices that we consider opposed to humanity.

'These employers of labour, these Christian adventurers who came into these valleys and exploited men and mountains until they had enough wealth to put their lives right side up, then withdrew their godheads and their profits, abandoned pits until our lives are now upside down, where are they now, I wonder?

The air might be cold and bitter for the poor bastards left
holding the kitty. But their country and city homes are probably
as warm as hell. Our throats might be dry. We might be
moaning for beer we can't buy, we might be yearning for milk
our mothers haven't got, but our late masters have a fine supply
of rich red wine. Oh Christ, Alf, I'm talking myself to sleep.
Perhaps that's what I was trying to do. It's a mess, a rotten hell
of a mess. You've had it for five years, me for six months. Not
much, not very much. Yet all the capitalists in all the world
could toil at their ledgers for a hundred years and never get
through enumerating all the kinds of pain those years and those
months have brought us.

'When a man falls out of work, society should dedicate every
dime of its surplus value to compensating him for that primal
curse. Instead, society dedicates every ounce of its mental
energy to persuade him that the curse is not a curse, but a
normally unpleasant incident, that will become tolerable when
life-conditions have become adjusted to it. Even you and I
might get used to it. I'll wake up one morning, after spending a
couple of years making a little loose change in the way of smaller
scale post-graduate adulteries and I'll find myself looking like
an eighty-year old peasant who had known only long hours of
labour in the field, servile torpor in the church, without ever
having felt one moment of either anger or revolt. That's a
bonny prospect, I'll be damned.'

'An eighty-year old peasant. Our generation won't live that
long, unless the government singles some of us out to keep alive
by artifical means, to experiment with artificial means of
starving us into subjection.'

'They might call in a witch from one of the Dominions and turn
us all into sugar-beet.'

'They say the unemployed are red now.'

'That's a start. All we need now is roots.'

'That's all we need . . . Roots. That's what we haven't got.'

'You're right, Alf. We haven't got much contact with life, have
we? We don't make much of a mark on life the way we are.
When a man's without a job he's only half-born. If I'd known
about this capitalist crisis twenty-two years ago I'd have jumped
from my mother's womb after the first six months. The last

three months were a dead loss. It was spent in taking a shape that no one would ever need and it was as dark as pitch in there.

'When society cannot use a man's capacity for being useful, it doesn't matter whether that man has the form of a man, a trolleybus, a jack-rabbit or the seat of a lavatory. Work is man. Man is work. Without work man is released from the responsibility of walking about looking as if he was made in God's image. Ask Charlie the Apostolic how many men who stand outside the Labour Exchange on a day of cold and rain present such an image as God would claim to be proud of. He'll give himself piles sitting down thinking out an answer to that one.

'The circle of God's images within society is getting narrower. Assuming, that is, that God would never face the public with a tail of dirty shirt sticking out of the seat of his trousers, with all the diseases of dirt, tedium and undernourishment sticking out a mile from the features of his face. As unemployment spreads, God's image will become more and more the exclusive property of the middle and upper classes. As the unemployed masses see that godliness is only another form of that jobliness which is denied them, the social and religious structure now standing are in for a walloping . . . What are you thinking about, Alf? You look like Elijah.'

'I was wondering how we'd be if we had never known this valley and everything that goes with it.'

'We are the valley. The valley is us. Nobody can alter us now, not even by Orders in Council. Either the world can like us or leave us, kiss us or kick us. We are here, fixed, unchangeable like those stars over the mountain there. The sum total of a dozen blind, lousy accidents, ranging from birth in the bosom of a still-enslaved proletariat to the greed and the business stupidity of a few coalowners.

'If we don't like ourselves, we can alter ourselves only by altering this valley. How? That's the question I stumble over in the dark. That's the question I've been trying like the devil to get away from me in the last few weeks. I doubt if it will ever change. In the days of wealth and plenty there was life enough in this valley, raw, real howling life to change not only the valley but the entire universe. The sun and stars could have been kicked out of their courses as easily as the money-grabbers and spell-weavers from their banks and temples. But the frost had killed that life. Ten years of unemployment for half the population and worsened conditions of labour for the other half, have proved that intelligence, energy and vision, are destructible, even if matter isn't.

'You've told me about demonstrations to the council. What did they demonstrate for? Extra relief. Thousands needed it, but only a few dozen were far enough away from snoring and animal hibernation to demonstrate. When people have learned to submit themselves to the rule of avoidable, unnecessary agony in that fashion they deserve to suffer. You think they'll create hell with these new Regulations. I don't think so.'

'I can almost hear them marching now. Ordinary poverty just injures poverty. This *Means Test* insults them. That might make a difference.'

'We've had religious revivalists insulting us for centuries. They have kidded us that we are the nation nearest in all the world to total damnation and most in need of redemption. We've certainly helped ourselves to redemption in bigger gulps than any other community. The religious revivals were a good basis for the *Means Test*. Our ancestors did so many damned silly things for the good of their souls there'll be some of their latter day descendants willing to take investigators and Labour Camps on the same basis. We might go to a Labour Camp and learn to be farmers. Our great-grandfather was a farmer. He took part in the Rebecca riots.'

'What grudge did Rebecca have?'

'That's just the name they gave the riots. Our great-grandfather wrapped a toll-gate round a bailiff's neck.'

'If the bailiff was anything like the brotherhood of bums we've got around here I bet he used it as a collar.'

'Wouldn't you like to be a farmer?'

'What the hell for? All the bloody seeds we ever planted never came to fruit. When I was a kid, I planted a handful of orange pips in the back garden. What came of it? The woman next door died of appendicitis and I was expecting orange trees. I planted a handful of dreams in Gwyneth. Same thing. No appendicitis this time. Dreams are soft and messy and they don't annoy the

Gwyn Thomas. (*Source: Welsh Arts Council.*)

stomach like orange pips. But there's death mixed up in it and it's coming closer than that woman next door. This time it's Gwyneth.'

'Mm. The world's making a special job of us two. They might pickle us and peddle us around under the noses of future generations to prove that bad as they may think things are for them things were a devil of a sight worse for us . . . Why shouldn't we go back to broad fields and empty valleys, anyway? Why should we stand still and see our lives taken away from us, dirtied and spoiled by a bunch of sanctimonious maniacs who are willing to sacrifice never-mind-how-many lives just in order to keep a few social relationships away from the cleaners. Why shouldn't we lead an exodus of all victims of the industrial revolution back to the pastures where they started.

'The Israelites did it, and they had steady jobs in Egypt, though nobody stamped their cards for it. Nobody needed a promised land more than we do. We could look for it. We could manure our fields with the distilled juices from the wrung withers of every politician who has ever given us lands of promise instead of promised lands, and we could use the priests to fetch us sweet water from the well when we are thirsty from singing and loving at night.'

'Better talk it over with Herbert. He knows a couple of priests.'

'Will he be in the house now?'

'Aye. This is his night for music and meditation.'

(Gwyn Thomas, *Sorrow for thy Sons*, London, 1986, pp.235-41.)

F.14   I was born in a large Welsh industrial town at the beginning of the Great War: an ugly, lovely town (or so it was, and is, to me), crawling, sprawling, slummed, unplanned, jerry-villa'd, and smug-suburbed by the side of a long and splendid-curving shore where truant boys and sandfield boys and old anonymous men, in the tatters and hangovers of a hundred charity suits, beachcombed, idled, and paddled, watched the dock-bound boats, threw stones into the sea for the barking, outcast dogs, and, on Saturday summer afternoons, listened to the militant music of salvation and hell-fire preached from a soap-box.

This sea town was my world; outside a *strange* Wales, coal-pitted, mountained, river run, full, so far as I knew, of choirs and sheep and story-book tall hats, moved about its business which was none of mine; beyond that unknown Wales lay England, which was London, and a country called 'The Front' from which many of our neighbours never came back. At the beginning, the only 'front' I knew was the little lobby before our front door; I could not understand how so many people never returned from there; but later I grew to know more, though still without understanding, and carried a wooden rifle in Cwmdonkin Park and shot down the invisible, unknown enemy like a flock of wild birds. And the park itself was a world within the world of the sea town; quite near where I lived, so near that on summer evenings I could listen, in my bed, to the voices of other children playing ball on the sloping, paper-littered bank; the part was full of terrors and treasures . . .

. . . .

Never *was* there such a town as ours, I thought, as we fought on the sandhills with the boys our mothers called 'common', or dared each other up the scaffolding of half-built houses, soon to be called Laburnums or the Beeches, near the residential districts where the solider business families 'dined' at half past seven and never drew the curtains. Never *was* there such a town (I thought) for the smell of fish and chips on Saturday nights; for the Saturday afternoon cinema matinees where we shouted and hissed our threepences away; for the crowds in the streets, with leeks in their pockets, on international nights, for the singing that gushed from the smoky doorways of the pubs in the quarters we never should have visited; for the park, the inexhaustibly ridiculous and mysterious, the bushy Red-Indian-hiding park, where the hunchback sat alone, images of perfection in his head, and 'the groves were blue with sailors'.

The recollections of childhood have no order; of all those every-coloured and shifting scented shoals that move below the surface of the moment of recollection, one, two, indiscriminately, suddenly, dart up out of their revolving waters into the present air: immortal flying-fish.

So I remember that never was there such a dame-school as

ours: so firm and kind and smelling of galoshes, with the sweet
and fumbled music of the piano-lessons drifting down from
upstairs to the lonely schoolroom where only the sometimes
tearful wicked sat over undone sums or to repent a little crime,
the pulling of a girl's hair during geography, the sly shin-kick
under the table during prayers. Behind the school was a narrow
lane where the oldest and boldest threw pebbles at windows,
scuffled and boasted, lied about their relations —
'My father's got a chauffeur.'
'What's he want a chauffeur for, he hasn't got a car.'
'My father's the richest man in Swansea.'
'My father's the richest man in Wales.'
'My father's the richest man in the world' —
and smoked the butt ends of cigarettes, turned green, went
home, and had little appetite for tea.

The lane was the place to tell your secrets; if you did not have
any, you invented them; I had few. Occasionally, now, I dream
that I am turning, after school, into the lane of confidences
where I say to the children of my class: 'At last I have a secret.'
'What is it? What is it?'
'I can fly!' And when they do not believe me, I flap my arms like
a large, stout bird and slowly leave the ground, only a few
inches at first, then gaining air until I fly, like Dracula in a
schoolboy cap, level with the windows of the school, peering in
until the mistress at the piano screams, and the metronome falls
with a clout to the ground, stops, and there is no more Time;
and I fly over the trees and chimneys of my town, over the
dockyards, skimming the masts and funnels; over Inkerman
Street and Sebastopol Street and the street of the man-capped
women hurrying to the Jug and Bottle with a fish-frail full of
empties; over the trees of the eternal park, where a brass band
shakes the leaves and sends them showering down to the nurses
and the children, the cripples and the out-of-work. This is only a
dream. The ugly, lovely, at least to me, town is alive, exciting
and real though war has made a hideous hole in it. I do not need
to remember a dream. The reality is there. The fine, live people,
the spirit of Wales itself.

(Dylan Thomas, *Miscellany*, London, 1963, pp.87 and 91–3.)

F.15 Saturday mornings, I used to climb into my mother's bed and lie between my parents and ask questions:
'Who made the world?'
'God.'
'Who made God?'

When Mam would go and prepare breakfast I would lie on the warm part where she had been. My father snored with his mouth ajar. His face was turned towards me and I could see the individual pores in the skin over his nose, clearly. His skin was like a used dartboard. He opened one eye fishily and saw me upside down. 'What are you looking at?' he said sleepily. 'Your nose,' I said. He closed his eyes again. The wallpaper in the bedroom was pinkish, so warm and kindly. He opened his left eye once more. 'What's wrong with my nose?' he asked. 'Nothing,' I said, but he turned over and I gazed at the back of his head. 'You're going bald a bit on the crown,' I remarked. Father grunted but he soon moved again, this time on to his back. 'You have quite a prominent Adam's apple,' I said. 'Be quiet.' he said. 'You have hair growing in your ears,' I continued. He pulled the bedclothes over his head. 'What are you doing that for?' I shouted.

Saturday was a grand day for there was not school . . . not until Monday. Saturday mornings Leo would often read me poetry from a little blue book.
'The one about the Merman, our kid.'
'No. And don't call me our kid.'
'The one about the Merman, and call once yet before you go, Marg-aret, Marg-aret.'
My brother sat up in his bed, so I lay down.
'This is by Gerard Manley Hopkins,' he said.
'Is he a revolutionary?' I asked.
'Well . . . in a way.'
'You always read revolutionaries,' I said.

Outside it was raining. Saturday morning rain and the slish, slish, slish of wet tyres over a shining patent leather street with its caged pieces of sky in puddles. They say Manchester is rainy. Have you ever been to Cardiff? It's the rainiest city in the world. Wilfred told me a story about that: when Noah looked out from his Ark so many years ago, he patted the nearest giraffe and said: 'Soon it will be dry everywhere, except of course in Cardiff'. In 1934, one Saturday morning, it was rain over my home town and my brother Leo was reading me poetry from a little blue book. 'Glory be to God for dappled things,' he read. Mama was downstairs cooking breakfast; in the front bedroom Dad lay back snoring, his arm dangling over the side of the bed near an empty teacup. Keith's mother was dead in the wet graveyard and Uncle Isidore was still alive reading Karl Marx in the Public Library. Oh the rain in 1934 that fell over all the map. In the valleys, thirty miles from Cardiff, the rain fell absently across the town square and the queue at the bus stop suddenly started singing into the rain — the rain that stretched itself across the blind windows, the rain that pattered on the black umbrellas, the rain that dived into the slagheaps — the chapel of voices *together*, ever rising higher into the thin rain. Others lounged at corners, in doorways, smelling of wet mackintoshes, listless, dull with unemployment — depression in the valleys and the orator thumping his fist — they only went on singing *together*, louder and higher into the rain — then the bus arrived. The red-coloured bus arrived and they stopped singing, became conscious of the rain, the dampness seeping right through to their souls, the Rhondda Valley naked, bony, the green dress pulled off, the pulleys stopped and a girl trembling near the coal-mine with a gentle fluttering movement under her heart. One of the queue had a fit of coughing — spat from his mouth a yellow viscid fluid, mixed with coal and blood. All the people in the queue watched his convulsion of coughing, and like prisoners they filed through the pin-striped rain into the red-coloured bus, terribly mute, wet, *lonely*. 1934.

'Glory be to God for dappled things,' my brother read.

Alun and Gwennie had climbed the hills in the early morning to pick mushrooms. Then the bad rain fell, and they found a cave to shelter in.

'Why shouldn't we go to London, Gwennie fach?' asked Alun. 'Work is more regular. Safe work. Safe to get married and 'ave kids.'

'We've been through it before, Alun.'

'You'd like it there,' he said vaguely. 'Theatre and things.' But they wouldn't go. He knew it. A man has to keep his roots or he's lost. Alun's father had been a miner. The family always had been miners. And that was his life too, to come up blinking into the sunlight, or the rain, with the coal dust lathered on his face and black lines under his fingernails. And the soapy water in the zinc bath before the smoky fire-grate, and the yellow canary singing in its cage. It was a simple life and a hard one, but it was his. The men with white scarves around their necks and caps tilted on their heads, working when they were allowed to work, singing when it was time to sing. The choirs, the rugby matches, the chapel, the pub, the billiard hall, and being born and being loved, and the coughing. The English were alien. England was alien and yet the boys were going up North or to London, losing their own tongue, their own language, their own customs. Going to an alien country and feeling clumsy and different and disliked.

'Bugger the rain', said Alun.

And Gwennie was thinking how one-third of a miner's life had to be spent away from the fresh air and sunlight. She didn't want Alun to get silicosis like her father and her grandfather. She didn't want to wake up in the morning hearing Alun coughing and gasping for breath. Only a week ago, she had heard one of the soapbox orators saying that four miners were launched into eternity every day, and nearly two hundred thousand were impaired every year. A hazardous calling, the orator had said. A hazardous calling, thought Gwennie.

They were at the foot of the hills when they heard the explosion. Gwennie and Alun joined the silent knots of people who waited in the rain at the top of the pit. A fire was burning fiercely at the coal face, and the rescue party went down the pit with the aid of oxygen cylinders and canaries in cages, and one by one, pitifully, painfully, the trapped men were brought to the surface. The faces of many were badly disfigured. The rain fell. Gwennie said, 'Yes, Alun, we'll go to London, there'll be theatres and things.' 1934.

'Glory be to God for dappled things,' my brother Leo read from his little blue book.

'Breakfast, breakfast — get up or I'll throw a bucket of water over you,' shouted mother laughing. *Amo, amas, amat, amamus, amatis, amant.* When I was born my brother Wilfred bought me a *Comic Cuts* to read. I couldn't read then. Wilfred touched me to see if I was real. I was.

(Dannie Abse, *Ash on a Young Man's Sleeve*, London, 1982, pp.29–31.)

F.16   I see now that I was born into the end of one era of Welsh Wales and Welsh Nonconformity. In Penuel Chapel when I was a boy, the age of the congregation was increasing; there were fewer and fewer young people and the Sunday School classes grew smaller and smaller in my lifetime until finally the building was demolished. The chapel and its religion declined because it ceased to appeal while the Welsh Language was like something to be cosseted as if used 'for best' on a Sunday, then put aside for the working week in the houses of all but a few stalwarts whose children — usually sons of the manse — were unexpectedly, and often undeservedly, to prosper in later years. For them, in broadcasting and other circles, the Welsh language became a caste mark, like an old Etonian tie, and people like myself became outsiders, easily excluded for a long while.

But my grandmother had known a flourishing and youthful congregation in the aftermath of the Revival, and Penuel people were for the most part old Pontypridd people who had struggled along against the competition and the invasion of outsiders in the great population explosion after the coal rush. Then the valleys were opened up; the industrial population doubled in a very short space of time, adding nearly a million souls to what had been a rural area. They came, like my grandfather, from the Welsh countryside and from the other side of the Bristol Channel like the parents of so many of my schoolmates who brought with them the names of remote Devon and Cornwall villages whose names were to puzzle me so much when I read them in obituaries. I was impatient with the lack of youth and vigour about my chapel, the plain foolishness of so much Welsh when the streets were alive with the vernacular; impatient at the do's-and-don'ts of simple people, even at their piety in a world which grew more violent every day, and my restlessness drove me into those same streets which seemed to me to be the real world. I had enough places in which to daydream, but my grandmother saw to it that I was the instrument of her chapel duties; for I became her messenger, first accompanying her when she took home-baked cakes and delicacies to invalids and others, all members of the chapel, and later when she was unable to walk, making the visits myself, a shopping basket forever under my arm. This I did all through my childhood, changing to a more masculine briefcase which I inherited when my mother's youngest brother was killed in the second war and, once again, these visits were a happy accident of my life since it meant that I crossed doorsteps I would not otherwise have crossed. They also led to some strange memories when I lay in hospital; for I was in a ward full of colliers, most of whom had silicosis and heart conditions as well as *tuberculosis*, and the images which returned to me were rich and varied — all to be sifted, even treasured if they hastened the endless slow procession of days.

As a child I had no direct knowledge of the colliery, only my grandmother's stories of her father's involvement, but I used to visit one old collier who had suffered an accident underground which had paralysed his hand. With the little compensation he received, he had opened a backstreet sweet shop, one of those tiny front-room businesses which sold humbugs and cough sweets and simple household requirements and whose trade was virtually confined to the terraced street in which it stood. Here you would sometimes see men who had come directly from the colliery, their white eyeballs and teeth gleaming in their black faces as they performed errands for their wives with simple requests. ('A packet of Reckett's Blue and ten Woods on the book!') The old collier, whose name was Rhys Jones, carried on with the shop after his wife died, struggling to lift the heavy sweet bottles with his withered arm, and every week I would make my journey with a plate of Welsh cakes or *Tiesion Lap* — a delicacy made with sour milk — and then I would listen while he told me stories of his struggles with stubborn horses underground. He never allowed me to see his withered arm which he kept wrapped up in a woman's black silk stocking, but he welcomed my company and even came to depend upon it as I listened gravely to his comments while the war approached.

'Myself,' he would say airily, shaking the screw of caster

sugar over the Welsh cakes, 'I think that Stalin is only bouncing!'

I grew used to the sound of his voice and was pleased at his excitement at my visits, for I was one of the few visitors he received and whenever he saw my grandmother, he would extol my virtues — once stating that in his view I was a likely candidate for the Nonconformist Ministry, which showed a shrewd judgement of what would please her. I was a good listener, he said, implying that it was a rare attribute in that calling.

In hospital I also thought about my schooldays and I would try to remember the names of the children who had sat next to me and the games we played in Infants' School. I suppose I was trying to recapture a sense of innocence and now, going back on it from afar, I realise that I am attempting to lay incidents of my life on paper like a card player would lay a hand upon a table — saying, as the autobiographer does with a flourish, 'Here I am. This is what made me and this is what I made of myself.' But I can detect no conscious pattern of events, and if there is any danger, it is the professional writer's curse — the dangerous habit of trying to please. I have always thought that every autobiography should contain something disgraceful, and yet the loyalties which bind you are like tentacles so that it is often painful to go back, each layer of memory having to be lifted and unstuck like an adhesion. The facts are easy but the least important. You ask yourself, how did you really feel? Perhaps the best guide is to watch your own children as they grow up, and then it is often a matter of revealing the contrast — then and now.

At first I see myself as a little cosseted pumpkin again, Grandma's boy still, standing at her side outside chapel, the sort of chummy little boy whose hair adults cannot help ruffling. I remember I had a tam at one time which I could pull down overy my mole like a paratrooper's beret, and I stretched it as much as I could to hide the mole; but when I went to school, it was the mole that interested everyone. There was also the embarrassing matter of my clothes since, by the bitter poverty-line standards of the 1930s we were well off and I had new shoes, a clean red jersey and short grey trousers from the town's largest emporium, kept by a wealthy man whose ill-fitting ginger wig was a source of constant fascination since it slipped continuously, revealing a totally bald pate. I was, I see now, the sort of nice little boy whom schoolmistresses were glad to have in their class. This was to change markedly but, on that first day wending my way into the Infants' School yard, the most obvious contrast was the condition of most of my schoolmates; while there were a few as tidy as myself, my difference was immediately noticeable in the newness of everything I wore and this became one of the first of the stigmas to mark me out from my fellows. I did not have boots which most of the other boys had, but shoes, and I did not have handed-down clothes some of which, I soon saw, had the advantage of being able to stretch over your extremities and could be very useful in wiping your nose. At first, there was not a darn in anything I owned.

Many of the boys wore rubber daps or plimsolls, some did not have socks, and now I became acutely aware, not of rickets, nor malformations of the limbs due to malnutrition, but clanking leg irons which were worn by several children in every class; and it soon became apparent that there were those who suffered from epileptic fits which fact was entered upon a card and the susceptible had to be placed in desks near the aisles so that the teacher could get at them quickly if they began to choke. Leg irons on top of fits constituted a special hazard since the braces could become jammed in the metal supports of the desks. Of course I cannot remember exactly and in what order my perceptions came, but within three days I had made a bosom pal and somehow I knew now beyond any doubt that it was my mole which drew him to me, just as his awkward comic gait had struck me from the moment I saw him in the schoolyard. His name was Albert. He came from the gypsy caravans. He had been run over by one of them when a horse bolted and his legs were permanently bowed so that he could not walk in a straight line. Instead he rolled, a comic opera roll like a sailor in a musical comedy — his whole body rolling, shoulders and legs moving from side to side, his head following as if bowled along by the wind. Albert always had a smile on his face, as if by way of apologising for his oddity and his face, an old man's even at five, which was swarthy, dark, gypsyish and — astonishingly —

a hint of his hair receding at the temples. I think he had unruly hair and his mother kept it firmly plastered down with grease. He was none too clean, bit his fingernails and was the owner of a multitude of boards and wheels and bits of broken skates which could be assembled rapidly into a wide variety of gutter transport which whizzed him down hills. He would never walk normally, somebody said. But he smiled, smiled, smiled, and went on smiling. He was a clown but with soft appealing eyes like a spaniel's. He would never hit anybody. He never shouted. He could do a kind of cartwheel, throwing himself sideways and landing on his little bent legs like a cartoon man. He could also whistle with two fingers in his mouth, giving out a real piercer. The first time I spoke to him, he put these two fingers in his mouth, wet them, then fingered my birthmark and we touched like dogs. I knew there was gypsy in him but it did not make any difference to my birthmark — he knew me straight away, from the very first playtime. Then we sat together, went home together, and he used to wait for me outside the house. Every day he had something different to show me, a gobstopper in a piece of rag, cigarette cards galore, a spider in a jar, and always bits and pieces of wheels which he hid in various hiding places along the road. I think some of his family collected and sold the debris at the back of the market. They were market totters, trading in scraps, and the last of the haul was Albert's. He got what nobody else wanted, the very dregs, but out of it all he created a wonderland of possessions and within a week he was calling for me.

'Is Al' in? C'mon, I got the bogey.'

Once my grandfather saw us on the road.

'Who is this?'

'This is Albert.'

My grandfather gave us money for sweets. We ran up to the shop, purchased an ocean of pear drops, shared them out; riches!

At first, Albert wouldn't come into the house but shouted over the wall.

'Is Al' in?' That was his cry and I loved it.

'Yes,' I said. I was always 'in' to Albert.

(Alun Richards, *Days of Absence*, London, 1986, pp.34–8.)

F.17   — You don't begin to deal in reality, see. I can't read your funny little magazine, but I can catch the drift, and I can read you. Take away the cultural trimmings , the sentimentality and soft soap and what have you left? Petit-bourgeois nationalism. That was out of date in 1848. You want to identify with the Welsh workers. And the irony is, mun, the irony is you are even more foreign than those do-gooding English Quakers. And that's a pretty bitter bloody pill for you to swallow, isn't it?

In spite of the vehemence of his utterance Pen was still smiling. The little boy's lips parted and the dummy fell on the dirty floor. Immediately he began to whimper. The two men towering above him had become frightening, threatening shapes. His mother bent down to pick up the dummy. She wiped it on the woven cloth of the baby's shawl and stuck it back in the little boy's mouth.

— Don't argue, Pen.

There was pleading in her tired voice.

— It upsets him, see. It always upsets him.

Pen moved outside. With an inclination of his head he invited Val to follow him. Val managed to squeeze his way past the wardrobe. He touched the little boy on the shoulder, but the child shrank back from the contact. On the pavement Pen was in the mood to conduct a public debate. There were idle men watching and willing to listen.

— While we are waiting I'll give you a lesson if you like in scientific thought.

His manner was jovial and relaxed.

— Look around you, Mr Gwyn. And what do you see?

He waited patiently for Val to answer.

— Poverty and misery, Val said. The suffering of our own people.

Men pushed forward to listen to them, looking from one to the other like spectators at a prize fight. Pen's smile had become a hungry grin. He was a seasoned and trained debater, poised to demolish his opponent.

— You see a black valley, he said. That's what you should see. And that black valley is a black crucible that contains the stark essentials of the class war. Now if your mind had the correct scientific training that's what you should see. That's the only way forward, my friend. Winning the war. That's the only foundation on which we can build a new society. A new civilization. A new world.

Pen's eloquence was fed by noises of approval from the men behind him.

— So when I look around me, see, I don't see despair. I don't see hopelessness. I don't even see misery. I see hope for the future. I see heroic possibilities. Even poverty can be a cloak of hope. I see the darkest hour before a glorious red dawn.

— That's it, Pen. Give it him, lad. You tell him, boy. We're behind you, boy. Every inch of the way.

The men looked expectantly at Val. As an opponent he was disappointing, lacking in fire, lacking in vision, without any spark of enthusiasm.

— Fantasies, he said. Fantasies. Not facts.

Val was sighing deeply and shaking his head as though he found it difficult to know where to begin. Pen seemed to be taking pity on him.

— What's the Welsh for 'victimisation'? he said. What's the Welsh for 'dialectical materialism'? What's the Welsh for 'bicycle' for God's sake?

He was encouraged by the laughter of the men standing behind him. Val pointed at him suddenly.

— What's your name? he said. What's your first name? What's your full name anyway, if it comes to that.

— Pen Lewis, man. What's the matter with you? Don't be so childish.

— Penry Aneurin Lewis.

Val spoke the name with a kind of possessive confidence that annoyed his opponent.

— This is ridiculous, Pen said. It's like children in standard two. Sticking names on each other.

— It's your proper name, Val said. You have every right to it.

Pen drew his flat hand backwards and forwards under his chin.

— You are up to here in it, he said. Medieval mumbo-jumbo. You're irrelevant, man. You're in the wrong century.

A disturbance in the crowd reached them. Three open vehicles filled with policemen were converging on the side of the road from three different directions. To clear a way the driver of the nearest was working energetically at his klaxon horn. The concourse of men began to move. The more nervous were already dispersing up the hillside.

— It's the Pats, mun. Coming in at the double. They're coming from all over. With their truncheons out. Look out for the buggers.

Pen jumped on the chair and raised his hands to restore calm.

— We've done nothing! Just keep calm and hold your ground. Let the inspector through there, please.

The police inspector's eyes were bloodshot and protruding. They swivelled about suspiciously. He was too hot in his uniform. When he stood by the chair, Val could smell his apprehensive sweat. He wore a flat cap and a strap which reached just under his first chin. He had a smudge of black moustache under his long fleshy nose. Val's presence seemed to displease and perplex him. He looked up at Pen Lewis on his chair. He spoke in a slow ponderous manner that was the fruit of a strange amalgam of experience and instruction.

— Agitation, is it? he said.

Smiling cheerfully Pen Lewis came down from his chair.

— Everything is in order, Inspector Davies. A little misunderstanding. It's been cleared up. I was just telling the lads here about a meeting to be held in the Miners' Welfare this afternoon. Very interesting lecture. 'Why Lenin dedicated 'Left Wing Communism' to Mr Lloyd George.'

Inspector Davies's eyes shifted about restlessly. The title of the lecture sounded improbable. And yet it was unlikely that Pen Lewis would risk making up lies in public just for the pleasure of making a senior police officer look a fool. The bailiff quickly assumed a stance that implied he had been engaged in prolonged and thoughtful discussion with Mrs Jenkins. The small child shrank away from the shadow of the policeman to suck his dummy, with his face to the wall. Inspector Davies frowned as he stared at the child's bare bottom. He was thinking hard. A cloud of cunning settled on his thick eyebrows. A course of action presented itself to him. He considered it and found it good. He came out of the house more lightheartedly than he went in.

— Where's your sparring partner?

The question he put to Pen Lewis was almost jovial.

— In communication with the Council Offices, Pen said. On the telephone. Everything is in order.

— What about the fine?

— Paid. First thing this morning.

The Inspector gave a slow nod that could have been interpreted as benign approval. His whole manner seemed to grow less ominous and threatening.

— Better tell them to disperse.

He muttered his advice in a manner that was almost informal: a hint from a referee well in control of the match.

— We don't want this to look like an Unlawful Assembly now, do we? Or incitement. Or defiance of Law and Order. Et cetera, et cetera.

— All right, lads! We can all go home. Now don't forget the lecture this afternoon. 'Lenin and Lloyd George.' Under the auspices of the N.C.L.C.

While Pen was speaking the Inspector touched Val lightly on the elbow. He spoke to him in Welsh.

— What are you doing with a lot like this? I've seen you in Chapel, haven't I? Let me give you a word of advice.

Val looked away. His cheeks were flushed with embarrassment and anger.

— Maybe you don't know the conditions around here as well as you should.

Inspector Davies made an effort to show he was being helpful and kindly.

— These two men are Moscow trained, he said. And of course there are others. We know who they are. Every single one of them. And they're Moscow paid as well. They've got no respect for anything. You come down to the station and I'll show you their records. Aggressive and dangerous. And these two are the worst of the lot. So take my advice, brother. Don't associate with them. And I mean that. If you do it will only land you in trouble.

Wes and the bailiff's assistant were pushing their way through the dispersing crowd. The pale young man looked relieved, his head swinging loosely on his long neck as he watched the men moving away. Alive with triumph, Wes' small features radiated puckish delight.

— You're too late, Inspector Davies!

He was no longer annoyed by his own croaking whisper.

— Unless you want to tell the bailiff to go home.

He gave the bailiff's assistant a push into the house.

— Go on, tell him, Wes said. Pass on the message.

Inspector Davies put his hands behind his back. He gazed innocently at Val and then at Wes.

— One or two with stones in their hands, I think you saw?

— Certainly not.

Wes Hicks hotly denied the allegation. Inspector Davies looked at Val again with the stern benevolence of a Sunday School Superintendent.

— One or two I'm sure. One or two wouldn't you say now? *Yn enw'r gwir.*

Val breathed deeply and shook his head.

— No rough stuff, Inspector.

Pen was grinning provocatively.

— No rough stuff at all. Pure justice it was and lovely to watch. Wasn't it, Mr Gwyn?

— You haven't given me much of a chance to say anything, Val said.

— Well here's your chance, man. You can tell the Inspector how you enjoyed every minute.

— We can do something about the rates, Val said. There should be a reduction.

— There you are, Inspector, Pen said. A big-hearted bourgeois who wants to help the working class. Not many of them left. Even in chapel these days.

The inspector did not enjoy being teased.

— You watch your tongue, Lewis, he said. It's funny how there's always trouble when you're around.

Pen made a face of childlike innocence.

— This isn't trouble, Inspector. This is a spontaneous celebration of the joy of living by the working people of Cwm Du. They've got so much to be thankful for.

Val burst out laughing. He was awarded with a glare of intense disapproval from Inspector Davies.

(Emyr Humphreys, *The Best of Friends*, London, 1978, pp.280–4.)

F.18   A large pair of binoculars lay on cotton wool in the box. Bert began fingering the strap.

'Are they yours?' Gwyn asked. 'I've never seen them.'

'No. I put all that kind of thing away.'

'From the war, are they?'

'No, not the war. They're much too good for them to give us in the war.'

'What, then?'

Bert pulled at the strap and held the binoculars flat in his palms. 'They're German glasses. The best.'

'Did you take them from the Germans?'

'No. They belonged to a boy from Cambridge. Paul he was called. Paul Howe.'

'How did they come to you, then?'

Bert turned the binoculars and gripped the long black barrels. He looked up at Gwyn. His damaged eye was almost closed.

'I want you, Gwyn, to hold on to these glasses. They come to me the year you was born. He was a boy of eighteen, nineteen. Straight from Cambridge. He'd never done anything hard in his life.'

'It was Spain, was it?'

'In Spain. His mother had given him the glasses. He was killed there in front of me. I've had them ever since.'

'Paul Howe, you say?'

'Aye, that was his name. There's now two of us remembering him.'

'Perhaps there are others.'

'Aye I expect his family. His Mam didn't want him to go. It was all very hard.'

Bert moved in the bed. He winced as pain shot through his knee.

'Can I get you comfortable?' Gwyn asked, anxiously.

Bert leaned back on his pillows.

'I want you to keep these glasses,' he said. 'I want you to

Raymond Williams. (*Source: Welsh Arts Council.*)

remember what a communist was like.'

'Remember? I don't need reminding.'

'Perhaps you do, perhaps you don't. But I read, you know, and I listen. I know what they think of us.'

'That's always so in politics.'

'Aye, politics! That's all they make of it. But this was a boy getting killed. If that mortar hadn't got him he'd be a man coming fifty. He'd be walking around to take part in their discussions.'

There was a long silence.

'The year you was born,' Bert repeated.

'Yes.'

'I took them with me, over to Normandie. I looked through them from old Cossack trying to see that bloody Death's Head.'

'Death's Head?'

'*SS Totenkopf.* They told me that's what it means.'

'When you were wounded?'

'Aye. More bloody fool me.'

He turned his head on the pillows. The damaged eye was now in shadow. He was breathing hard. Gwyn stayed silent, hoping he would rest or even sleep.

'Only when I was in that fight with the scabs down Bettws,' the hoarse voice came again.

'Rest now a bit, Dad.'

'Old Vanny Prosser it was, an old chap of sixty. And he give me this pick handle, a dirty old thing, and he said he'd had it against the horses, 1910, 1911.'

'Horses?'

'Police horses.'

'So why did he give it to you?'

'He didn't say. He just give it me.'

'So you could use it?'

'No, no, we had plenty of picks.'

'What did you think, then?'

'I didn't. At that age you don't.'

He rolled again on the pillows. He felt for the binoculars and grasped them.

'You'll know better than me,' he said, with his eyes closed, 'but I don't reckon much to this memory they call history.'

'Why's that?'

'History, I don't know. Your aunt Emma's always saying it. Only what I've noticed is you get this story, this record, this account they call it. And of course you can soon take it in. Aye that was Tonypandy. That was Bettws. That was Spain. That was Normandie. You know it all, you know what I mean?'

'Aye.'

'And you know nothing. Like a birth certificate, or a diary. Accurate, granted ...'

'Not always even that.'

'Aye but still when it is you know what it means you to know. And it still isn't none of it what it was. That was why old Vanny give the pick handle.'

'To feel it? Through the actual thing?'

Bert sighed.

'Aye. I suppose that's what he meant.'

'And did you?'

Bert opened his eyes.

'No. Not then.'

'And the glasses?'

'I expect so. I mean I can feel it, but it isn't in them.'

'It is now you've told me.'

Bert smiled.

'I'm glad to hear you say that.'

(Raymond Williams, *Loyalties*, London, 1985, pp.251–4.)

Debating the Evidence

The historian cannot avoid using literature as a source. He is not concerned, as such, with the structure of a novel or the rhyme scheme of a poem. But neither can he endorse Duke Theseus in *A Midsummer Night's Dream*:

> The lunatic, the lover and the poet
> Are of imagination all compact.

Unlike Theseus, the calculating historian wants to tap into that poetic imagination with its heightened perceptions and its new insights and its richness of imagery — even the imagery of distress — especially in a period like that of the Depression when the issues themselves are starkly defined, politically, socially, even morally. In David Smith's rich sentence, 'Perhaps only in the reaches of the literary imagination can lives be made whole again'.

Source F.1
What kind of insights into education, socialism and religion are furnished by this extract from *Kate Roberts*'s novel about the Wales of the years before the First World War?

Source F.2
In discussing education, Goodwin's points all have substance. The intermediate schools were unique to Wales where they existed all over the country. *Matriculation* was needed to go to a college — to a university college — and the most popular job for university products in the inter-war years was teaching. How far does the corroboration of such facts influence our attitude to this extract as a historical source?

Sources F.3, F.4, F.5
Of what significance would the authors' political affiliations be to the historian's interpretation of these extracts?

Source F.6
What does this poem tell us about the *General Strike*? And what does it tell us about the poet?

Source F.7
This famous, to some, infamous, poem is as powerful a statement about the industrialization of Wales as there is. What is it saying? Why is it so much more powerful as poetry than it would have been as prose?

Source F.10
It is easy to catch the mood of this poem — one of intense bitterness — and to see how the mood is generated by richness of language or riveting metaphor. What avenues of strictly historical research are suggested by the poem?

Sources F.12, F.13
For this historian one of the novelist's most illuminating gifts is that of

creating the atmosphere of the past, generating an empathetic awareness of the sights and sounds of the event and the period. It is a dangerous gift though. Are there any danger signals for the historian in these extracts?

Source F.16
This extract is autobiographical. There is much in it which is valuable to the social historian of Wales but the information needs to be used with considerable caution. Why?

Discussion

There was no great Welsh novelist of the nineteenth century, with the possible ·exception of Daniel Owen. But the selection which David Smith makes demonstrates the quality and talent of the genre in both languages in the twentieth century. The traumas of industrial decline, whether in the slate industries of north Wales or the steel and coal industries of the south Wales valleys, have generated a literature of outrage, despair, bitterness and humour of the highest order. Such is the grip which Depression took by the enormity of its consequences on vital communities that fact provides all the necessary ammunition for fiction. *Kate Roberts*'s insights in this passage are as significant as those of any historian. English did allow you to make your way in the world — something which was readily apparent to parents of pupils of the intermediate schools established after 1889. The end of the nineteenth century did see Welsh politicization along lines very different from those of the Liberalism of the previous generation. Around the turn of the century social Christianity did tend to replace the Evangelical message of earlier Nonconformity. *Kate Roberts*, and Goodwin in F.2, therefore command immediate attention from readers whose concern is to empathize with the people of late nineteenth- and twentieth-century Wales. These novelists are significantly sensitive to historical realities. To this they then bring that marvellous historical imagination which creates a deeper reality, in the best historical novels, than the historian is allowed.

At the same time the reader has to be more careful using these sources than conventional historical sources. The Depression, as much as any event in Welsh history, has generated its mythology, partly because so many writers expressed their moral outrage so brilliantly. Sometimes this outrage has been coupled with a specifically left-wing political stance. But, almost inevitably, it has invariably been on the attack, goaded on by the tragedy of the 'locust years'. It is left to the historian to point to some elements of balance, meagre though they be — rather more prosperity in the western coalfield and certainly more in Cardiff, with consumer society open to those in employment.

The poet's use of language is yet more concentrated and evocative. It can be yet more illuminating, and, indeed, dangerous. Idris Davies's insights into the inter-war years show the masterly perception of the poet and the committed polemicist. But there were other views based on different philosophies. To *Saunders Lewis* (F.7) the industrialization of Wales, not the Depression, was the disaster. Here is an insight into one basic philosophical strand of Welsh nationalism, its emphasis on the theory of leadership emanating from Welsh-speaking rural Wales and drawing on the independent small farmer for sustenance. Here is poetic expression of what was, for a time, party policy — the de-industrial-ization of Wales. Whatever reaction there is to *Lewis*'s vitriolic language, the ambiguity of the industrial experience for Wales in the nineteenth and twentieth centuries is not only that of prosperity and depression, or exploitation and progress, but also of the validity of the whole process for the people of Wales.

Further Reading

Roy Armes, *A Critical History of British Cinema*, London, 1978.

C. Baber and L. J. Williams, *Essays in the Economic History of South Wales*, Cardiff, 1986.

Colin Baker, *Aspects of Bilingualism in Wales*, Clevedon, 1985.

Deirdre Beddoe, *Women in Britain between the Wars*, London, 1988.

T.E. Brennan, E. Cooney and H. Pollins, *Social Change in South-West Wales*, London, 1954.

Tony Curtis (ed.), *Wales: The Imagined Nation. Essays in Cultural and National Identity*, Bridgend, 1986.

D. Hywel Davies, *The Welsh Nationalist Party 1925–1945*, Cardiff, 1983.

John Davies, 'The End of the Great Estates and the Rise of Freehold Farming in Wales', *Welsh History Review*, Volume 7, Number 2, December, 1974.

H. Francis and D. Smith, *The Fed: A History of the South Wales Miners in the Twentieth Century*, London, 1980.

J.B. Hilling, *The Historic Architecture of Wales*, Cardiff, 1976.

Arthur Horner, *Incorrigible Rebel*, London, 1960.

A.V. John, 'A miner struggle? Women's protests in Welsh mining history', *Llafur*, Volume 4, Number 1, pp.72–90.

A.Y. Jones and D. Beddoe, *The Welsh Maid: A Study of Welsh Women in Domestic Service 1919–1939*, London, 1988.

Gareth Elwyn Jones, *Controls and Conflicts in Welsh Secondary Education 1889–1944*, Cardiff, 1982.

Gwyn Jones, ed., *Oxford Book of Welsh Verse in English*, Oxford, 1977.

Gwyn Jones, *Profiles*, Llandysul, 1980.

R. Brinley Jones and Meic Stephens (eds.), *Writers of Wales*, Cardiff, 1970 — a series on individual authors including: Saunders Lewis, Lewis Jones, Gwyn Thomas, Dylan Thomas, Geraint Goodwin, Jack Jones, T. Rowland Hughes, Gwyn Jones, Dannie Abse, Kate Roberts, Emyr Humphreys, Gwenallt, Idris Davies, Raymond Williams, Alun Lewis.

E.D. Lewis, *The Rhondda Valleys*, Cardiff, 1959.

Saunders Lewis, *Is There an Anglo-Welsh Literature*, Cardiff, 1939.

M. Llewellyn Davies, *Maternity: Letters from Working Women*, London, 1978.

H. Marquand, *South Wales Needs a Plan*, London, 1936.

Kenneth O. Morgan, *Rebirth of a Nation: Wales 1880–1980*, Oxford, 1981.

Kenneth O. Morgan, *Wales in British Politics 1868–1922*, Cardiff 1980.

R. Page Arnott, *South Wales Miners, 1898–1914*, London, 1967.

Thomas Parry, *Llenyddiaeth Gymraeg 1900–1945*, Liverpool, 1945.

Alwyn D. Rees, *Life in a Welsh Countryside*, Cardiff, 1950.

Geoffrey Richards, *The Age of the Dream Palace: Cinema and Society in Britain 1930–1939*, London, 1984.

J. Richards and A. Aldgate, *The Best of British: Cinema and Society 1930–1970*, London, 1983.

Eric Rowan, *Art in Wales 1850–1975*, Cardiff, 1978.

D. Smith and G. Williams, *Fields of Praise: The Official History of the Welsh Rugby Union 1881–1981*, Cardiff, 1980.

M. Spring Rice, *Working Class Wives*, London, 1981.

Peter Stead, 'Wales and Film' in Tony Curtis, ed. *Wales: The Imagined Nation*, Cardiff, 1985.

Meic Stephens (ed.), *The Oxford Companion to the Literature of Wales*, Oxford, 1986.

Elizabeth Sussex, *The Rise and Fall of the British Documentary*, London, 1975.

Brinley Thomas, ed., *The Welsh Economy*, Cardiff, 1962.

David Walker, ed., *A History of the Church in Wales*, Cardiff, 1976.

Llafur, Volume 2, Number 2, 1977 — special number on the General Strike.

Note: The best resource for the history of film in this country is the British Film Institute Library, 127 Charing Cross Road, London.

Glossary

1935 Demonstrations	Marches of *c.*300,000 people in south Wales protesting against the new *Unemployment Assistance Board Act* which enforced strict limits on the amount local *Boards of Guardians* could give in unemployment benefit.
Addison, Christopher	Liberal reforming politician. Minister in Lloyd George's 1918 government, responsible for an important housing and town planning act under which large numbers of houses were built. The programme suffered from the Geddes economies of 1922. (See *Geddes' Axe*).
Asquithian Liberals	Those members of the Liberal party who remained loyal to H.H. Asquith when he was replaced as Prime Minister by Lloyd George in 1916.
Baptists	Christian Nonconformists of the Baptist Denomination, characterized particularly by the practice of adult baptism by total immersion in water.
Bedwellty Guardians	The local body in the district of Bedwellty in south-east Wales charged with administering poor relief. They incurred the wrath of central government for spending more on poor relief than the government allowed. The Bedwellty Guardians were replaced by the government.
Beveridge, Sir William	The civil servant whose report on social insurance in 1943 was the blueprint for the post-Second World War welfare state.

Boards of Guardians	Local organizations responsible for the administration of poor relief. See, for example, *Bedwellty Guardians*.
Bolshevik	The name generally applied to the post-1917 Russian communist state, or its party members. Originally applied to the majority group led by Lenin who defeated Martov and Trotsky in a crucial ideological debate in 1903 on the nature of the communist party in Russia.
Calvinistic Methodist	Christian Nonconformist denomination particularly strong in Welsh-speaking north Wales.
Coalition Liberals	Those Liberals who supported the coalition government of Liberals and Conservatives under Lloyd George after the 1918 election.
Collectivist	A term often applied to that co-operative activity, for example in wartime, which draws the resources of virtually all classes and groups in the nation into collective or co-operative action.
Congregational	Christian Nonconformist denomination particularly characterized by its democratic government.
Coupon Election	The 1918 election in which approved candidates from both Liberal and Conservative parties were given a letter of endorsement — the coupon.
Fed, The	The *South Wales Miners' Federation*, founded 1898 — the south Wales coalminers' trade union.
Geddes' Axe	The economy measures of 1922 formulated by Sir Eric Geddes.
General Strike	The strike of all the major trade unions in May 1926. The TUC called off the strike after nine days and the miners were left to fight on alone.
Gold Standard	The means of regulating the currency and money supply suspended during the First World War. Restored by Winston Churchill, Chancellor of the Exchequer, in 1925. It led, effectively, to a ten per cent rise in the external value of sterling.

Glossary

Gwenallt — D. Gwenallt Jones. Published his first volume of poems in 1935. One of Wales's most distinguished twentieth-century Welsh-language writers.

Horner, Arthur — A founder member of the Communist party in Great Britain and one of its most important members. President of the *South Wales Miners' Federation*.

Hunger Marches — One of the most popular forms of protest against unemployment and its consequent privations. The first from south Wales was in 1927 and they continued in the 1930s, mainly to London.

Independent Labour Party — One of the major movements which resulted from and became part of the foundation of the Labour party. Spread quickly in south Wales after 1898.

Independent Liberals — The Liberal MPs who refused to support the National (in practice Conservative) government after the election of October 1931.

Insured Workers — Those workers who, in partnership with their employers, had paid unemployment insurance contributions under the 1920 Unemployment Insurance Act. Included almost all categories of workers except domestic workers, agricultural labourers and civil servants.

Keynes, John Maynard — Distinguished economist. Co-operated with Lloyd George in the 1930s to produce programmes by which government spending could be made to alleviate unemployment and re-vitalize industry.

Lewis, Saunders — The major literary figure in the Welsh language of twentieth-century Wales as poet and playwright. Founder member and first President of *Plaid Cymru*.

London Welsh Girls Friendly Aid Society — During the 1920s and 1930s large numbers of young girls from Wales went to London as domestic servants. This Society was established to help ease the often traumatic transition.

MacDonald, Ramsay	First Labour Prime Minister in 1924. Prime Minister again in 1929, continuing as head of the so-called National government which was created in the financial crisis of 1931.
Malthusian	The Reverend Thomas Malthus, professor of political economy at a Haileybury college. Formulated the so-called Malthus Law in the 1790s, which argued that population growth would outstrip the means of subsistence.
Marriage Bar	Bar against the employment of married women in some jobs — teaching was a prime example until after 1944.
Marxist/ Marxism	Adherent of Marxist philosophies of society promulgated by Karl Marx which postulated the coming of the Communist revolution.
Matriculation	Effectively, a university entrance qualification. Applied, in the inter-war years, to those who gained a five-subject certificate at credit level (significantly higher than pass level) of an authorized examining board — in Wales, for most schools, this was the Central Welsh Board.
Means Test	The system by which welfare benefits, including money for the unemployed, the 'dole', was cut in line with income brought in by any member of the household.
Miners' Lock-Out	After the collapse of the *General Strike* in 1926 the miners were locked out by the owners for six months.
Miners' Federation of Great Britain	The union of British coalfield unions. In 1908 it affiliated to the Labour party.
Orange Book	*We Can Conquer Unemployment* — part of a major Liberal party programme (when in opposition in the late 1920s) to come to grips with unemployment and industrial decline. Inspired by *J.M. Keynes* and Lloyd George.
Plaid Cymru	The Welsh Nationalist party, founded in 1925.

Poor Law Commissioners	Those responsible for administering the Poor Law centrally. Involved regulations for elections of Boards of Guardians who adminstered unemployment relief locally.
Popular Front	Attempts from the mid-1930s to mobilize anti-Conservative elements in Britain and unite Socialist League, Communists and the Labour party against Fascism and the National government.
Popular Guardians	See *Poor Law Commissioners.*
Progressivism	A synthesis of Liberal and Gradualist Socialist ideas for social reform.
Protection	A system of imposing tariffs (taxes) on imported goods in order to nurture and protect home-produced goods.
Representation of the People Act	The 1918 reform act which gave votes to many women over thirty. Only in 1928 were women granted voting rights on the same terms as men.
Roberts, Kate	An outstanding Welsh novelist of the twentieth century. Wrote mainly in Welsh of the quarrying districts of north Wales. Also a notable literary and social critic.
Sankey Commission	The Royal Commission on the coal industry which in 1919 advocated state ownership of the industry. The report was rejected by the government.
Sex Disqualification (Removal) Act 1919	Theoretically outlawed the exclusion of women from the professions on grounds of their sex alone. The act was often ignored and, in any case, women were excluded, on marriage, from, for example, the teaching profession.
Shonis	Shon is one Welsh version of the name John. Shonis is a slang, partly anglicized, version of the name.
South Wales Miners' Federation	The union of the miners of the south Wales coalfield founded 1898.

Spanish Civil War	Fought from 1936 to 1939 between right-wing generals under Franco and the left-wing Popular Front government. About 2,000 Britons fought for the International Brigade against Franco. The biggest contingent in terms of national population came from the ranks of unemployed south Wales miners, though north Wales was represented too.
Spencer Union	1930s' coal miners' union in the English Midlands which broke away from the official old-established coalfield union.
Stopes, Marie	Most famous of twentieth-century advocates of birth control. Founded the first United Kingdom birth control clinic in 1921.
Tuberculosis	Infectious disease in man and animals. Most common form is pulmonary tuberculosis. Economic conditions have a notable effect on its rate of occurrence, with the working class being most susceptible to the disease. High death rate until effective drug therapy was developed in the 1940s and 1950s.
Unemployment Assistance Act	See *1935 Demonstrations*.
University of Wales Constituency	In the inter-war years the University of Wales, like other universities, had separate representation in the House of Commons, with the vote available to graduates of the University.
Vidor, King	Hollywood film maker.
Welsh National Memorial	Launched by David Davies, MP, with a gift of £125,000 in 1910. Concerned with investigating social deprivation in Wales, especially to counter the high incidence of tuberculosis in Wales.
Williams, Emlyn	Welsh actor and playwright.
Women's Social and Political Union	A movement set up to campaign for women's rights.

Index

Index